MINING THE BIG BUG

ARCHAEOLOGICAL INVESTIGATIONS AT TWELVE HISTORIC
STATE ROUTE 69 BETWEEN MAYER AND DEWEY, Y

by

PAT H. STEIN
ELIZABETH J. SKINNER

with contributions by

STEWART DEATS
JOHN D. GOODMAN II

SWCA, Inc.
Environmental Consultants
Flagstaff, Arizona

SWCA Anthropological Research Paper Number 5

1997

Prepared for

Arizona Department of Transportation
Environmental Planning Section
Phoenix, Arizona

under

Contract No. 94-08
TRACS No. H2369-05L

and

Bureau of Land Management Cultural Resources Use (ARPA) Permit No. AZ-000113
Arizona State Museum Project-Specific Permit No. 94-5

With special thanks to

Stan, Jenni, and Pepper Young

of Young's Farm

General series editor - Robert C. Euler
Assistant editor - Richard V. N. Ahlstrom
Copy editor - Jean H. Ballagh
Cover design - Christina Watkins

1997
SWCA, Inc., Environmental Consultants
Flagstaff

TABLE OF CONTENTS

List of Figures

List of Tables

ACKNOWLEDGMENTS

The authors would like to thank the many individuals who assisted in these investigations and in the preparation of this report. Bettina Rosenberg, C. Marshall Hoffman, Robert Gasser, and Sally Atkinson administered the project on behalf of the Arizona Department of Transportation. David Greenwald acted as Project Administrator for SWCA. SWCA staff who participated in the testing or excavation phases were: crew members Andy Arias, Matt Caouette, Stewart Deats, John Goodman, and Preston Payton; crew chiefs Lynne Gardner and Robert Haynes-Peterson; field director Lynn Neal; laboratory director Mary-Ellen Walsh-Anduze; laboratory technicians Janet Hagopian and Allison McComiskey; draftsperson Jill Caouette; and technical typists Pat Donnelly and Ginger White. Special thanks are extended to SWCA employees Bernadette Slater, who analyzed historic artifacts during the testing phase; Stewart Deats, who assumed that task during the excavation phase; and to John Goodman, who recorded and reported on linear historic resources and analyzed faunal material from the excavations. Ms. Neal and Jean Ballagh of SWCA edited the final report of the investigations. Mr. Deats, Randy Fox, and Laura Jones assisted in report assemblage. Ms. Ballagh, Dr. Robert Euler, and Richard Ahlstrom of SWCA prepared the manuscript for the SWCA publication series.

Reviewers of the testing report were Ms. Rosenberg and Mr. Hoffman (on behalf of ADOT), Connie Stone (District Archaeologist, Phoenix District, Bureau of Land Management), and Mr. Gasser (then on behalf of the State Historic Preservation Office). Reviewers of the final report of the investigations were Ms. Rosenberg and Mr. Gasser (on behalf of ADOT); Ms. Stone (for the BLM); Jim McKie (Forest Archaeologist, Prescott National Forest); and William Collins, Carol Griffith, and Joanne Miller (Historian, Historical Archaeologist/Deputy SHPO, and Compliance Coordinator, respectively, for the State Historic Preservation Office).

People who generously contributed their expertise to the project (but were not formally associated with it) included: Jack Basham (former President, Camp Verde Historical Society); Mason Coggin (Director, Arizona Department of Mines and Mineral Resources); Donald Hardesty (Professor of Anthropology, University of Nevada at Reno); Kevin Harper (former Tribal Archaeologist, Yavapai-Prescott Tribe); Jeff Hathaway (Archaeologist, Archaeological Research Services); Karolyn Jensen (Historical Archaeologist, Archaeological Consulting Services); Ken Kimsey (Forest Historian, Prescott National Forest); Lonnie Morgan (former Tribal Para-Archaeologist, Yavapai-Prescott Tribe); David Myrick (author, *Pioneer Arizona Railroads*); Nyal Niemuth (Mining Historian, Arizona Department of Mines and Mineral Resources); Pat O'Hara (mining consultant, Prescott); Ken Phillips (Chief Engineer, Arizona Department of Mines and Mineral Resources); George Teague (Division Chief, Western Archeological and Conservation Center); Norm Tessman (Historian, Sharlot Hall Museum); and Michael Wurtz (Archivist, Sharlot Hall Museum). Their knowledge greatly enriched the project; to them, the authors extend a special debt of gratitude.

ABSTRACT

In December of 1993 the Arizona Department of Transportation (ADOT) contracted with SWCA, Inc., Environmental Consultants, to conduct investigations at archaeological sites that could not be avoided by a proposed highway widening project along State Route (SR) 69 between Mayer and Dewey, Yavapai County, Arizona. Sites that would be impacted by the proposed construction were two prehistoric sites, eight historic sites, one multicomponent (prehistoric and historic) site, and three linear historic resources. The federally funded project was to be on existing and newly acquired ADOT right-of-way (ROW) across Prescott National Forest, Bureau of Land Management, Arizona State Land Department, and private lands. The project area consisted of an 11.1-mile corridor varying between 300 feet and 900 feet in width and extending from milepost 269.7 south of Mayer to milepost 280.8 just north of Dewey along SR 69.

The first phase of the investigations required testing to determine the extent, condition, and significance of cultural deposits at each site within the ROW. Based on the testing results, SWCA recommended no further work at the prehistoric sites and components. However, ADOT requested additional investigations at the prehistoric component of the multicomponent site, and SWCA personnel completed this work between March 27 and 31, 1995. On the basis of testing at the historic sites and the historic component of the multicomponent site, SWCA recommended that nine of these sites be formally determined eligible for the National Register of Historic Places. Of these nine properties, only two contained significant subsurface remains within the ROW. SWCA submitted a data recovery plan for these two sites to ADOT in 1994 and conducted data recovery investigations from March 20 to April 10, 1995. SWCA submitted two reports on the results of the SR 69 investigations, one on the prehistoric sites and one on the historic sites.

This document, the final report on investigations at the historic sites in the SR 69 project area, describes testing at 12 sites and components (9 properties and 3 sets of linear segments) and data recovery at the 2 sites with subsurface remains. The nine sites investigated were AR-03-09-03-238 (the Poland Junction Substation), AZ N:11:19(ASM) (the Bay View Placer Mining Claim), AZ N:11:20(ASM) (the Princes Placer erosion control device), AZ N:11:23(ASM) (Huron Station and the Montezuma and Eagle Fraction lode claims), AZ N:11:25(ASM), AZ N:12:29(ASM), AZ N:12:30(ASM) (the Treadwell [Great Western] Smelter), AZ N:12:39(ASM), (the Gray Eagle Reduction [Mayer Custom] Plant), and AZ N:12:40(ASM). Data recovery was conducted at AZ N:11:19(ASM) (the Bay View Placer Mining Claim) and AZ N:11:23(ASM) (Huron Station and the Montezuma and Eagle Fraction lode claims). The linear resources were seven segments of the historic Prescott & Eastern Railway (Sites AZ N:7:44[ASM], AZ N:8:29[ASM], AZ N:11:28[ASM]/AR-03-09-03-365, AZ N:12:41[ASM]), nine segments of the historic Phoenix (Rock Springs)–Prescott Highway (Sites AZ N:8:30[ASM], AZ N:11:29[ASM]/AR 03-09-03-366, AZ N:12:27[ASM]), and a series of unidentified road segments in a small area 0.2 miles north of Poland Junction (Site AZ N:11:27(ASM)/AR-03-09-03-364).

SWCA investigated the sites in the context of three thematic categories from the Prescott National Forest's overview: Demography, Technology and Industry, and Transportation and Communication. Under Demography, archival and archaeological data from the SR 69 sites provided evidence for the presence of Yavapai, Chinese, Hispanic, and Euroamerican residents in the Mayer-Dewey area in the late nineteenth and early twentieth centuries. Archival data indicated that the persons associated with the Euroamerican sites came from far-flung areas and suggested the factors—opportunities in mining, agriculture (homesteading), and transportation (railroading)—that attracted them to the area. Under Technology and Industry, the information obtained through testing revealed how mines and mining plants were organized, how the tasks of mineral exploration and processing were phased, what equipment was used, and how technologies differed through time and among sites. Under Transportation and

Communication, SWCA researchers assembled an interesting and valuable body of information regarding historic railroad and highway construction methods and materials, providing insight into a neglected aspect of the history of the project area.

The State Route 69 investigations provided the opportunity to study mining and related activities within one of Arizona's 246 mining districts, the Big Bug. An interesting finding of the study was that ethnicity was sometimes expressed in the archaeological data set from a site but not in archival data, underscoring the importance of looking at both of these data sets when studying historical-archaeological properties. Using both types of data, SWCA archaeologists were able to shed light on the complex and tenuous nature of mineral extraction and processing within the Big Bug Mining District and the factors that made those activities moderately successful in some localities and less successful in others.

CHAPTER 1

INTRODUCTION

Pat H. Stein
Elizabeth J. Skinner

PROJECT HISTORY

In December of 1993 the Arizona Department of Transportation (ADOT) contracted with SWCA, Inc., Environmental Consultants, to conduct archaeological investigations at two prehistoric sites, eight historic sites, one multicomponent (prehistoric and historic) site, and three linear historic resources that were to be impacted by a proposed highway widening project along State Route (SR) 69 between Mayer and Dewey, Yavapai County, Arizona. The sites could not be avoided by the proposed construction. The proposed project was federally funded and took place on existing and newly acquired ADOT right-of-way (ROW) across Prescott National Forest (PNF), Bureau of Land Management (BLM), Arizona State Land Department (ASLD), and private lands.

The project area consisted of an 11.1-mile corridor along SR 69 in central Arizona (Figure 1.1). The corridor varied between 300 feet and 900 feet in width and extended from milepost 269.7 south of Mayer to milepost 280.8 just north of Dewey.

The first phase of the investigations required testing to determine the extent, condition, and significance of cultural deposits at each site within the ROW. ADOT staff needed this information to help determine whether and where data recovery would be necessary and thus to define the scope of the data recovery effort. SWCA field crews conducted testing during a three-week period from January 17 to February 4, 1994. SWCA submitted to ADOT two reports describing the results of testing, one for prehistoric sites and components (Mitchell 1994) and the other for historic sites and components (Stein 1994). Based on the testing results, SWCA recommended no further work at the prehistoric sites and components. However, ADOT requested additional investigations at the prehistoric component of the multicomponent site; SWCA personnel completed this work between March 27 and 31, 1995. SWCA submitted a report describing the testing and data recovery at the prehistoric sites and components in 1995 (Mitchell 1995). On the basis of testing at the historic sites and the historic component of the multicomponent site, SWCA recommended that nine of these sites be formally determined eligible for the National Register of Historic Places. Of these nine properties, only two contained significant subsurface remains within the ROW. SWCA submitted a data recovery plan for these two sites to ADOT in 1994 (SWCA 1994), conducted data recovery investigations from March 20 to April 10, 1995, and submitted an interim report on the results of the data recovery in 1995 (Stein 1995).

This document, the final report on investigations at the historic sites in the SR 69 project area, describes testing at 12 sites and components (9 properties and 3 sets of linear segments) and data recovery at the 2 sites with subsurface remains. All appropriate permits and agreements were obtained.[1]

---

[1]Permits and agreements acquired for the project included a Cultural Resource Use (ARPA) Permit (No. AZ-000113) from the BLM; a Project-Specific Permit (No. 94-5) from the Arizona State Museum (ASM); a Special-Use/Nondisturbing Permit from PNF; and a Notice of Intent to Provide Repository Services (dated December 12, 1993) from ASM.

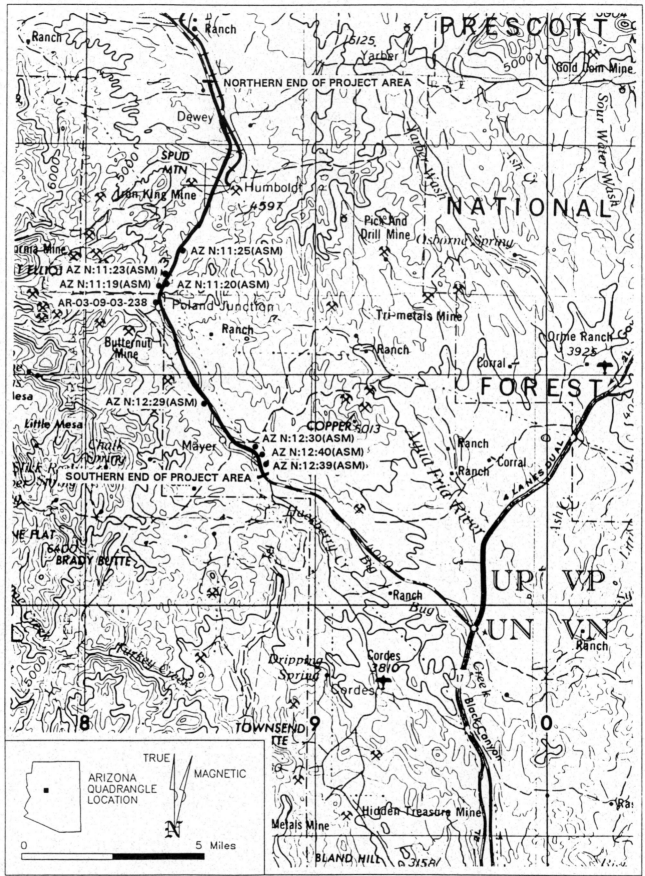

Figure 1.1. Location of the State Route 69 Mayer to Dewey project area. Base map is Prescott, Arizona, USGS 1:250,000 scale topographic map, 1954 (revised 1970).

ENVIRONMENTAL SETTING

The project area is in eastern Yavapai County in the northeastern foothills of the Bradshaw Mountains, at distances between 16.5 miles and 27.6 miles east of Prescott, the county seat. This area is in an ecotone between the Sonoran Desert of southern Arizona and the Colorado Plateau of northern Arizona. Elevations in the general area range from 4300–4600 feet in the valleys to approximately 6500 feet on nearby peaks. The immediate area consists of a series of east-west-trending ridges with drainage to the southeast. The major washes adjoining and crossing the project area are the Agua Fria River and four of its tributaries: Big Bug Creek, Galena Gulch, Chaparral Gulch, and Green Gulch.

Two distinct vegetative zones characterize the area (Lowe and Brown 1973). From Mayer to Poland Junction, a Plains and Desert Grasslands community dominates, with native vegetation consisting mainly of assorted grasses, shrub oak, acacia, creosotebush, narrow-leaf yucca, prickly pear cactus, cholla cactus, and various composites. Non-native vegetation includes Russian thistle, grapes, and alfalfa. From Poland Junction to Humboldt, the project area is characterized by an Interior Chaparral community consisting mainly of shrub and emory oak, manzanita, acacia, mesquite, juniper, bear grass, agave, yucca, mountain mahogany, devil's claw, prickly pear cactus, pincushion cactus, and various grasses and composites. From Humboldt to Dewey, the project area re-enters a Plains and Desert Grasslands community. These vegetative zones are occasionally broken by riparian and attenuated riparian communities along the washes that cross the project area.

Much of the history of the project area has been determined by its geology. The area lies in the Big Bug Mining District, a region endowed with workable deposits of gold, silver, copper, lead, and zinc. The predominant formation is schist, with intrusions of diorite, granodiorite, granite, and dikes of rhyolite-porphyry. The schist is mainly of sedimentary origin but also contains some igneous members. The schist is intruded on the west by the Mount Union belt of granite and, southwest of McCabe, by a stock of granodiorite. Basalt flows postdating the mineralization form Big Bug Mesa, where they rest on a late Tertiary or early Quaternary pediment. Elsewhere in the mining district, post-basalt erosion has extensively dissected this pediment (Lindgren 1926:126–127; Wilson, Cunningham, and Butler 1967:35).

The ore deposits of the Big Bug Mining District belong to five classes: (1) pyritic copper deposits, represented by the Blue Bell, Hackberry, Butternut, and Boggs mines; (2) Precambrian quartz veins, such as the old Mesa Mine, near Poland; (3) the Iron King gold-silver replacement deposit; (4) veins of later date, probably connected genetically with rhyolite-porphyry dikes, mainly near the Poland and Providence mines; and (5) placer deposits in gulches around McCabe and Mayer (Lindgren 1926:127; Wilson, Cunningham, and Butler 1967:35).

HISTORICAL SETTING

In the past, portions of Yavapai County have been the subject of study by ethnographers (such as Gifford [1936] and Schroeder [1974]) and historians (such as Henson [1965], Pape [1987], and Sayre [1979, 1985]). Studies by historical archaeologists (such as Hoffman [1985] and Keller and Stein [1985]) —mandated in many instances by federal and state preservation laws—have contributed new perspectives on the region's past. The resulting literature documents a rich tapestry of human activity in the area from the point of Euroamerican contact through recent times.

The first contact between native and non-native peoples in the area was in 1582–1583 as the result of a Spanish *entrada*. A wealthy *don*, Antonio de Espejo, offered to finance and lead an expedition westward from New Mexico on behalf of the Spanish realm. The expedition reached the Hopi Mesas, then turned southwest in search of rumored mines. Hopi guides led the Espejo party through Chavez Pass and along the Palatkwapi Trail to the Verde Valley. At that location, native groups, likely the Yavapai, were encountered. Espejo was followed by Captain Marcos Farfán de los Godos, who entered the Verde Valley in 1598 by nearly the same route (Bartlett 1943). Farfán was under the command of Juan de Oñate, a wealthy nobleman with orders to conquer and colonize the region on behalf of New Spain. In 1604 Oñate himself entered the Verde Valley, continuing southwestward to the Bill Williams River, the Colorado River, and the Gulf of Mexico (Bolton 1919). All of these early expeditions sought gold and silver. When the explorers failed to encounter these minerals in lucrative quantities, Spanish interest in the area waned.

When Mexico won its independence from Spain in 1821, the area passed from Spanish to Mexican rule. During the Mexican Period (1821–1848), the Santa Fe Trail opened a lively commerce between Mexican Santa Fe and American St. Louis. The trail brought a tide of American merchants who freighted goods between the two cities (Weber 1982). With the traders came trappers—"mountain men"—who scoured the rivers of central Arizona in search of beaver. Mountain men known to have ranged to and through the Yavapai County area include Pauline Weaver, William Wolfskill, and Ewing Young. Their most intense period of activity was in the late 1820s and early 1830s. As the market for beaver pelts crashed in the mid 1830s, most trapping came to an abrupt end. However, when Mexico ceded much of Arizona to the United States in 1848, it was from this body of knowledgeable mountain men that the U.S. Army recruited guides for southwestern expeditions (Walker and Bufkin 1986:17).

If Yavapai County—indeed, all of central Arizona—had a defining moment in history, that moment came in 1863 when a prospecting party organized by mountain man Joseph Reddeford Walker and guided by John W. "Jack" Swilling discovered gold along Lynx Creek, southeast of present-day Prescott. A mining camp named Walker quickly grew at the location. Although this was not Arizona's first gold strike (the mineral had been found in 1858 at Gila City on the lower Gila River), the Walker discovery was the first strike of substantial size and great economic promise in central Arizona (Gilbert 1983). As the Walker party scoured the Hassayampa River and Granite Creek, the A. H. Peeples party, a group consisting mostly of Californians led by Pauline Weaver, prospected Arizona's virgin interior by way of La Paz on the Colorado River. A Mexican member of the group, Bernardo Freyes, literally stumbled across gold nuggets atop what would soon be called "Rich Hill," near present-day Wickenburg. Other finds quickly followed and sparked "gold fever" in the mountains of central Arizona (Spude 1976:15–16; Keane and Rogge 1992:43–44).

The initial gold discoveries were in *placer* form. A placer deposit is an alluvial formation in which a mineral weathered out of nearby bedrock has become concentrated by stream action. The simplest method for extracting placer gold used pans or rockers (also called "cradles") to wash nuggets directly from creek beds. Slightly more advanced methods involved the digging of ditches to divert streams into "long toms" (sluices or troughs); such efforts usually involved several miners acting in concert to form and manage ditch companies. Where water was scarce, miners used the painstaking "dry wash" (also called dry concentrating) system, employing screens and bellows rather than flowing water, to separate the heavier gold from the lighter waste rock. Still more labor intensive was the hydraulic method of mining placer gold. This technique used water pressure to break down, wash, and transport placer deposits into a sluice box, where the gold could be trapped and collected. By 1868 at least one such system was in operation along Lynx Creek near the project area (Spude 1976:16).

Placer mining systems usually involved little skill to operate. Unskilled laborers flocked to each "boom" camp, then moved away as boom turned to "bust." Demographic change associated with early placer mining is difficult to measure because camp populations often swelled and collapsed between ten-year federal censuses. However, it does appear that the majority of early placer mine laborers in central Arizona were Mexican (Servin and Spude 1975:44; Spude 1976:18). Their lot was not easy; wherever Mexican *placeros* went, they encountered discriminatory mining regulations. In each new gold field, including Gila City, Walker, and Weaver, the Euroamerican miners passed regulations forbidding Mexicans from owning claims. Sometimes the discrimination took more violent form:

> In at least one recorded instance, at Walker, force was used to expel unwanted Mexican *placeros*. If a Mexican did work in one of the mining districts, it was either in the employ of a Anglo-American claim owner or in the less profitable ravines. Otherwise, the *placero* left the mines with only meager returns [Spude 1976:18].

Discrimination was often embedded in the charters of mining districts. A mining district was a quasi-political entity created by isolated mining communities as a form of self-government; each district chartered its own laws and mining regulations, similar to the incorporation of a new town (Keane and Rogge 1992:127). Fully realizing the value of the minerals they controlled, Euroamerican miners and prospectors near the project area acted quickly to protect their interests by forming the Big Bug Mining District. Although the exact date is not known, incorporation had definitely occurred by July of 1866 (*Arizona Journal-Miner (AJM)* 25 July 1866). Big Bug was one of the earliest mining districts formed in Arizona Territory (Lindgren 1926:126).

Gold fever soon led victims "bitten by the bug" to discover not only placer but also *lode* (vein) deposits of the precious mineral in central Arizona. When the placer camps were still prospering, experienced individuals scouted nearby hills and began to find promising veins. Although Lindgren (1926:3) stated that lode mining in the Big Bug Mining District first occurred around 1875, a variety of historical records indicate that it began a decade earlier (Spude 1976:21).

To work lode deposits, early "hardrock" miners would often consolidate their labor and capital, dig into the vein with pick and shovel, stockpile a few tons of ore, then hire a Mexican or experienced miner to build an *arrastra*, a mule-powered device that dragged milling stones in a circular motion to crush the ore. Quicksilver (mercury) was then added to absorb the crushed gold particles. The amalgam of gold and mercury was drawn off and the mercury was retorted (vaporized), leaving the gold. A more sophisticated technology called stamp milling was installed if a hardrock vein became productive and profitable. A stamp mill, operated by animal, water, or steam power, used descending pestles to crush ore. The arrival of the first stamp mill in a mining district was a much-heralded event. The first such device near the project area may have been the twenty-stamp mill installed at the Bully Bueno Mine in the Bradshaw Mountains in 1864 (Spude 1976:23).

As miners flocked to central Arizona, the U.S. government perceived the need to protect them and the riches they extracted and established a chain of military forts at strategic transportation and mining locations. Among them was Fort Whipple, founded at Del Rio Springs in 1863, then moved to Granite Creek the following year. The latter location became the nucleus for Prescott, the capital of Arizona Territory from 1864 to 1867 and from 1877 to 1889 (Henson 1965).

A symbiotic relationship developed between miners, the military, and the farmers, ranchers, and merchants who supplied them with essential goods. Conspicuously absent from this economic equation were American Indians. As increasing numbers of Euroamericans staked mines, established homesteads, and claimed watering holes, native peoples lost access to traditional hunting and gathering areas. Conflict ensued and quickly escalated.

The Bully Bueno Mine early came to symbolize this conflict and the struggle to make mining profitable. In 1864 George H. Vickroy purchased the Bully Bueno and other gold claims in the Bradshaws and obtained backers in Philadelphia to purchase equipment, including a stamp mill. From the start, high costs and American Indians plagued Vickroy. He paid the phenomenal fee of $118,000 to freight the mill from Leavenworth, Kansas. As his men were establishing camp and erecting the works, Yavapai Indians attacked the Bully Bueno. Raids continued during ensuing years. Vickroy estimated that between 1866 and 1869, American Indians killed or stole 347 mules and killed 11 of his workmen. When Vickroy asked for military protection, he was rebuffed. Finally, in June of 1869, American Indians burned the mine and its camp, including the stamp mill. Vickroy's investors had only charred remains to show for the $426,000 they had invested in the operation (Spude 1976:24).

As the result of such encounters, mine owners frequently said they hired more guards than miners (Henderson 1958:104). Civilians who retaliated against American Indians gained the status of folk heroes. Perhaps the best known of these "Indian fighters" was King S. Woolsey, who in 1864 led a party of 93 civilians on a mission to destroy native encampments (Farish 1916 Vol. 3: 258-272). Today the remains of Woolsey's ranch and stage station can be seen east of the project area near Dewey.

Continuing conflicts between natives and non-natives culminated in the military campaign led by General George S. Crook in the winter of 1872-1873. Crook fought the American Indians using shrewd and innovative tactics. He chose a winter offensive because cold weather would necessitate the use of fires, making native encampments easier to pinpoint, and would decrease the fugitives' mobility. Crook carefully organized pack trains to increase the range of his troops and make them less reliant on fort supplies (Gates 1967:311). Moreover, he incorporated into his forces American Indian scouts who knew the location of traditional encampments. Crook's strategies were effective, resulting in subjugation of most Yavapai and Apache by the spring of 1873. Two years later the Army forcibly removed American Indians from Yavapai County and marched them to the San Carlos Indian Reservation in eastern Arizona.

Following the removal of their foe, miners confronted new challenges. As many placer deposits played out, miners realized that lode deposits were not easily worked. They could literally pluck placer gold from the detritus of river gravel; in contrast, lode gold was laboriously coaxed from Mother Earth. Productive veins were difficult to identify; mines could yield rich returns at the surface but then "pinch out" at depth.

Veins that did not pinch out usually revealed complex ores of lower grade beneath the surface. At the water table, ores became low-grade sulfides, a complex (called "sulphuretts") of base metals including copper, zinc, and lead. Such ores required a more advanced technology for their economical recovery. That technology was smelting, a process accomplished through pyrometallurgy, the application of heat to cause chemical reactions though which end products are obtained. Shipping central Arizona's ores to smelting centers in California and Colorado was too expensive, and there was no reliable and cheap source of power for installing that technology locally. The dilemma of complex ores and what to do with them sent the hardrock mining industry of Yavapai County into a doldrums. Many miners gave up and left the county in the 1860s and 1870s. Those who devised home remedies for working the complex ores—Big

Bug Mine, for example, experimented with elaborate milling techniques—invariably emerged from the experience deeply in debt (Spude 1976:25, 28).

Miners received some relief through the Mining Law, a series of legislative acts that evolved between 1866 and 1872 (Henderson 1958; Leshy 1987). The law clarified the process for establishing a valid claim and obtaining a mining patent from the government. It gave the General Land Office (GLO), the precursor of the BLM, the authority to register claims, coordinate surveys, refer disputes to courts, and facilitate the issuance of patents. The law stipulated that a single claim was not to exceed 1500 feet in length by 600 feet in width and was to have parallel opposite sides (that is, only square, rectangular, or parallelogram-shaped claims were allowable). In the case of lode claims, the apex of the vein (that is, the top of the vein as it protruded from the ground) was to be included within the boundaries of the claim. The miner could follow the vein to the boundaries of the claim but could not go beyond them without filing extension claims for this purpose. For any vein opened on the face of a tunnel, the miner was given exploratory rights extending for 3000 feet; however, the miner was required to follow the extralateral vein down and not surface on another party's claim. Any claim on the face of a tunnel left undeveloped for six months could be declared abandoned and reopened to location. To patent a claim, the miner had to file a survey plat and surveyor's field notes with the GLO, post a notice on the claim, file proof that $500 worth of improvements had been made, and provide two witnesses testifying to the improvements. The GLO was required to publish a notice of the claimant's application for a patent.

Smelting reached eastern Yavapai County in the mid 1870s but had a fitful start. The first smelter appears to have been a 20-ton furnace built in 1876 on the Agua Fria that processed about $350,000 worth of silver from the small but rich Silver Belt Mine before it played out in 1884. The year 1882 witnessed the erection of three smelters: at the United Verde Copper Company's Jerome mine; at the Howells Mine, on Lynx Creek near Walker; and at Stoddard, six miles north of Mayer on the north side of the Agua Fria River. The well-capitalized Jerome operation retained profitability by upgrading its equipment through the years as deeper, lower-grade ores were encountered. The Howells smelter was quickly rendered unprofitable by the high cost of hauling fuel (coke) 60 miles from the nearest railroad, at Ash Fork; it processed $173,825 of lead and silver before closing in less than a year. The 40-ton Stoddard furnace closed in 1884 due to its isolation and low copper prices that year. In 1889 Phelps Dodge, through a subsidiary called the Commercial Mining Company, opened a 50-ton smelter at Boggs, two miles northwest of Mayer on Big Bug Creek, but closed the plant during the Financial Panic of 1893 (Rickard 1987: 191–205).

As fitful as these attempts were, they marked the first truly large scale infusions of capital into the mining industry of eastern Yavapai County. The industry witnessed rapid growth during the period 1880 to 1900 through such capitalization and more astute management. Williams millionaire Edward B. Perrin backed and promoted the Blue Bell Mine and attracted eastern capitalists. The United Verde Extension Mining Company of Jerome branched into ownership of the Red Rock Mine. Other prosperous mines with substantial backing included the Iron Queen, Butternut, Galena Dividend, McCabe, Hackberry, Little Jessie, and Poland (Pape 1987:79–80). In 1899 the local mining industry achieved a milestone when the well-financed Val Verde Smelting Company built a smelter at Val Verde (now Humboldt). Designed to process copper, the smelter had a capacity of 250 tons daily. It burned in September of 1904 but was rebuilt in 1906, then closed, reopened, and changed ownership several times before it was finally dismantled in 1937 (Rickard 1987:204; Swenson 1988:11–13).

Arguably the greatest achievement related to mining near the project area was the building of the Prescott & Eastern Railway in 1898 by a group of investors led by Frank M. Murphy (Pape 1987; Sayre 1985). Murphy and associates had recently completed the Santa Fe, Prescott & Phoenix (SFP&P) Railroad from Ash Fork through Prescott to Phoenix. Connecting the project area to the SFP&P via the Prescott & Eastern gave miners of the area an economical and fast way to import needed goods and to export ore. In addition to machinery and smelting fuel, miners imported large quantities of Oregon pine to construct pipes resistant to corrosion from the sulphuric acid that developed in deep ores and ate through iron and steel pipes (Sayre 1979:50–51). Via Murphy's railroads, area settlers were also able to connect with two transcontinental carriers: the Atlantic & Pacific in northern Arizona Territory and the Southern Pacific in the southern part of the territory. A branch line called the Bradshaw Mountain Railway extended the Prescott & Eastern to the Poland Mine in 1901 and to the Crowned (also called Crown) King Mine in 1904. In 1907 the railway company extended the Poland Branch farther west to tap into the Hassayampa Mining District and thus increase the number of substantial customers ("feeders") along its route (Spude n.d.:7–8).

The Prescott & Eastern Railway gave rise to new settlements and infused life into existing ones. In the project area, small communities developed at shipping points such as Huron and Chaparral stations, while existing towns continued to grow at Dewey, Humboldt, and Mayer. Miners and merchants needed food, and ranches and farms developed in response to their needs. Many of the agricultural properties that dotted the landscape around the turn of the century were acquired pursuant to the Homestead Act and its amendments.

With the arrival of the railroad, the project area and the mines of the Bradshaw Mountains were poised for unprecedented success. In response to national consumer demand for electrical products, copper became the dominant metal of the area. As predicted by Murphy and other capitalists, the copper industry of eastern Yavapai County boomed beginning at the turn of the century. A 1902 map (Figure 1.2) shows the locations of the mines, towns, smelter, and railroad that played main roles in that industry.

According to Sayre (1979), twentieth-century copper mining in the Bradshaw Mountains became the domain of the skilled miner. In response to new technologies, many Northern Europeans with mining experience came to populate the area, while the proportion of unskilled Mexican laborers decreased markedly. The workers who lived in the mining camps of the Bradshaws during its years of copper mining were predominantly young, single, and white. Over forty percent were either foreign born or first-generation Americans of European parentage. Of the foreign-born individuals, over half came from Great Britain, although Italy, Germany, Canada, and the Scandinavian countries were also well represented. Few Mexicans lived in the area; those who did found work as woodcutters, farm laborers, or housekeepers. Also present were a small number of Chinese, who worked almost exclusively as cooks or launderers (Sayre 1979:4–5, 108).

The copper miners of Yavapai County, including those of the Bradshaw Mountains, supported the Western Federation of Miners (WFM). Created in 1893 as a result of violent labor wars in Colorado and Idaho, this union did not reach Yavapai County until the early twentieth century. One of the county's strongest chapters, in McCabe just west of the project area, supported the WFM's 1903 demands for an eight-hour work day and played a leading role in community social and benevolent activities (Sayre 1979:110).

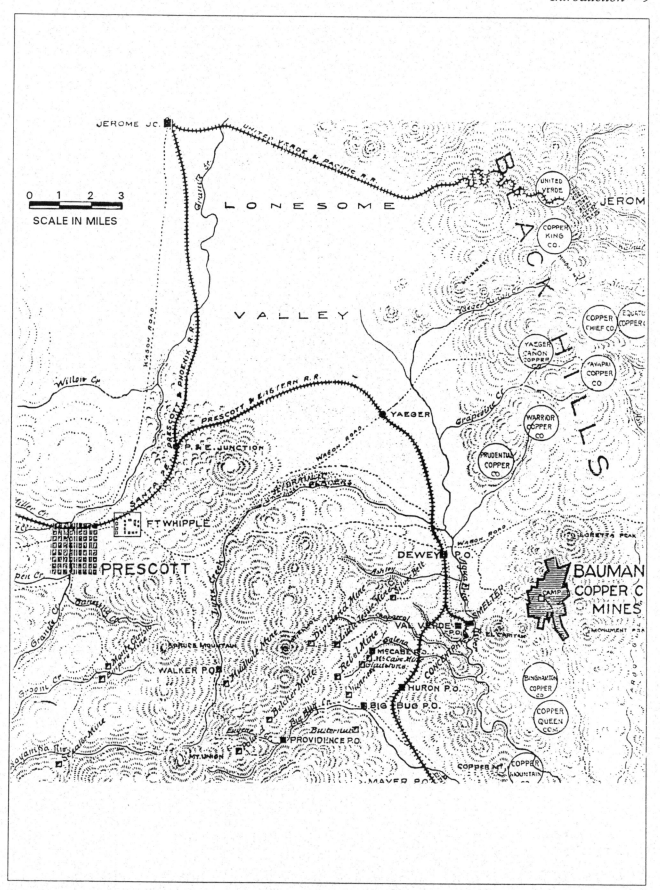

Figure 1.2. Copper mines and related facilities in eastern Yavapai County, 1902 (*The Prospect* 1902).

On the fringes of the copper industry were American Indians. In the late 1890s, many Yavapais and Apaches requested permission to leave the San Carlos Indian Reservation and return to traditional homelands in Yavapai County. Their request was granted in part because cheap labor was needed for the rapidly developing mines. Many American Indians returning to the area lived precariously on the outskirts of towns where they could find employment: Prescott, Mayer, Humboldt, Dewey, Clarkdale, and Jerome (McPherson 1914:1–4). Although agricultural communities were eventually established for the Yavapai and Apache within the county at Camp Verde and Clarkdale, many members of these tribes continued to live and pursue work off-reservation (Morris 1971).

Mining in Yavapai County always walked a fine line between profitability and nonprofitability. Miners were ever-aware of what was known in the industry as "the cut-off point," the point below which it became impossible to run a mine profitably. Numerous factors could affect the cut-off point: a drop in metal prices, a rise in shipping costs, a decrease in the purity of the ore being mined, the repair or replacement of mining equipment, new demands by labor, and so forth. Between 1905 and 1910, mining activity near the project area declined rapidly when complex forces made operations fall below the cut-off point.

Complications involving smelting played a major role in this economic downturn (Spude n.d.:6–7). With the burning of the Val Verde Smelter in September of 1904, ore shipments had to be sent to El Paso in Texas, Silver City in New Mexico, and other distant smelter cities. The increased cost of shipping was a burden most mining companies could not afford. When the smelter was rebuilt in March of 1906, mining again resumed. Unfortunately, the smelter had stockpiled ores at high prices in 1905 and early 1906. When over-production in other regions of the nation cut ore prices in half during the summer of 1907, the smelting company found itself saddled with a financial burden from which it could not recover. The Arizona Smelting Company (the owners of the Val Verde Smelter) went bankrupt and formed the Consolidated Arizona Smelting Company in its place. Financial problems were settled and the smelter was "blown in" (first fired) again in April of 1910. By that date, however, mines in the district were not producing well. Capitalists accordingly lowered their investments in the mines; lower capitalization meant that equipment, lumber, and other needed supplies could not be purchased. Decreased shipping activity in turn lowered railroad revenues. The entire infrastructure of mining near the project area slipped into a state of decay from which it never fully recovered.

Mining witnessed a brief resurgence during World War I, when the demand for industrial metals again stimulated the copper market. However, by 1920 the majority of mines were again dormant. In the mid 1920s, a geologist inspecting ore deposits noted that the mining infrastructure of the area lay in a state of "striking decay" (Lindgren 1926:134). Only the McCabe and Arizona National mines remained in copper production. The Iron King Mine retooled its equipment in the late 1930s and became central Arizona's single largest producer of zinc and lead (Anderson and Blacet 1972:71; Pape 1987:82).

One unusual "mini-boom" occurred in the area from 1933 to 1942. Breaking all precedent, President Franklin D. Roosevelt in 1933 elevated the price of gold to $33.00 per ounce. His action touched off a burst of renewed activity for Arizona's small gold mines, particularly those around Kingman in Mohave County and those near Mayer in Yavapai County (Fagerberg 1989:1). "Low-tech" placer mines in particular prospered during the mini-boom; in the late 1930s and 1940s, hundreds of "cradles" could be seen rocking placer deposits along the Agua Fria River and Big Bug Creek near Mayer (*Phoenix Gazette* 16 November 1940). The boom ended when a 1942 federal action cut off essential materials and equipment for gold mines so that critical war industries of World War II could be better supplied (Fagerberg 1989:1).

During the 1940s, largely as a result of World War II, a few lode mines near the project area produced industrial rather than precious metals. Those producing copper were the Boggs, Lone Pine, Binghampton, Copper Queen, Stoddard, and Hackberry mines; Hackberry produced lead and zinc as well. All large-scale mining activity in the area ceased with the closure of the Iron King in 1969 (Anderson and Blacet 1972:71; Pape 1987:83).

As mining declined, agriculture became the economic mainstay of the area and remained so throughout the rest of the historic period (to 1945) and into the modern period. Cattle and goat ranching became important agricultural activities; truck farming was also practiced. Mayer became a major shipping point for cattle, while Chaparral Siding was used mainly for the shipment of goats (*Phoenix Gazette* 16 November 1940). The most important truck farm of the postwar period has been Young's Farm, a prosperous enterprise at the northern end of the project area.

REPORT ORGANIZATION

This report has 13 chapters. This chapter has introduced the project and described the study area. The second chapter discusses project goals and methods. Chapters 3 through 12 describe testing results at each historic resource and data recovery results at two sites. The final chapter (Chapter 13) provides a summary and discussion of research goals as they are addressed by the data. A number of terms familiar to analysts of historical artifacts but not necessarily to others appear in the site descriptions. These terms are listed and explained in a Glossary following Chapter 13.

A certain amount of redundancy has been built into the report so that each chapter can stand alone. The reason is a conviction that few people read a report such as this one in one sitting, or from cover to cover. Therefore, those interested only in project methods, the project summary, or information pertaining to a specific site need look no further than the appropriate chapters to find the information that most interests them.

The reader may note that all measurements of historic sites and artifacts are in the English system, and the English system *only*. That is because the historic sites described in this report were made in a world that measured objects in feet and inches, and distances in miles. It would be pedantic to describe the sites using metric equivalents.

CHAPTER 2

PROJECT GOALS AND METHODS

Pat H. Stein
Elizabeth J. Skinner

SWCA archaeologists conducted investigations for the State Route 69 project in accordance with clear management objectives and research goals. This chapter describes the objectives and goals and the methods used to address them.

MANAGEMENT OBJECTIVES

Several archaeological studies have been undertaken in and near the SR 69 Mayer to Dewey project area in past and recent years. They range from surveys (Cantley 1988; Dosh 1988; Macnider 1990; Weaver 1989) to excavations (Barnett 1970, 1974, 1975; Caywood 1936; Jeter 1977; Rogers and Weaver 1990; Stone and Kisselburg 1991; Weed and Ward 1970) to overviews (Macnider, Effland, and Ford 1989). However, the most focused archaeological study of the project area was the intensive (Class III) cultural resource survey conducted by Archaeological Research Services, Inc., (ARS) on behalf of the Arizona Department of Transportation (ADOT). The ARS report (Hathaway 1992) described 14 archaeological sites, 16 artifact scatters, 40 isolated occurrences, 19 isolated features, and 34 areas with isolated mining features within the project area.

A Memorandum of Agreement (MOA) for all segments of the SR 69 project was executed in 1993 among ADOT, the Southwest Region of the U.S. Forest Service, the Bureau of Land Management (BLM), the Arizona State Lands Department (ASLD), the Arizona State Historic Preservation Office (SHPO), the Federal Highway Administration, and the Advisory Council on Historic Preservation. In accordance with the terms of the MOA, ADOT (the lead agency) used the Class III survey report for Section 106 consultation on the Mayer to Dewey segment.

The consultation process led to a determination that 13 of the 14 archaeological sites between Mayer and Dewey identified by Hathaway (1992) were potentially eligible for the National Register of Historic Places (National Register/NRHP). The potentially eligible sites were a prehistoric habitation with masonry structures (AZ N:8:27[ASM]); a prehistoric lithic site (AZ N:11:24[ASM]); a multicomponent site (AZ N:11:19[ASM]); eight historic sites (AZ N:11:20, N:11:23, N:11:25, N:12:29, N:12:30, N:12:39, and N:12:40[ASM]); and three *linear* historic sites (each including multiple segments and each known by several site numbers; see Chapter 12). These 13 sites appeared to have the potential to yield important information about the past and were therefore considered eligible under National Register Criterion D. The fourteenth site—AR-03-09-03-238, the Poland Junction Substation—was considered ineligible because of modern disturbance and consequent loss of integrity.

The sites could not be avoided by construction. Therefore, ADOT staff developed a program of archaeological investigations to include two phases: testing and data recovery. The goals of the testing phase were to determine the extent, condition, and significance of each site within the ROW. ADOT specified that the ineligible site was also to be investigated during the testing phase, although minimally and for documentation purposes only.

The SWCA researchers originally envisioned the testing phase as culminating in a single report. However, during the course of the project it became clear that it would make more sense to divide the testing results into two separate reports, one dealing with prehistoric sites and the other dealing with historic sites. With ADOT's approval, SWCA took this approach because: (1) the two categories of sites related to vastly different themes and historic contexts; (2) testing initially appeared to have exhausted the data content of the prehistoric sites but not of the historic ones; and (3) separate reports permitted full discussion of all sites while facilitating the presentation of focused arguments for data recovery.

The testing report for historic sites (Stein 1994) recommended that nine sites be formally determined eligible for the National Register: AZ N:11:19, N:11:20, N:11:23, N:11:25, N:12:30, N:12:39, and N:12:40(ASM), and two linear sites, the Prescott & Eastern Railway segments and the Phoenix to Prescott Highway segments. The report additionally recommended further investigations at two of the eligible sites (AZ N:11:19 and N:11:23[ASM]), as they appeared to contain significant subsurface remains within the project right-of-way (ROW). The testing report included a data recovery program that would mitigate adverse impacts to the two sites. SWCA also submitted to ADOT a cost estimate for the data recovery work (SWCA 1994). The lead agency (ADOT), the SHPO, and other parties to the SR 69 MOA approved the plan with minor revisions. SWCA conducted the data recovery program from March 20 to April 10, 1995, and prepared an interim report of the research findings (Stein 1995). The present report integrates data recovery results from the two excavated sites with testing results from those sites and the other ten original sites, thus summarizing all investigations conducted at the historic sites and providing detailed descriptions of the work and findings at each resource.

Throughout these investigations, SWCA personnel consulted several sources to ensure that management objectives were achieved in accordance with current professional standards. The *Secretary of the Interior's Standards and Guidelines for Archeology and Historic Preservation* (*Federal Register* 1983) provided general guidance concerning how a project of this nature should be conducted. To assess site condition (integrity) and significance (importance)—qualities that relate closely to NRHP eligibility—SWCA consulted *National Register Bulletin 15: How to Apply the National Register Criteria for Evaluation* (USDI National Park Service [NPS] 1991a); *National Register Bulletin 16A: How to Complete the National Register Registration Form* (NPS 1991b); and *National Register Bulletin 36: Guidelines for Evaluating and Registering Historical Archeological Sites and Districts* (Townsend, Sprinkle, and Knoerl 1993). Since several sites in the project area related to historic mining, *National Register Bulletin 42: Guidelines for Identifying, Evaluating, and Registering Historic Mining Properties* (Noble and Spude 1992) was also helpful. Other useful guides for assessing site extent, condition, and significance were the historic context studies recently published by the Arizona SHPO. The SHPO contexts of greatest applicability to the SR 69 project were those related to railroading (Janus 1989) and gold and silver mining (Keane and Rogge 1992).

RESEARCH GOALS

In its proposal for archaeological investigations, SWCA (1993) articulated a number of research goals that appeared from the outset to be potentially addressable with data from the project area. ADOT (1993:23) had instructed bidders to relate research goals to the thematic categories defined in the Prescott National Forest (PNF) *Cultural Resources Overview* (Macnider, Effland, and Ford 1989). Based on the survey report (Hathaway 1992) and a preproposal visit to the sites, SWCA investigators predicted that the

SR 69 historic sites could yield data relating to the themes of Demography, Technology and Industry, and Transportation and Commerce as defined in the PNF overview.

Research Issues Related to the Theme of Demography

Demography is the statistical study of the dynamics of human populations in terms of quantities, distribution, and composition. "This would include topics such as ethnicity, continuity of populations, population movements, age and sex composition, functional (work related) and nutritional stress on a population, abandonments, and the nature of population distribution" (Macnider, Effland, and Ford 1989:9). In the PNF overview, thematic categories associated with demography are growth and decline of population, population aggregation and/or dispersion across a landscape, population movements, ethnicity of population, and quality of life.

From the beginning of the archaeological investigations, the project area appeared capable of yielding an interesting and important set of demographic data relating to the late nineteenth and early twentieth centuries. Sources such as Thorpe (1978) and Swenson (1988) indicated that the study area was a cultural mosaic during this time period. An imported Greek and Italian workforce built the Prescott & Eastern Railway, members of Chinese *tongs* served in Euroamerican establishments, and a large Yavapai Indian camp flourished at Mayer. A major research goal was to establish a demographic profile of the historic Mayer-Dewey area in general and of project area sites in particular. By studying archival, oral-historical, and archaeological data, SWCA archaeologists hoped to determine the ethnicity of persons associated with the cultural resources, the ages and genders of these persons, the approximate length of their association with the sites, where they came from, and what became of them when they left the sites.

The project area also appeared potentially capable of yielding data relating to issues of acculturation. Specifically, SWCA proposed to measure the degree to which American Indians were assimilated into Euroamerican material culture in comparison with other areas of historic Arizona (Jones 1969; Rogge, Keane, and McWaters 1994; Teague 1980).

In addition, the project area appeared capable of yielding significant demographic data relating to quality-of-life issues. Survey data suggested that some of the sites were associated with mining, while others related more directly to railroading or homesteading. Therefore, a goal of the research was to compare the quality of life of a mining site, for example, with that of a contemporaneous homestead, as reflected in material remains such as food-related items and proprietary/medicinal artifacts. Archival sources (including but not limited to historic-era newspapers) were deemed likely to reveal rich details about these issues.

Research Issues Related to the Theme of Technology and Industry

The Prescott National Forest overview defined this theme as the study of the development of techniques and processes by which a society controls or modifies the natural environment. Technology, the material means of adapting to an environment, includes both the techniques used to make artifacts and the methods used to acquire materials for manufacturing (Macnider, Effland, and Ford 1989:11). Thematic categories within the Technology/Industry theme include modification of the landscape, engineering technology, exploitation of raw materials, food preservation and storage, architecture, and material culture.

Historic sites in the project area appeared to have the potential to yield significant data relating to the technology and industry of late nineteenth and early twentieth century mining and railroading (for a discussion of the latter subject, see the third research theme, discussed below). In particular, SWCA archaeologists thought that data from the project area could make an important contribution to the rapidly growing body of archaeological literature on mining in the West (Ayres 1984; Hardesty 1988; Keane and Rogge 1992; Teague 1980). Per definitions in *National Register Bulletin 42* (Noble and Spude 1992:9–12), the SR 69 sites appeared to represent the three major stages of ore processing: extraction, beneficiation (upgrading of ore to increase its value), and refining. Therefore, site data appeared likely to contribute to an understanding of how work spaces were organized, how the various tasks of mineral exploitation were phased, what equipment was used, and how technology differed through time and among sites.

Survey data suggested that the project area contained small-scale, informal mining operations as well as large and intricate processing plants. Larger, more complex mining operations were engineer-designed systems with every part working in harmony to reduce costs, increase production, and maximize profits:

> Especially after the 1890s, mining engineers developed standard systems for mine operation. *The Mines Handbook* [sic] by Peele [originally published 1918] describes in detail most of the components of the mine engineers' system. This system, which integrated massive operations to produce economies of scale, corresponded with the rise of big business in America. Massive operations created phenomenal profits, which often went into bigger plants. These engineer-designed complexes help define the twentieth-century operations at Minnesota's iron ranges, the copper mines of the Far West, the lead and zinc of the tri-state region of the Mississippi Valley..., and the big gold mines of Cripple Creek, Colorado, and the Homestake of Lead, South Dakota [Noble and Spude 1992:13].

With this statement in mind, SWCA researchers proposed to compare small, informal mining sites with larger, engineer-designed sites in terms of site longevity, productivity, and contribution to the economic growth of the Mayer-Dewey area. A second goal was to compare and contrast the large, engineered systems of the study area to those described in *The Mining Engineers Handbook* (Peele 1927), looking at the interpretation of standard systems and their application to local conditions.

At the conclusion of the testing phase, SWCA researchers defined an additional goal related to this theme. Testing revealed the presence of significant subsurface features at Sites AZ N:11:19(ASM) and AZ N:11:23(ASM), roughly contemporaneous sites located at Huron. The former property represented placer mining, while the latter represented, in part, lode mining (it was also the site of a train depot). Therefore, the two sites presented the opportunity to conduct an interesting comparative case study of two different mining technologies at one locality in the early twentieth century. SWCA estimated that through additional archival, archaeological, and oral-historical research, comparison of the material culture and quality of life of the two sites would be possible, permitting a deeper understanding of factors that contributed to the success or failure of mining claims at Huron at the beginning of this century. Data recovery would also yield information on how space was organized and utilized at these two different types of mining sites.

Research Issues Related to the Theme of Transportation and Communication

The PNF overview defines this theme as the study of "the development trends related to travel as well as the conveyance of materials from one place to another" (Macnider, Effland, and Ford 1989:13). Thematic categories within the theme of Transportation and Communication are transportation routing, nodes of transportation (stage stations, railroad stations, and so forth), and methods for the transfer of materials and information. Survey data indicated that the project area could yield an important body of data concerning changes wrought in the Mayer-Dewey area by the arrival of the railroad and the improvement of roads.

October 15, 1898, marked a milestone for the project area: the arrival of the Prescott & Eastern Railway's first train to Mayer. Historians have convincingly maintained that the railroad had a profound effect on the development of Yavapai County:

It gave direction and impetus to the development of the mining industry in the area south of Prescott. The rail brought in almost as much Eastern capital as it shipped out ore. The mineral deposits in the area were vast and spread out southwest like a large fan from Jerome. The P. & E. delivered shipments of heavy equipment and mining machinery to hundreds of Bradshaw Mountain mines. A large mill and smelter were constructed near Bowers' Ranch on the Agua Fria River. The sound of stamp mills, gasoline powered hoists, and general construction soon filled the Bradshaw Range as mining operations expanded [Sayre 1985:9].

The railroad exerted a profound influence not only on mining but also on other industries and the material culture of everyday life. "The P. & E. didn't transport just mining supplies and ore. The number of passengers and amount of personal freight carried on the line were substantial at the turn of the century" (Sayre 1985:9).

Many changes came to Mayer with the railroad. For instance, we could now have ice....The railroad was, of course, good for business. Cattlemen and sheepmen felt the difference. Twice a year 300,000 sheep passed through Mayer and shearing pens were set up close to town where the greater part of the sheep were sheared....The railroad made business easier for the ranchers [Thorpe 1978:155].

Resources in the project area appeared to have the potential to yield significant data regarding railroads and roads as agents of culture change. Using archival records and historic artifacts, SWCA archaeologists proposed to date each historic site closely and tightly and to compare pre-railroad and post-railroad sites. If the data did not allow division of sites along this temporal scale, then pre-automotive sites would be compared with post-automotive ones. The hypothesis to be tested was that artifact diversity would increase and supply networks would expand as transportation systems were improved.

SWCA researchers also thought that segments of the railroad and roads within the project area had the potential to yield valuable information concerning construction methods and materials. For example, previous writers (Myrick 1968; Robertson 1986; Sayre 1985) had provided much information about the history of the Prescott & Eastern Railway but little information about the material culture of this important historic property. By consulting references such as Barry (1876), SWCA proposed to describe and identify railroad hardware and features along the right-of-way portions of the line and thus provide insight into a neglected aspect of the railroad's past.

SWCA defined an additional research goal related to this theme at the conclusion of the testing phase, recommending data recovery at AZ N:11:23(ASM), the Huron Station site, which appeared to contain significant subsurface remains. Archival research conducted during the testing phase indicated that few, if any, historical photographs of this stop along the Prescott & Eastern Railway had survived. Sayre (1985:55) produced a sketch map of the facility's plan, but long after the station was abandoned and its buildings had been removed. Excavation of station remains encountered during testing would provide the opportunity to learn specific details about its buildings and structures and to understand how the work space was organized to accommodate various activities.

PROJECT METHODS

The archaeological investigations sought information from three data classes (data sets) to address the management objectives and research goals of the project. The SWCA investigators studied archival data in conjunction with archaeological and interview data to try to gain a balanced and broad understanding of the SR 69 historic sites. The initial phase of the work was testing of twelve sites, followed by data recovery at two of the sites.

Testing Phase

The first step in the testing program was checking the accuracy of the legal description of each historic site recorded in the Class III survey report (Hathaway 1992). The Principal Investigator briefly visited each site, checked its plot on topographic maps in the survey report, and determined whether each location was correctly described. This step was of crucial importance for the historical research to follow, as some of the main research repositories (such as the BLM State Office) would refer to historic properties primarily by legal description. The check revealed that the legal descriptions of all but one of the historic sites were correct in the survey report.

The next step was historical research to learn about the project area and its sites. Sources included historic-era maps, photographs, manuscripts, newspapers, published and unpublished sources, and miscellaneous other data. These materials were in repositories that included the Sharlot Hall Museum (Prescott), the Yavapai County Recorder's Office (Prescott), the BLM State Office (Phoenix), the Prescott National Forest (Prescott), the Arizona Department of Library, Archives, and Public Records (Phoenix), the Region 3 Forest Museum (currently in storage at the Prescott National Forest), the Jerome Historical Society (Jerome), the Arizona Mines and Minerals Museum (Phoenix), Arizona Public Service Company (Phoenix), the SHPO (Phoenix), the Arizona Historical Foundation (Tempe), the Arizona Historical Society (Tucson), and the state's three universities.

A list of keywords and key names relevant to the project area (for example, "Big Bug," "Dewey," "Mayer," "George Hull") facilitated the search for archival material in the manual or automated card catalogs at the libraries, museums, universities, and historical societies. As SWCA's knowledge of the project area grew, the list expanded to include approximately 50 entries and proved of great use in locating archival material efficiently.

The search for additional details concerning historic sites in the project area led SWCA researchers to several repositories distant from Arizona. Case files for the two homesteads represented by sites in the project area came from the National Archives in Washington, D.C. The Kansas State Historical Society (Topeka), which houses a collection pertaining to the Atchison, Topeka & Santa Fe Railroad and its affiliates, provided more information about the Prescott & Eastern Railway, and the Illinois State Historical Society and the Springfield Public Library were sources of information regarding the Gray Eagle Reduction Plant (Site AZ N:12:39[ASM]), a facility once owned by an Illinois firm.

Historical research was followed by on-site investigations. Bearing in mind that the management objective was to determine significance, condition, and extent of remains within the ROW but not to exhaust such remains, and that ADOT engineers might make design changes before beginning construction, SWCA attempted to assemble the data needed while disturbing the sites as little as possible.

Field personnel cleared each site of vegetation as necessary to better define features and artifact distributions, then used an alidade and plane table to map each site, including portions of sites inside as well as outside the ROW so that resources could be appraised in their entirety. The crews established secure datum points to allow the mapping system to be re-established later if necessary, then photographed, measured, and described in field notes every feature and artifact cluster.

Portions of sites within the ROW required additional investigative techniques. Hand testing of ROW features or artifact areas that indicated the potential for depth was by means of test pits, test trenches, or occasionally shovel pits. The decision to use a trench rather than a pit or shovel test in any given instance depended on the nature and size of the feature or artifact area being tested. Excavation of trenches, pits, and tests was in arbitrary 6-inch levels unless natural strata were present that could be used for vertical control. Documentation of test units included stratigraphic descriptions, plan views and profiles, and photographs. The soil from test units was generally not screened unless it contained rich cultural remains; in such instances, 1/4-inch mesh was used. Field personnel gridded and collected portions of sites within the ROW unless the ROW area contained so few artifacts that gridding was counterproductive (for example, several ROW areas contained fewer than 100 artifacts). In these cases, the Principal Investigator conducted an in-field analysis of every ROW item. Virtually all of the artifacts at the historic sites were mass-produced, mechanically made items that were readily identifiable.

Artifact collection focused on diagnostic artifacts, but "diagnostic" was broadly defined to include artifacts indicative of function, dating, or, in the case of containers, size, form, and contents. For example, included in diagnostic artifacts were cans or can fragments bearing all or an identifiable portion of a maker's mark, a trade name, or a distinctive seam or method of closure. All test units were backfilled at the conclusion of testing.

Three criteria guided laboratory analysis of collected material: compatibility with project goals, ease of data manipulation, and facility of use by future researchers. The analyst first sorted the artifacts by material (glass, metal, ceramic, and other) and then analyzed them by function and form. Functional interpretations, deemed most relevant to the research goals stated above, used the Sprague (1981) classification, as modified by Hull-Walski and Ayres (1989:36). This classificatory scheme consists of 17 functional categories: Food, Food Preparation and Consumption, Household Furnishings, Household Maintenance, Architecture (construction-related), Leisure and Recreation, Medical and Health, Personal Items, Coins and Tokens, Religious Articles, Transportation, Tools and Hardware, Machinery, Mining and Quarrying, Communication, Miscellaneous (artifacts with functions that do not readily fit into any other category), and Unidentified (cannot be identified as to function, or cannot be identified at all).

The analyst took great pains to identify collected artifacts as closely as possible in order to place them in accurate functional categories. For example, a wagon-bow staple could easily be misidentified as merely a staple and then misclassified by placing it in the Tools and Hardware category, missing its "true" function in relation to the site. Wagon-bow staples are used in wagons; thus, in the SR 69 analysis the staple would be placed in the Transportation category. However, if the wagon-bow staple had been noticeably modified for another use (if, for example, it had been reworked into a chisel), then the staple would be placed in the Tools and Hardware category.

Numerous references were consulted to identify the function and dating of the artifacts, including but not limited to Ayres (1984), Fontana and Greenleaf (1962), Gates and Ormerod (1982), Godden (1964), Goodman (1993), Herskovitz (1978), Hull-Walski and Ayres (1989), Lehner (1980), Periodical Publishers Association (1934), Rock (1981, 1987), Simonis (1992), Steward (1969), Teague (1980), Toulouse (1971), Ward, Abbink, and Stein (1977), and Zumwalt (1980). In the following chapters, all artifact identifications are from these sources unless otherwise noted. The testing phase did not yield any faunal or botanical remains requiring special analysis.

Data Recovery Phase

Testing results indicated and the consultation process confirmed the need for data recovery at the two historic sites that appeared to contain significant subsurface remains within the right-of-way: AZ N:11:19(ASM) and AZ N:11:23(ASM), both at the historic community of Huron along the former Prescott & Eastern Railway. Subsequent archaeological investigations therefore focused on these resources.

The data recovery phase began with more in-depth archival research on Huron and its environs than had been attempted during the testing phase, and examination of additional archives yielded new data. Several sources proved especially productive: U.S. Census Enumeration Records (microfilmed copies are on file at Northern Arizona University [NAU] and the Flagstaff-Coconino County Public Library); Santa Fe Railroad right-of-way maps (currently owned by the Old Trails Museum and housed at La Posada, both in Winslow); issues of the former Prescott newspaper called *The Arizona Journal-Miner* (microfilmed copies on file at NAU); issues of *The (Prescott) Prospect*, a mining news supplement published once each year in the early twentieth century (on file, Sharlot Hall Museum); records pertaining to the Wingfield family (housed at the Camp Verde Historical Society); and a prospectus from the Poland Mine near the project area (copy on file at the Sharlot Hall Museum). Through information in the Poland Mine prospectus, SWCA located and obtained (from the Western History Department of the Denver Public Library) a copy of a rare historical photo taken between Huron and Poland Junction in the early twentieth century (see Figure 4.4).

The first step in data recovery fieldwork was re-establishing the grids used during the testing phase and gridding in 10 × 10-foot units those portions of the sites within the ROW known from testing to contain subsurface cultural material. At AZ N:11:19(ASM) the gridded area totaled approximately 40 × 40 feet. At AZ N:11:23(ASM) the three gridded areas—the remains of the train depot platform (Feature 1), a terrace containing a depression (Feature 3), and a trash concentration (Trash Area A)—totaled approximately 200 × 150 feet. Field crews manually stripped (hand-stripped or HS units) deposits within the grids in arbitrary 6-inch horizontal levels, as no natural strata could be detected, and screened the soil through 1/4-inch mesh. In general, cultural materials at both sites were confined to the top four inches of soil, a medium to coarse loamy sand. Known features and any features found during stripping were excavated; the methods used depended on the type and depth of the feature (details are in the site descriptions in this report). Field records included excavation unit forms for each unit, plan view drawings of each feature, profiles of features with depth, and photodocumentation in black-and-white prints and color slides. Feature fill was collected for faunal and botanical analyses.

Analysis of excavated artifacts began in the field with separation by material type. Nondiagnostic artifacts (for example, scrap metal, nails, window glass, and bottle body shards) were described, classified, and tabulated in the field by material type, form, and use; these artifacts were not collected. Diagnostic artifacts (as defined above for the testing phase) from HS units and other areas within the ROW underwent laboratory analysis. To ensure compatibility with testing phase data, for the data recovery phase artifact analysis the analyst used the same laboratory procedures and reference sources. A glossary of terms used to describe historical artifacts, such as can types and special units of measurement, follows the body of the report.

Data recovery at the two sites yielded a small amount of faunal material but no botanical material other than trace amounts of ash and charcoal. John Goodman, SWCA faunal analyst, sorted and counted the bone and examined each specimen for diagnostic characteristics and alterations due to burning, gnawing by rodents or carnivores, digestive processes, water wear, mineralization, and butchering and other cultural modifications. Goodman based taxonomic classifications on external macromorphological attributes of identifiable specimens, in all cases identifying specimens to the lowest taxonomic category possible. Unidentifiable bone fragments were categorized by diaphysial thickness and curvature or other characteristics. The analyst's comparative vertebrate collection facilitated identification of diagnostic specimens.

Throughout the project (testing and data recovery phases), the investigators also collected interview data by questioning persons knowledgeable about the project area, its environs, or mining and railroading history/technology. The following individuals graciously shared their knowledge with SWCA: Ken Kimsey (Forest Historian, PNF), Jim McKie (Forest Archaeologist, PNF), Nyal Niemuth (Mining Historian, Department of Mines and Mineral Resources), Mason Coggin (mining technology expert, Department of Mines and Mineral Resources), John Sayre (author, *Ghost Railroads of Central Arizona*), David Myrick (author, *Pioneer Arizona Railroads*), Norm Tessman (Historian, Sharlot Hall Museum), Karolyn Jensen (Historical Archaeologist, Archaeological Consulting Services), Jeff Hathaway (Historical Archaeologist, ARS), Stan Young (co-owner, Young's Farm), Pat O'Hara (mining consultant, Prescott), Kevin Harper (former Tribal Archaeologist, Yavapai-Prescott Tribe), Lonnie Morgan (former Tribal Para-Archaeologist, Yavapai-Prescott Tribe), and Donald Hardesty (Professor of Anthropology, University of Nevada/Reno).

The Arizona State Museum is the permanent repository for all data associated with the State Route 69 Mayer to Dewey project. Materials curated included all field records and photographs, analyzed artifacts, and interview data.

CHAPTER 3

AR-03-09-03-238
THE POLAND JUNCTION SUBSTATION

Pat H. Stein
Elizabeth J. Skinner

MANAGEMENT HISTORY

Site AR-03-09-03-238, the Poland Junction Substation, constructed in 1909, was substantially modified in 1969 and is still in use. Arizona Public Service Company owns the substation, which occupies land administered by Prescott National Forest.

The site is in the N½SE¼NE¼ of Section 5, Township 12 North, Range 1 East, on the USGS Poland Junction, Arizona, 7.5 minute quadrangle (Figure 3.1). It is at the junction of Forest Road (FR) 261 and current State Route 69, approximately 4 miles southwest of Humboldt and 3.5 miles northwest of Mayer. This location has relatively little vegetation and low local relief. The archaeological property measures 525 feet north-south by 300 feet east-west and encompasses a total of 3.6 acres.

Cantley (1988) first inventoried the site during an archaeological survey of a proposed access road to the substation. The survey report included two concentrations of cultural material: Locus 1, consisting of concrete features believed to be the remains of the original substation and associated structures; and Locus 2, consisting of concrete remnants thought to mark the former location of a building and retaining wall related to the substation. Cantley recognized that Poland Junction Substation formed part of the Childs-Irving Hydroelectric Generating System, a historic resource then (1988) in the process of being evaluated for eligibility to the National Register of Historic Places (NRHP) (Macnider, Effland, and Howard 1988). Noting that the original components of the substation had been removed in 1969 and that all original buildings and most historic trash had been taken from the site, Cantley concluded that the site lacked integrity and therefore could not be considered a contributing element of the Childs-Irving system. This conclusion resulted in a "no effect" determination for the proposed access road (McKie 1988).

Archaeological Research Services, Inc., (Hathaway 1992) recorded the site in more detail during the Class III survey for SR 69. Hathaway produced a good site map depicting 10 features: two roads, a cairn, a concrete basin with trash, two low-density artifact scatters, concrete remnants of structural foundations, two small concrete pads believed to be bases for transmission-line towers, and the modern substation. ADOT staff determined that the proposed widening of SR 69 would impact only Feature J, one of the possible transmission tower pads, and specified that archaeological investigations were to be limited to documentation of Feature J, with no subsurface testing.

SWCA investigators conducted archival research on the facility and the electrical system of which it was a part, plane-table mapped the entire site, recorded Feature J by cleaning, photographing, and sketching it, and analyzed all artifacts found within the proposed (right-of-way) ROW. SWCA also discovered and documented an additional feature within the ROW (Feature L).

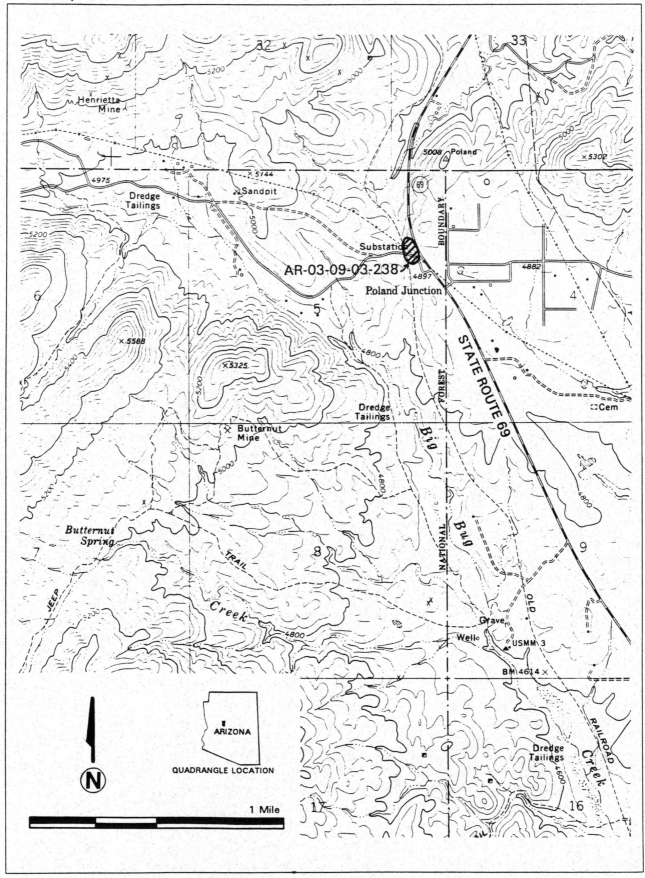

Figure 3.1.   Location of Site AR-03-09-03-238, the Poland Junction Substation.   Base map is Poland Junction, Arizona, USGS 7.5′ quadrangle, 1975.

HISTORICAL DATA

The Poland Junction Substation is part of a power generation and transmission system that has served central Arizona in historic and modern times. To understand the substation's function and to appreciate its significance, it is important to look at the system as a whole in historical perspective.

The story of the Poland Junction Substation begins in the Verde Valley. In the 1880s a Yavapai County cattleman named Lew Turner discovered immense springs that gushed from rocks one hundred yards or so from the Apache Trail (a U.S. military road that paralleled the Verde River). Turner noted that objects dropped in the waters of the springs became coated with travertine and named the spot Fossil Creek (Biddle 1976). Twenty years later, in February of 1900, Turner filed for water rights to the springs. By that time the technology for generating electricity from running water had become well established, and the cattleman-turned-entrepreneur wanted to apply that technology to Fossil Creek by developing a power plant to serve the Verde Valley (Masson 1910).

Turner needed two things to launch his plan, working capital and a feasibility study, and he addressed both issues without delay. His preliminary studies drew the attention of investors by late 1901. Engineers employed by the investors made more accurate measurements of the waters and found that 43 cubic feet per second (28,000,000 gallons per day) flowed regularly from the springs, day after day, season after season. An often-recounted tale is that the man employed to gauge the springs, J. C. Palmer, gave up in disgust after taking measurements three times a day for two years. The springs, he concluded, ran with monotonous regularity, the volume of water varying only during episodes of rainfall (Biddle 1976; Masson 1910).

The feasibility study demonstrated that a large potential market for electricity existed in the mines and towns of Yavapai County. Fifty-five miles west-northwest of the construction site lay Prescott, a populous county seat and popular health resort. Forty-five miles to the northwest lay the town of Jerome, where Senator W. A. Clark of Montana was expanding his United Verde Mine, the richest individually owned copper mine in the world (Cleland 1952:239). Fifty miles southwest were the Bradshaw Mountains, one of the richest mineral belts in Arizona.

The need to use powered equipment to procure and concentrate the area's low-grade ores before shipment meant that lack of a reliable and inexpensive power source hindered the mining industry in this region. Even small mines needed from 100 to 200 horsepower to drive their stamp mills, air compressors, or hoists. Fuel (coal, oil, or wood) could be imported to generate power on-site at mines, but this was expensive, thanks in no small part to the tendency of railroads to charge exorbitant freight rates. A mine using a small coal-, oil-, or wood-fired engine could expect to pay over $250 per year to generate its own power. Such high costs exacted their toll on many a mine and could bankrupt marginally productive ones (Effland and Macnider 1991).

Senator Clark saw the advantages of water power in a locality where on-site power generation was expensive and therefore contracted for more than one-third of the capacity of the proposed plant. With the United Verde contract in hand, the Electric Operating Construction Company began work on the plant in April of 1908 (Effland and Macnider 1991:8.8; Masson 1910:4). A month earlier, the assets of the company had passed to the Arizona Power Company (APC), a corporation based in Maine.

Building the power plant was no easy matter. The nearest rail station was Blue Bell, a siding on the Bradshaw Mountain Railway. A wagon road 50 miles long had to be built so that material and equipment could be hauled from the railroad to the construction site. Hauling equipment alone required more than three hundred men (Sayre 1985:75), plus mule teams. The hauling of the largest piece of apparatus, the generator stator, required a 26-mule team (Biddle 1976:5).

Generator 1 of the powerhouse went on-line in June of 1909, followed later that year by Generators 2 and 3 (Biddle 1976:6). The powerhouse was named "Childs" for a local rancher (Granger 1960:337). The resulting system was a technological marvel that employed many innovative features. It included an intake, a 12,000-foot flume, tunnels, a syphon, a storage reservoir (named Stehr Lake), a 4800-foot pressure pipe, the powerhouse, transmission lines, and substations. No company in the United States could manufacture steel pipe strong enough to withstand the pressure of the Childs penstock, so engineers had pipe custom-made by the Krupp Company in Germany and then shipped via Cape Horn to Los Angeles, Blue Bell, and finally Fossil Creek. Towers for the transmission line also required creative engineering. Wooden ones could not be carried by burro, and steel ones had not yet been invented, so engineers adapted steel windmill towers to the task at hand, purchasing them from the U.S. Wind Engine and Pump Company of Batavia, Illinois (Biddle 1976:5; Masson 1910:11).

Engineer Raymond S. Masson designed a delivery system praised for its simplicity and logic (*Electrical World* 1910a). From Childs, 44,000 volts of power flowed along two sets of towers arranged side by side but operating somewhat independently. At the Poland Junction Substation the lines forked, with one branch continuing to Prescott and the other going to Jerome. The Poland Junction Substation, and others at Walker (on the Prescott fork), Prescott, and Jerome, had two basic functions: they relayed voltage (via high-tension transmission lines) to the next substation, and they reduced voltage so that it could be distributed (via low-tension distribution lines) to customers in the vicinity. The substations reduced power to 11,000 volts and delivered it to customers at 440 volts, 60 cycles, three-phase (Masson 1910:11–12). In designing the Childs-Irving system, Masson observed that power failures in other systems were caused more by "engineer error" (miscommunications between powerhouse and substation operators, resulting in accidental or unintentional openings of switches and circuit breakers) than by technical malfunctions. Therefore, he devised a system in which only the powerhouse operator could control the whole system and, if necessary, switch power from a failing line to a functioning one (Masson 1910:10–11).

Sayre (1985:57) suggests that the Poland Junction Substation was built in 1911. However, a 1910 map (Figure 3.2) indicates that the facility was operating at least a year earlier, while a newspaper article (*Jerome Miner News* [*JMN*] 1909) hints that the facility was functioning by June of 1909. The map indicates that the substation transmitted power to Prescott and Jerome and delivered power directly to the Mount Elliott Mine. According to the same document, the substation was about to start delivering power to the Little Jessie, McCabe, and Lelan mines. The 1909 newspaper article stated that the Arizona Smelting Company of Humboldt had also become a customer. It is thus reasonable to conclude that the Poland Junction Substation was built not in 1911 (as Sayre suggests) but two years earlier.

The hydroelectric system immediately injected new life into the faltering mining industry of eastern Yavapai County. "The availability of dependable and cheaper power sources enabled the mining industry to expand in several directions: (1) larger, up-to-date smelters and stamp mills were built that could process larger amounts of ore more efficiently, (2) many mining companies could focus on the upgrading of their machinery, and (3) miners could develop deeper portions of their mines" (Effland and Macnider 1991:8.10–8.11).

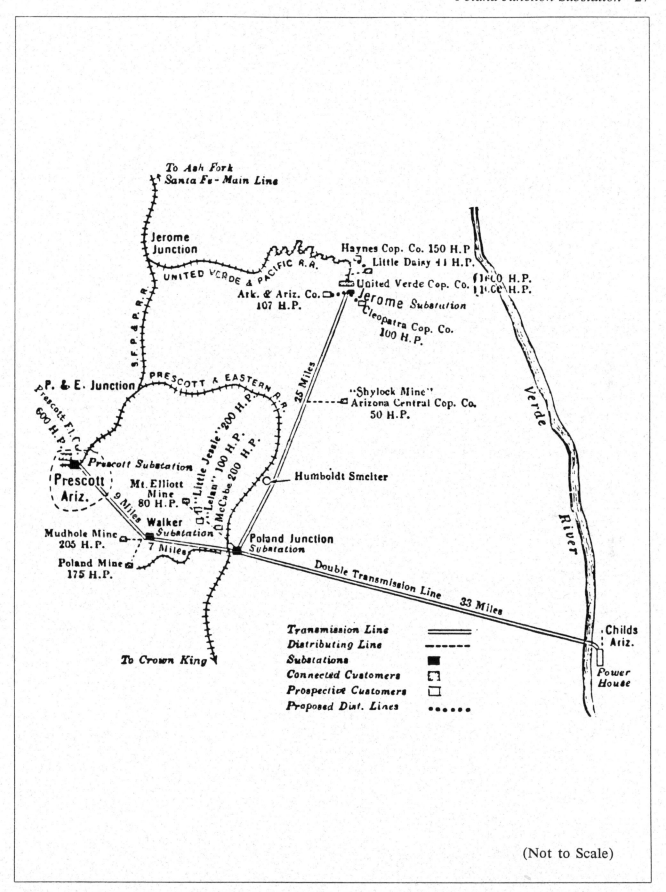

Figure 3.2. 1910 map of Childs Power Plant and transmission system (*Electrical World* 1910b).

Archival sources document innumerable ways in which the power system benefited the area. After becoming a customer in 1909, the smelter at Humboldt purchased and installed thousands of dollars worth of equipment and hired a workforce exceeding 60 laborers (*JMN* 1909). By the end of 1912, the smelting company had added one of the biggest concentrating mills in the state (*Prescott Journal Miner* [*PJM*] 6 December 1912). In 1910 the United Verde Mine used some of its new current to power a gigantic compressor that provided air to the deepest tunnels of its mine (*PJM* 28 November 1910). United Verde converted all its machinery to hydroelectric power and petitioned the power company for additional horsepower (Effland and Macnider 1991:8.11). Perhaps the companies that benefited most were the smaller mines that had been unable to produce power economically enough to exploit their finds. By February of 1910 the manager of the power company recognized that although the company had few large customers, it had myriad small ones who were desperate to receive power and could therefore be assessed higher rates per kilowatt hour (Effland and Macnider 1991:8.11).

The power company expanded the system during 1915 and 1916. The impetus for the change was the decision by United Verde to construct a new smelter that would require additional power. War had broken out in Europe, leading to higher prices for copper and greater profits for copper mines such as United Verde. Agreements between the copper and power companies led to the construction of a second powerhouse and a direct, 40,000-volt transmission line from Childs to Jerome and to the new smelter at Clarkdale. A 1916 map (Figure 3.3) shows the resulting system. The new powerhouse, designated Irving, went on-line in May of 1916.

Although the new plant approximately doubled the output of the hydroelectric system, demand outpaced supply. By February of 1917 the system had more potential customers on its waiting list than it could possibly accommodate, and during that year the company built an auxiliary, 10,000-horsepower steam plant on the Verde about three miles from Clarkdale. The plant was called TAPCO, the acronym of its builder, the Arizona Power Company.

The end of World War I brought a decline in the copper industry and a slump in the economy of eastern Yavapai County. With a surplus of energy in its Childs-Irving system, the APC arranged to divert some of the voltage to rapidly growing Phoenix. In 1919 the company constructed a transmission line between Fossil Creek and Phoenix, a distance of 72 miles, at the expense of the Pacific Gas and Electric Company (PG&E). By 1920 the Childs-Irving system was meeting an estimated seventy percent of the power needs of Phoenix (with a population of 44,000). Increasing demands by the metropolis led to an upgrade of the system in 1926 (Effland and Macnider 1991:8.14).

Other changes followed. In 1927 a new 44,000-volt transmission line from the Prescott Substation to Constellation supplied mines in the Wickenburg area. In 1929–1930, following its purchase of the Ash Fork and Seligman electric works, APC built a transmission line from the Prescott Substation northward to those towns. In 1933 the contract between APC and PG&E's successor, the Central Arizona Light and Power Company (CALAPCO), was canceled; however, even after that date, the Childs-Irving system delivered power to the Phoenix area in times of critical power shortage. In 1949 CALAPCO purchased APC and in 1952 merged with Arizona Edison Company to form Arizona Public Service Company (APS).

Designation of the Fossil Creek property as a National Historic Mechanical Engineering Landmark marked recognition of the technological significance of the Childs-Irving system (Biddle 1976). The property received further recognition in 1992 with listing on the NRHP (Effland and Macnider 1991) for its historical importance (Criterion A) and its engineering significance (Criterion C).

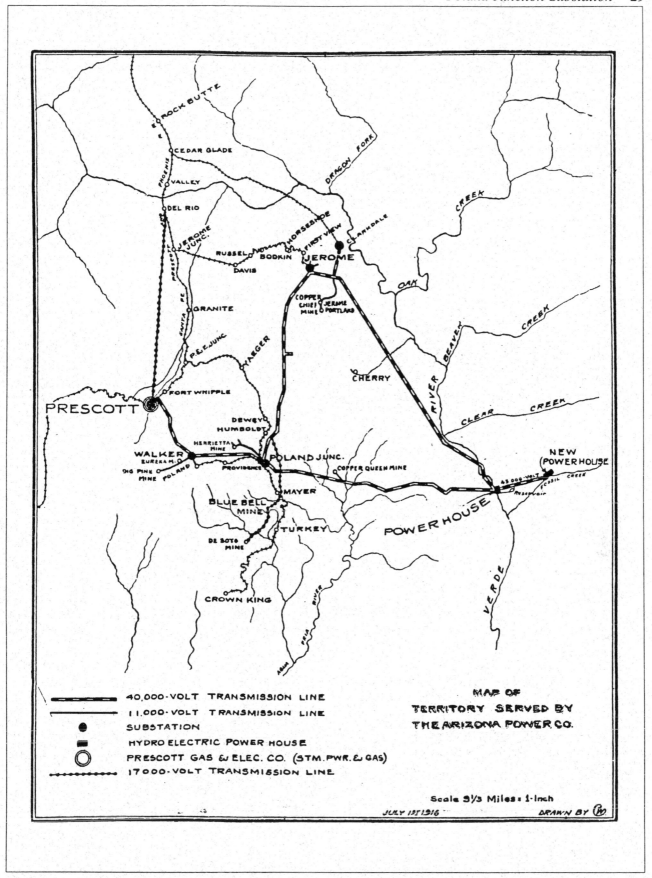

Figure 3.3. 1916 map of Childs-Irving Power Plant and transmission system (*Yavapai Magazine* February 1917). Childs plant is shown as "powerhouse," Irving plant as "new powerhouse."

Published and unpublished sources revealed further specific information about Poland Junction Substation and its historical setting. The facility received its name from its proximity to the Poland Mine, a gold and silver lode mine. The mine (as well as a creek and a canyon) were, in turn, named for Davis Robert Poland, a Yavapai County prospector who discovered mineral deposits in the headwaters of Big Bug Creek circa 1864. Near his Poland Mine (in Section 28, Township 12½ North, Range 1 West) he built a cabin, residing there until his death in 1882. Despite flurries of activity in 1887 and the mid 1890s, Poland Mine did not become a viable mineral property until industrialist Frank M. Murphy and his associates acquired it in 1900. Murphy was a railroad baron who had built the Santa Fe, Prescott & Phoenix Railway in 1891–1893 and the Prescott & Eastern Railway in 1898. In 1901 Murphy built a branch line from the latter railway to the Poland Mine; Poland Junction served as a base camp for construction crews when the branch line was being built. Officially known as "the Poland Branch of the Bradshaw Mountain Railway," the branch line originated at Poland Junction, wound 5.5 miles westward through narrow Poland Canyon, and terminated at Poland Mine. The branch line gave the mine life, and a town (named, of course, Poland) was born (Sayre 1985:56–57 and 131–141; Spude n.d.; Spude and Paher 1978:34).

A national economic recession slowed production at Poland Mine in 1907. Economic recovery after 1907 and the arrival of electrical power via Poland Junction Substation in 1909 stimulated a new round of production at the mine, but soon it became obvious that the vein was "playing out." The Poland Mine closed in 1912. Nearby mines continued to ship ores in 1914 and 1916 but soon, they, too, became exhausted. The railroad discontinued regular service on the Poland Branch in 1920, then reconditioned the line and resumed service in the late 1920s when production began again on Lynx Creek. However, the line's new life was short-lived. The railroad abandoned the track in 1932, salvaging rails and rail hardware from the Poland end of the line in November of 1932 and from the Poland Junction end in 1939 (Sayre 1985:57, 139–140).

The abandoned and salvaged rail line became an automotive route known today as Forest Road (FR) 261. The Poland properties (mine, town, and canyon) witnessed activity in the 1940s when a developer bought them, subdivided them into lots, sold the lots to seasonal residents, and named the subdivision Breezy Pines. Soon the cottages of summer visitors replaced the former mining community (Sayre 1985:140).

The history of Poland Junction Substation did not closely parallel that of the mining community. As the mine declined, the substation assumed increasing importance. If the mine no longer needed electrical power, other points in Yavapai County did, and the little substation stood ready to serve them. Prior to or during the 1920s, the Arizona Power Company constructed housing for substation workers at the facility (Figures 3.4 and 3.5). Resident employees monitored the substation equipment and served as linemen, patrolling the transmission and distribution lines. The Works Progress Administration performed improvement work of an unspecified nature in 1939. ADOT engineers made the only known map of the substation (Figure 3.6) in 1954 during engineering studies along SR 69. In 1969 APS bulldozed the original facility and replaced it with a modern substation. The Poland Junction Substation has remained a vital nexus in the electrical transmission system of central Arizona (Cantley 1988; Sayre 1985).

Figure 3.4. Circa 1935 photo of the Poland Junction Substation; view north, with worker housing in rear. (Photo courtesy Sharlot Hall Museum.)

Figure 3.5. Circa 1935 photo of the Poland Junction substation; view southwest. (Photo courtesy Sharlot Hall Museum.)

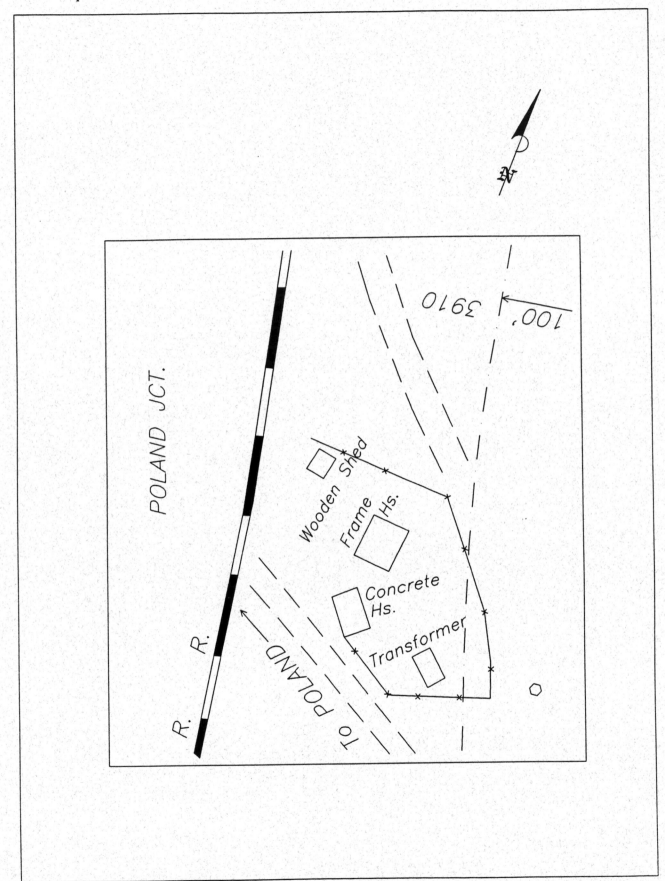

Figure 3.6. 1954 map of Poland Junction Substation (from ADOT 1954).

ARCHAEOLOGICAL DATA

The archaeological survey (Hathaway 1992) and preliminary design work by ADOT indicated that only one feature of Site AR-03-09-03-238, designated as Feature J during the Class III survey, would be impacted by construction. Therefore, ADOT limited subsequent archaeological investigations to that feature, with no subsurface testing to be conducted. Accordingly, SWCA proposed to document the facility archivally (see historic context provided above), map it, document Feature J, and identify all artifacts located within the proposed ROW.

The field crew mapped the entire site and each of its features, easily relocating features discovered during Hathaway's (1992) survey. The present investigations retained the designations assigned by Hathaway (Features A through J) but also discovered two additional features and labeled them K and L. The present investigations followed Hathaway's lead in not assigning feature designations to portions of an abandoned highway and an abandoned railroad grade that cut through the site, since these were parts of larger, linear resources that were to be treated specially and separately during the course of the investigations (see Chapter 12). Brief descriptions of Features A–I and Feature K follow, with more detailed descriptions of Features J and L, the features in the ROW; Figure 3.7 shows the site and the locations of the features. Please refer to the Glossary for definitions of terms used to describe historical artifacts.

Feature A was an unpaved dirt road varying from 10 feet to 12 feet in width in the southwest quadrant of the site. The road extended along a utility line, suggesting that it was used to service the line. The length of the feature within the site was 280 feet; however, the field crew was able to trace the road for short distances west and south of the site.

Feature B was a cairn of granite and basalt cobbles measuring 4 feet in diameter by 2.5 feet in height. The rocks of the cairn bore no inscriptions, and the cairn contained no identifying marker. The feature likely denoted the boundary of a survey for a mining claim, road ROW, railroad ROW, or other property tract.

Feature C was an unpaved dirt road varying from 12 feet to 14 feet in width. It was in the southern half of the site and appeared to be an earlier alignment of FR 261. In the survey report Hathaway (1992) stated that the feature cut through a trash area or dirt pile; SWCA's investigations found no trash in this area.

Feature D was a 6 × 10–foot concrete basin with walls varying from 6 inches to 12 inches in thickness. The basin was at least 5 feet deep; a trash deposit, approximately 1 foot thick and dating from the 1930s to the 1950s, had accumulated in the base of the feature.

Feature E was the poorly preserved remains of at least two foundations approximately 15 feet apart in an artificially leveled area. The southern foundation was of concrete and appeared to be a wall and corner of a structure that had been at least 24 × 20 feet in extent. The northern foundation was of concrete and stone and appeared to be the foundation of a building measuring at least 30 × 25 feet. A jumble of rocks lay 25 feet northwest of the northern foundation. This feature coincided with the location of "Locus 1," described in Cantley's (1988) report. At this locus, Cantley noted a concrete fragment bearing the inscription "U.S.A. / W.P.A. / 1939." Neither the Class III ADOT survey (Hathaway 1992) nor the present study relocated the inscription. Cantley suggested that this area once contained housing for em-

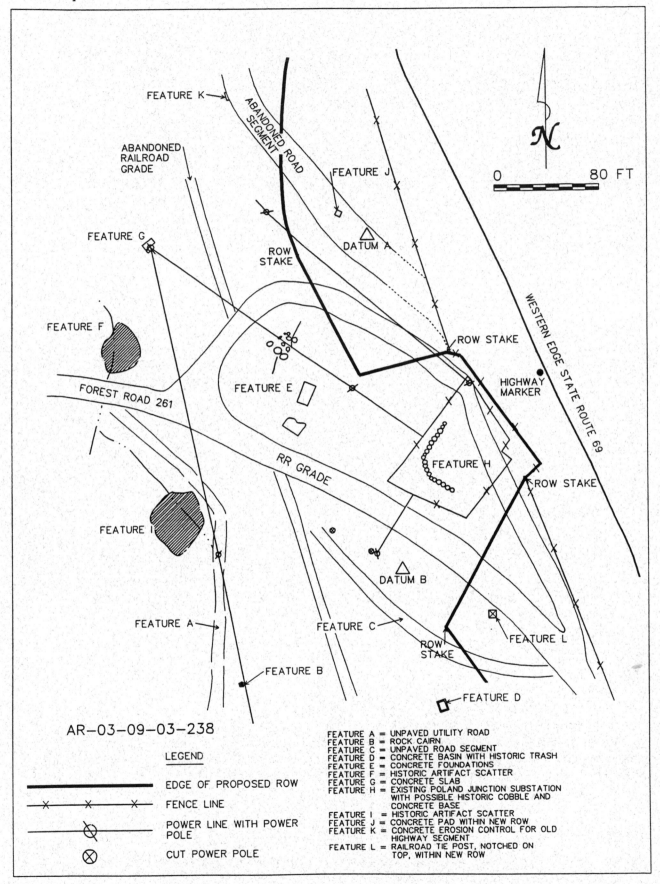

Figure 3.7. Site AR-03-09-03-238, the Poland Junction Substation.

ployees of the Poland Junction Substation. A comparison of this location with historical photos (see Figures 3.4 and 3.5) suggested that this was, indeed, the case.

Feature F was a low-density artifact scatter measuring 35 feet north-south by 30 feet east-west on the western edge of the site. Artifacts included approximately 50–100 fragments of glass containers, 10 tableware sherds, several can fragments, various lengths of baling wire, stove pipe, sheet metal, red brick fragments, barrel hoops, automobile parts, and ceramic insulator fragments. The material dated from the early twentieth century to the 1950s.

Feature G was a broken concrete slab measuring 12 feet northeast-southwest by 6 feet northwest-southeast in the northwest quadrant of the site. The slab anchored a power pole connected by power lines to the modern substation and to a line running along the western side of the site.

Feature H is the modern Poland Junction Substation, built in 1969. Electrical equipment is enclosed by a chain-link fence within a trapezoidal area measuring $100 \times 70 \times 62$ feet. The substation rests on a concrete pad that sits, in turn, on an artificial terrace composed of earthen fill retained by a masonry wall. The wall is of coursed rubble with concrete mortar.

Feature I was a low-density artifact scatter measuring 50 feet north-south by 40 feet east-west in the southwest quadrant of the site. Artifacts included approximately 15 fragments of probable blasting powder cans and one sanitary can. The sanitary can suggested a twentieth-century association for the trash; the artifact could not be dated more closely because it was not intact enough to be measured precisely and lacked temporally diagnostic attributes.

Feature K was a concrete retaining wall at the northern edge of the site. The wall, which measured approximately 3 feet in height by 6 feet in length, retained the downslope side of an abandoned segment of SR 69.

Feature J was a concrete pad (Figure 3.8) in the northeast quadrant of the site within the proposed ROW (not southwest of it as the survey report stated). The pad was friable and eroded, and its poor state of preservation made accurate measurement difficult; however, its original size appeared not to have exceeded 5 feet northeast-southwest by 4.6 feet northwest-southeast. Its top was flush with the present ground surface and was only one inch thick, as revealed by broken fragments of concrete in association with the pad. In the survey report, Hathaway (1992) concluded that Feature J represented the remains of a steel transmission line tower. Unfortunately, the only known historical map of the substation (Figure 3.6) does not depict this feature.

To test the notion that Feature J was a transmission tower base, SWCA's draftsperson made a scaled composite drawing of a typical Childs-Irving transmission line tower based on historical photographs and archival descriptions that cited the height of the towers as 45 feet. The historical records and photos indicated that there were actually two types of towers: with and without basal structures housing lightning arrestors (Figure 3.9). The conclusion from this exercise was that Feature J could not possibly have been the base for either type of transmission line tower; it was far too small. Transmission tower bases in the Childs-Irving system were at least two and perhaps three times the size of Feature J. Feature J may, however, have been a *distribution* line base. Power distribution lines were "lite" versions of transmission lines that used low-tension lines strung on poles to deliver power directly to customers in the Childs-Irving system.

Figure 3.8. Site AR-03-09-03-238, Feature J, concrete pad; view northeast.

Indirect data suggested the date of Feature J. Assuming that the feature performed an electrical function of some sort, it would not have been built earlier than 1909–1910, when the hydroelectric system started transmitting power to the area. The feature may have continued to function until the 1930s. During that decade, an upgrade of the transportation system of the area replaced a wagon road that had been used since the nineteenth century and that passed well to the east of Poland Junction Substation (General Land Office [GLO] 1914) with an automotive route that closely skirted the eastern edge of the power facility. The 1930s route went through Feature J, at which point the feature likely ceased to function as an electrical pole. The road work in this area may have been conducted by the Works Progress Administration, which would explain the "W.P.A." inscribed on a fragment found at the substation by Cantley (1988). Today the road (an abandoned, unpaved segment of SR 69) can still be seen running through Feature J.

Feature L was an upright railroad tie with a notched top (Figure 3.10) standing immediately on the west side of FR 261 only 100 feet from its junction with current SR 69. The tie measured 8 × 6 inches in cross section, projected 3 feet above the ground, and had a 1-foot-long notch cut into one half of its top. The size of the tie suggested that it was manufactured for a standard rather than a narrow-gauge railroad (Bryant 1913). The tie had been treated with creosote (a coal-tar-based preservative) and was in good condition. Its form and location suggested that it once supported a forest road sign.

Investigations at this site included analysis of all 38 whole or fragmentary artifacts found within the proposed ROW. The artifacts were scattered evenly and thinly throughout the proposed ROW and did not cluster in any particular area. Metal objects included 12 crushed sanitary-type fruit or vegetable cans, a coffee can and lid, 4 beverage cans, baling wire, rebar, strap metal of various sizes, a metal plate, sheet metal (galvanized and ungalvanized), 1/32-inch screening, an oil can, and an antifreeze can. Glass objects

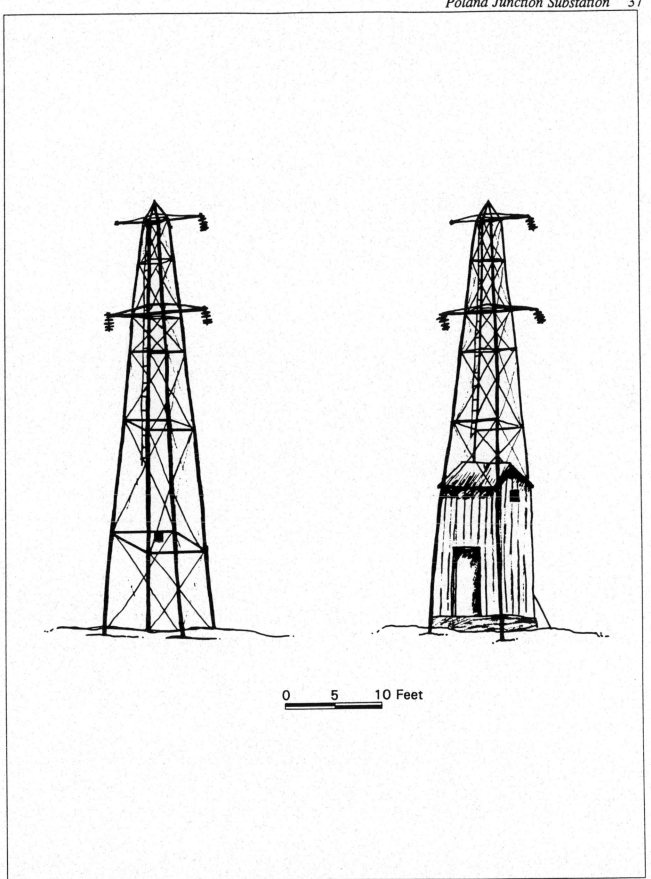

0   5   10 Feet

Figure 3.9. Transmission tower of Childs-Irving power system. Composite drawing from historical photographs published in *Yavapai Magazine*, 1917 and 1926.

Figure 3.10. Site AR-03-09-03-238, Feature L, upright railroad tie with notched top; view southwest.

consisted of a windshield fragment and fragments from three clear glass bottles (one of which had contained Puerto Rican rum). Ceramic fragments were from a porcelain plate, a Homer Laughlin Fiestaware bowl, a brown-glazed insulator, and a sewer tile. Other artifacts included a rubber gasket and pieces of two rubber hoses. The artifact assemblage represented a wide variety of functional categories: food (17 items), food preparation and consumption (4 items), architecture (2 items), leisure and recreation (1 item), transportation (1 item), tools and hardware (4 items), machinery (5 items), and miscellaneous (4 items). In terms of temporal affiliation, all objects appeared to date from the twentieth century. The most closely datable items were the Fiestaware bowl fragment (1936 ff.), a Glass Containers, Inc., bottle basemark (1945 ff.), an Owens-Illinois Glass Company bottle basemark (1929–1954), and a Puerto Rico Distillery bottle basemark (1940 ff.). Either travelers along the abandoned SR 69 segments or substation employees could have deposited the post-1930 items.

SUMMARY AND RECOMMENDATIONS

Modest archaeological features sometimes have rich historic contexts. This was indeed the case for Feature J of Site AR-03-09-03-238, a small concrete platform that was likely the base for a power distribution line pole associated with the Childs-Irving hydroelectric system. The line was a small yet vital link in a larger transmission system that brought water-generated electricity to the communities of Prescott and Jerome and to mines including the United Verde, Walker, Henrietta, Big Pine, Poland, Copper Chief, Crown King, and Blue Bell.

The effect of the Childs-Irving system on the mining industry of central Arizona should not be underestimated. The system brought power to the mines, and it did so cost effectively. Lower power costs reduced mine operating costs, making it possible for miners to exploit low-grade ores and small claims that might otherwise have been unprofitable. The "juice" from this system infused life into the mining town of Jerome, where rugged topography effectively prohibited power generation by any other means. The Childs-Irving system played a major role in making eastern Yavapai County a leading producer of gold, silver, and copper in the State of Arizona. The system was remarkable both for its innovative technology and for the skill with which it was constructed across rugged topography.

Despite their rich historic context, neither the Poland Junction Substation as a whole nor Feature J appear eligible for the National Register of Historic Places. Modernization of the facility in 1969 substantially modified the site and the feature. At that time APS removed all buildings and historic structures and bulldozed several building foundations. Historic trash may also have been removed during modernization to clean the facility; in any case, historic artifacts are not abundant at the site now. The Poland Junction Substation has historical significance but no physical integrity relating to its period of significance. Therefore, the property is not eligible for the NRHP. SWCA researchers documented Features J and L, the only elements that will be impacted by the widening of SR 69, and placed them in a historic context through archival research during the testing phase. SWCA did not recommend or conduct additional work during the data recovery phase.

CHAPTER 4

AZ N:11:19(ASM)
THE BAY VIEW PLACER MINING CLAIM

Pat H. Stein
Stewart Deats
Elizabeth J. Skinner

MANAGEMENT HISTORY

Site AZ N:11:19(ASM) is in the SE¼NW¼SW¼SW¼ and SW¼NW¼SW¼SW¼ of Section 33 in Township 13 North, Range 1 East, on the USGS Poland Junction, Arizona, 7.5 minute quadrangle (Figure 4.1). It is on the western side of current State Route 69, approximately 3.3 miles southwest of Humboldt and 0.5 mile north of Poland Junction. The site measures 240 feet north-south by 140 feet east-west, encompassing a total of 0.8 acre, and is on Bureau of Land Management (BLM) land and an Arizona Department of Transportation (ADOT) easement. Elevations at the site range from 4790 feet to 4800 feet above mean sea level. The site area is in attenuated riparian woodland, below the level of the existing highway grade. Several minor washes have dissected the area; the largest is the drainage known historically as Post Office Gulch (unnamed on the USGS Poland Junction quadrangle). Post Office Gulch adjoins the site on the east and was channelized when SR 69 was improved in 1954.

GPI Environmental, Inc., first recorded AZ N:11:19(ASM) during a preliminary survey of SR 69 (GPI 1991:13). The GPI surveyors noted historic artifacts in association with ground stone and flaked stone and categorized the resource as an "Anglo-Indian Habitation Site." Hathaway (1992:16–20) re-examined the site during the intensive cultural resource survey of SR 69 from Mayer to Dewey. Noting the presence of historic trash in association with sherds, flaked stone, and ground stone, Hathaway concluded that the site was multicomponent and recommended testing to determine the relationship of the two components. He assessed the site as potentially eligible for the National Register of Historic Places (NRHP), as it appeared capable of yielding scientific information pertaining to the historic and prehistoric occupation and utilization of central Arizona.

Engineering analysis by ADOT determined that the entire site would be impacted by the proposed construction and that avoidance was therefore not feasible. The testing program, the first phase of the archaeological work undertaken by SWCA, included archival research, removing vegetation, mapping, photodocumentation, establishing grids over the loci and collecting surface artifacts from them, and subsurface testing.

Testing of the historic component of the site revealed a moderate density of historical material, in general of a date consistent with the dating of the site through historical research. The site yielded important information about mining history in the area, especially concerning life on a turn-of-the-century gold placer claim, and appeared capable of yielding further information on this history. SWCA investigators therefore determined that the site was eligible for the NRHP under Criterion D and recommended data recovery. This chapter presents a description of SWCA's investigations at the historic component. Investigations at the prehistoric component appear in a separate report (Mitchell 1995).

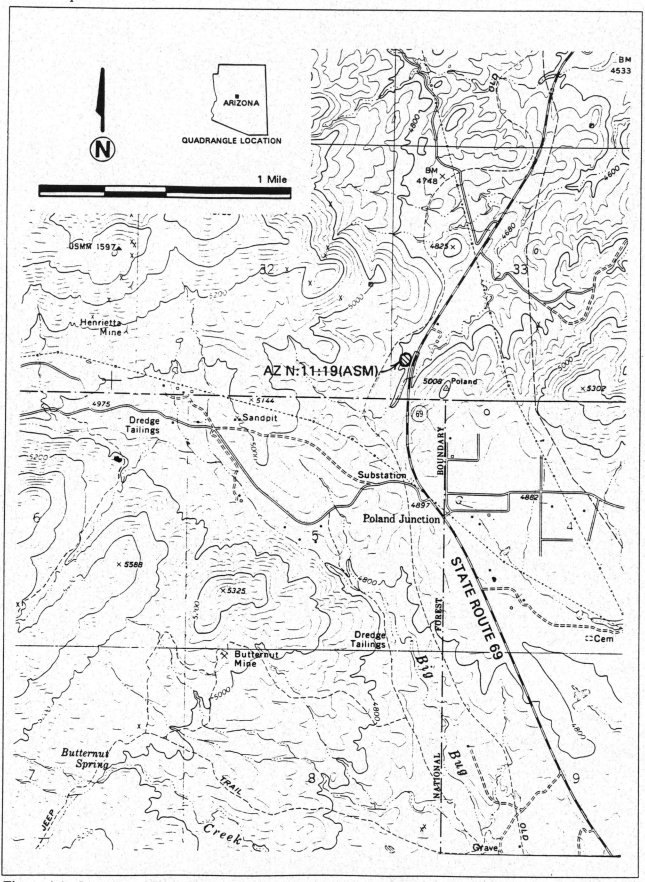

Figure 4.1. Location of Site AZ N:11:19(ASM), the Bay View Placer Mining Claim. Base map is Poland Junction, Arizona, USGS 7.5′ quadrangle, 1975.

HISTORICAL DATA

A thorough search of archival material revealed one period of historic use at the site: it was the location of a gold mining claim. In May of 1900 Mrs. Mary L. Van Patten located (filed) the claim (Yavapai County Recorder [YCR] Book of Mines [BM] 55:252–253). According to the notice of location and entry filed with the County Recorder, the claim measured 1500 feet north-south by either 300 feet or 600 feet east-west; both of the latter figures appeared in the same legal notice. Mrs. Van Patten called her claim "Bay View," a rather fanciful name for a property in high and dry Arizona.

Little is known about Mrs. Van Patten or the Bay View Placer. The Index to Mines at the County Recorder's office suggested that Bay View might have been her only mining claim; that is, she did not locate or file other claims in Yavapai County. The Twelfth Census of the U.S. Bureau of the Census recorded that in June of 1900 Mary resided in the vicinity of Huron Station with her husband Ezekiel, who listed his profession as "prospector." The census enumerator noted that Mary was born in Ohio in 1845, Ezekiel was born in New York in 1836, and the couple had no children, or at least none living with them in 1900. Mary's brief obituary (Sharlot Hall Museum [SHM] Obituary Book [OB]:3031) stated only that she was a former resident of the Verde Valley when she died on July 7, 1904. By September of 1904 her widowed husband was living in Skull Valley (approximately 25 miles west of Huron Station), where he opened a store for the sale of "groceries, provisions, hay, grain, etc." (*Arizona Journal-Miner [AJM]* 21 September 1904).

Mrs. Van Patten held mineral rights to the Bay View property for less than a year. In April of 1901 she and "E. Van Patten" (undoubtedly Ezekiel) sold their mineral rights in the Bay View property to John W. Nelson for $250 (YCR Book of Deeds [BD] 53:598). The quitclaim deed for this transaction indicated that the claim was approximately 1000 feet long (not 1500 feet, as previously recorded) and that it lay south of C. P. Wingfield's claim (see Chapter 5).

Little more is known about Nelson than about the Van Pattens. The earliest located record pertaining to John W. Nelson dates to September of 1896, when his wife, Essie, gave birth to a baby boy in Prescott (SHM Document Book [DB] 131, Folder 10, Item 128a). In June of 1900, when the Twelfth Census was conducted, Nelson was a neighbor of the Van Pattens in the Huron Station area. The census enumerator also recorded that Nelson was born in 1853 in Sweden, immigrated to the United States in 1864 but was not, by 1900, a naturalized citizen of the U.S., was a prospector by profession, had been married for eight years, and was still married but living alone on his Huron land when the 1900 census was taken. When he acquired the Bay View property in 1901, Nelson also held several other mining properties in central Arizona. A short time after 1901, Nelson moved to Illinois. (John Nelson of the Bay View claim bore no relation to a Prescott resident of the same name who committed suicide in 1910 by swallowing carbolic acid. A gardener suffering from the "white plague" and tuberculosis, this individual also came from Sweden but reportedly had no family living in the United States [*Arizona Journal* Miner (*AJM*) 4 November 1910 4:3].)

In May of 1905 John Nelson, then a resident of Christian County, Illinois, drafted a will bequeathing all property to his wife and also naming her as executor. Upon her husband's death on December 28, 1906, Essie Nelson filed the will with the probate courts of Christian and Yavapai counties (YCR Book of Wills [BW] 1:26). Settling the decedent's business affairs took over two years. His remaining assets were worth $10,000 in real estate but virtually nothing in personal property.

It appears that Nelson's mineral rights to the Bay View Placer lapsed during the probate process. To keep the claim active and valid, the claimant had to make minimal mining improvements. Apparently Mrs. Nelson, the will's executor, never took this precaution and lost all rights to the Bay View Placer Mining Claim. When the probate period ended, Essie Nelson sold all remaining mining claims of the Nelson Estate to the Nelson Mining Company; Bay View was not listed among them (YCR BD 93:274). According to BLM records, the Bay View Placer Mining Claim was never patented and has remained in the possession of the U.S. government.

No Mineral Entry Survey of the Bay View Placer Mining Claim was ever made; thus, no mineral entry survey plat for the claim was generated. The only map referring to Bay View is a 1901 Mineral Entry Survey map for the Princes Placer (see Figure 5.2). The 1901 map does not indicate the size or boundaries of the Bay View claim, only that it was immediately southwest of the Princes Placer.

ARCHAEOLOGICAL DATA

Testing

SWCA's field crew began testing at AZ N:11:19(ASM) by clearing the site of dense vegetation and mapping it, in the process confirming two of Hathaway's (1992) impressions of the site: it contained two loci of historic material (Locus A and Locus B) and was confined to the proposed ROW (Figure 4.2). Both loci were in a small, shallow sand dune, with cultural material eroding from the dune.

The crew gridded the two loci in 20-foot squares and collected all artifacts except bulky items, which were analyzed in the field, and prehistoric material, which they collected following completion of the historic investigations. The researchers suspected that the large quantity of architectural items—mostly flat glass and nails—observed at the site could mark the location of a dismantled wood-frame structure and that foundations might lie beneath the surface. They therefore pinflagged all architectural items before beginning artifact collection and found that the glass and nails were in linear configurations. The location of these configurations guided the subsequent placement of test trenches and test pits. The following paragraphs describe the results of the investigations at each locus. Please refer to the Glossary for definitions of the terms used to describe historical artifacts.

Locus A

Locus A was a medium-density scatter of historic artifacts measuring 110 feet east-west by 90 feet north-south in the northern half of the site. This locus included the one feature of the site, Feature 1, a cluster of schist slabs on the surface of the ground. The cluster measured 2 feet in diameter by 6 inches in height and appeared to be the remains of a footing or other building support (Figure 4.3).

Surface artifacts included ceramics, glass, and metal. The ceramic artifacts represented two functional categories, food preparation/consumption (a minimum of 13 items) and leisure/recreation. Eleven food-related items were of hard-paste earthenware (representing 5 plates, 1 cup, 1 bowl, 1 teapot, 1 saucer, and 2 vessels of indeterminate form) and two were of porcelain (from a cup and a plate). The leisure/recreation item was a piece of what may have been a porcelain doll, suggesting the presence of a child at the site. None of the fragments bore a maker's mark or patterns that could be closely identified and dated.

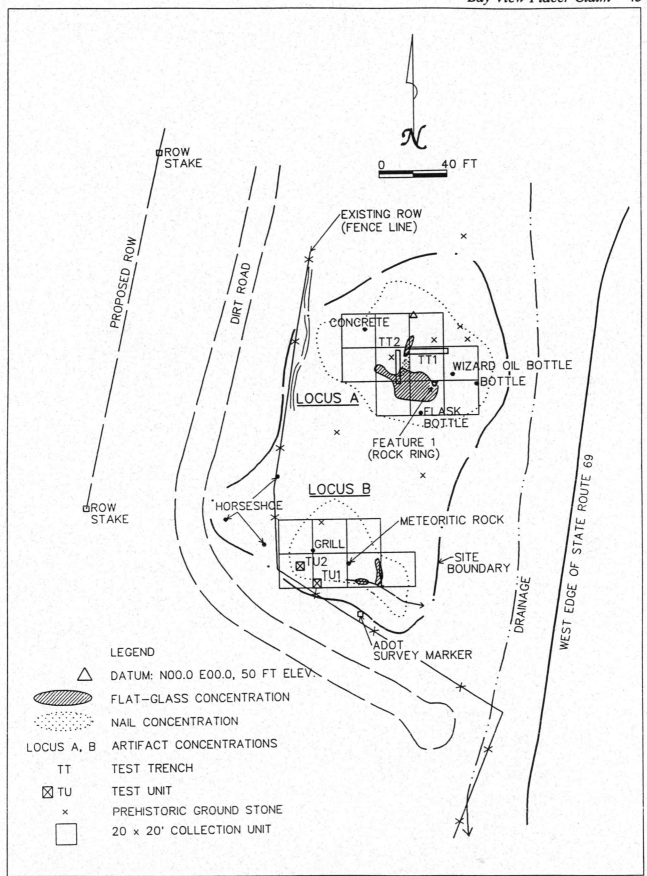

Figure 4.2. Site AZ N:11:19(ASM), the Bay View Placer Mining Claim.

Figure 4.3. Site AZ N:11:19(ASM) Locus A, Feature 1, rock pile possibly marking building support; view east.

Glass artifacts from Locus A represented the functional categories of architecture, leisure/recreation, and medicine/health. The architectural items were a large number of fragments of flat green glass (window glass). The leisure/recreation items were a picnic-type whiskey flask (sun-colored amethyst [SCA]), a champagne bottle (SCA), a beer bottle (amber), and a possible wine bottle (olive green). Medicinal/health items included two patent medicine bottles (SCA and aqua) and a possible Mentholatum bottle (cobalt blue). The glass colors and technology suggested a late nineteenth-early twentieth century date of manufacture. Only one of the vessels bore a mark that could be closely identified and dated: the pale green bottle had once contained Hamlin's Wizard Oil, a product manufactured circa 1871–1923.

Metal items were especially abundant in Locus A and represented a number of functional categories. Architectural items included numerous wire nails ranging in size from 4d to 60d. A single cut nail had been purposely bent to form a hook. Items representing food preparation/consumption were fragments of hole-in-cap cans (from vegetable/fruit, meat, and milk containers) and a coffee pot; one of the cans had been punctured many times through its base to form a sieve-like device. Tools and hardware present were pieces of strap iron, rebar, and a chisel. A fire grate represented household furnishings. A pick head represented mining/quarrying, while several bolts represented the machinery category. Personal items included suspender clasps, a buckle, and a jeans rivet. Miscellaneous items included a fragment of a horseshoe, three barrel hoops, and a pedal fragment. The most closely datable object was a milk can; its size and method of manufacture suggested a date circa 1885–1903.

The field crew excavated two test trenches through the areas of Locus A containing linear configurations of dense nails and window glass in anticipation that these surface concentrations marked subsurface structural remains. Test Trench 1 measured 25 × 2 feet and Test Trench 2 measured 20 × 2 feet (Figure 4.2). Although neither trench exposed any structural features, both revealed moderate densities of subsurface historic artifacts. Test Trench 1 yielded window glass, fragments of jars and bottles (SCA, pink, and pale green), pieces of plates and bowls, a garter-belt clasp, a rebar, a hinge, bolts, can fragments, a crown-cap opener, a cut nail, and numerous wire nails. Test Trench 2 yielded window glass, SCA and pale green bottle glass, a possible piece of a lamp chimney, a square-headed bolt, a wire handle, miscellaneous pieces of sheet metal, and many wire nails. Most of the historic cultural material was within the upper 6 inches of the soil; prehistoric material was present in Test Trench 2 below the historic material. At a depth of 1 foot the soil changed to a sterile matrix, and the trenching effort was discontinued.

Locus B

Locus B, 55 feet south of Locus A, was an area with sparse historic artifacts measuring 75 feet east-west by 50 feet north-south. The surface of this area also contained ceramic, glass, and metal objects, as well as a nodule of meteoritic iron.

The meteorite was the most unusual object observed during testing. While it was impossible to tell whether the celestial object had fallen to the site or someone had carried it there, the mining context of the site supported the latter notion. Meteorites were recognized by and of interest to miners in the late nineteenth and early twentieth centuries because the nodules contained potent concentrations of precious and semiprecious metals. Around 1890 Fred Volz, an entrepreneur at Canyon Diablo in neighboring Coconino County, hired Mexican laborers to collect meteorites (Nininger 1956:15; Richardson 1968:15). The workers accumulated two flatcar loads in a short time, and Volz sold the material to a Los Angeles iron dealer at $0.75 a pound. Unbeknownst to Volz, the iron in his meteorites was worth a pittance compared to other metals they contained. Just after Volz sold his meteorites, he learned that each pound of meteorite contained $36 in platinum alone (Richardson 1968:15); he had thrown away a fortune.

The only historic ceramics from the surface of Locus B were two fragments from the same hard-paste earthenware plate. The glass objects were fragments of an amber beer or liquor bottle and an SCA bottle of indeterminate form and function. Metal objects were most numerous and included many wire nails (ranging in size from 5d to 30d), two cut nails, several hole-in-cap cans (for meat, vegetables/fruit, and milk), a lard bucket, washtub fragments, sheet metal, a jeans rivet, baling wire, and a folding wire meat grill. One of the cans bore the lettering""THE MOST PERFECT MADE DR. PRICE'S CREAM BAKING POWDER / 2½ LBS FULL WEIGHT"; the analyst could not determine the date of this object. The most closely datable object was a .44-caliber cartridge case that had been issued by the U.S. Army circa 1871–1873. The artifact assemblage was otherwise consistent with a late nineteenth century–early twentieth century association for the site.

A few artifacts were near the western edge of Locus B: a mule shoe, a reutilized partial mule shoe, three fragments of a horseshoe, a 20d wire nail, and the lid of a paint pail or lard bucket. These artifacts might have been associated either with Locus B or with an ephemeral trail that ran along the west side of the site.

The field crew excavated two 5 × 5–foot test pits (Test Units 1 and 2) in the portions of Locus B with the greatest numbers of surface artifacts (Figure 4.2). Test Unit 1 was about 6 inches in depth, with a 1 × 1–foot window excavated in the northeast corner of the unit an additional 6 inches. Test Unit 2 was 1 foot in depth. Neither unit yielded any subsurface historic features or artifacts, but a possible prehistoric occupation surface was present (Mitchell 1994).

Testing revealed that Site AZ N:11:19(ASM) contained a moderate density of historic material representing the Bay View placer. The investigators could not date the artifacts closely enough to determine whether they were associated with the Van Patten, the Nelson, or both occupations of the site.

Since the proposed construction would impact the entire site, SWCA recommended data recovery, to include stripping the site horizontally and in a controlled manner to recover subsurface artifacts and excavating any features that might be revealed through this process. Although testing failed to reveal any subsurface structural remains (that is, foundations, footings, or piers), the researchers expected to find such remains during data recovery, as suggested by the high numbers of nails and window glass at the site.

Data Recovery

As data recovery began, SWCA's Principal Investigator located and obtained from the Western History Department of the Denver Public Library a copy of a rare historical photograph of the general site area taken at approximately the turn of the century (Figure 4.4). Although the exact date of the photo is unknown, it clearly depicts the Prescott & Eastern Railway (built in 1898) and was published in a 1901 mining prospectus (American Finance & Trust Co. 1901), placing it between those two dates. Using the railbed, a railroad trestle, vegetation patterns, and hillside contours as reference points, SWCA field personnel located the point from which the photograph had been taken and rephotographed that viewshed as it appears today (Figure 4.5). Close examination of the earlier image indicated one building in the site area. The structure was front-gabled, was substantial in size, had several windows along at least its south side, had a light-colored or reflective roof (probably sheet metal or tin), and may have had one-and-a-half stories. Comparison of Figures 4.4 and 4.5 suggested that construction of SR 69 by the State Highway Department (now ADOT) in 1954 probably destroyed the structural remains of the building. Photo analysis further suggested that data recovery might not locate the foundation of the building but would likely unearth at least the trash associated with it and therefore shed light on its residents.

Data recovery at Site AZ N:11:19(ASM) focused on Locus A (Figure 4.6), known through testing to contain Feature 1 as well as subsurface material. The field crew began data recovery by re-establishing the grid across the portion of Locus A that had yielded dense artifacts during testing and subdividing this grid into 10 × 10–foot squares. The excavators manually stripped to a depth of 6 inches the surface of 14 squares in Locus A in an area measuring 40 × 40 feet, pedestaled any possible structural support stones, and screened the soil through 1/4-inch mesh. In two units (HS 6 and HS 7) 1/8-inch mesh was used experimentally; the finer mesh did not increase artifact recovery appreciably and slowed the rate of recovery considerably, so the experiment was not repeated in the other units. The soil matrix consisted of a medium to coarse loamy sand; historic cultural material was generally within the top three inches of soil. The excavators collected diagnostic artifacts (see Chapter 2) for laboratory analysis and described and counted nondiagnostic artifacts in the field.

Data recovery found numerous artifacts (see analyses below) but no structural remains. The three small rocks the field crew pedestaled were in no apparent configuration and could not have been part of a building foundation; they appeared to be natural.

The first step in investigating Feature 1, a surface cluster of schist slabs, was excavation of the southern half (which exposed another layer of rocks), followed by excavation of the northern half. The feature was a rock-lined hearth composed of approximately 40 rocks (Figure 4.7), most of them schistose slate and phyllite, but some quartz and diorite as well. The hearth measured 2.6 feet in diameter, had two courses of rock, and was approximately 6 inches deep. No artifacts were in direct association with the hearth. A flotation sample collected from within the hearth yielded only trace amounts of ash and charcoal.

A charcoal concentration in the east-central portion of HS 9 consisted of a light scatter of intact charcoal and a charcoal stain measuring 58 × 25 inches, with charcoal mottling extending into HS 12. The concentration had a depth of only 3/4 inch, with no fire-affected rocks, soil, or artifacts, and was interpreted as a possible trash burn of paper items.

When the field crew had completed excavation of the historical component, they investigated the prehistoric component by excavating a series of backhoe trenches at 5-m intervals throughout Locus A. Each trench was 25 m long, approximately 2 m wide, and 1–1.3 m deep. The trenching revealed a prehistoric feature, described by Mitchell (1995). These backhoe trenches did not reveal additional historical features or other historical materials.

ARTIFACT ANALYSES

Metal

Metal was the most abundant material type recovered from AZ N:11:19(ASM), with 1945 artifacts in this category. SWCA field personnel studied most of the metal artifacts in the field but retained 350 of them for laboratory analysis. When necessary, the artifacts were brushed clean to help in their identification. The state of preservation of the metal artifacts varied considerably. Artifacts made mostly of iron were more corroded and oxidized than those of brass, copper, and other metals. Very few artifacts had deteriorated beyond recognition. In general, when the analyst could not identify an artifact, it was because the artifact was highly unusual, not because of its state of preservation. The metal items represented 13 of the 17 functional classifications.

Food

The majority of the metal artifacts in this functional category were food containers. Most of these cans were crushed and heavily corroded. The many different kinds of cans recovered included 8 round hole-in-cap food cans, 5 rectangular meat cans, 2 sardine cans, 1 coffee can, and 27 evaporated/condensed milk cans. Two of the hole-in-cap cans had been opened by using a knife to quarter an end. At least one of the rectangular meat cans was a hole-in-cap can, and at least two others had been opened using a score-strip and key. This method of opening meat cans dates to as early as 1895, according to Rock (1992). According to the condensed/evaporated milk can dating chronology developed by Simonis (1992), 2 of the milk cans date between 1875 and 1903, 5 date between 1885 and 1903, 11 date between 1903 and 1914, and 5 date between 1908 and 1914. The four other milk cans were too incomplete for dating, but three had been opened with parallel knife blade punches through opposite sides of one end. Eighteen round cans with soldered end seams may have been milk cans, but they were too incomplete to identify with certainty.

Figure 4.4. Circa 1898-1901 photo of general area of Site AZ N:11:19(ASM); view northeast toward Huron Station from a point northwest of Poland Junction. Trestle and railbed are part of Prescott & Eastern Railway. Arrow indicates location of site, with house. (Photo by the Denver Public Library, Western History Collection.)

Figure 4.5. SWCA's 1995 photo of view shown in Figure 4.4, with remains of trestle and railbed still visible. Arrows indicate location of trestle, railbed, and site. Structural remains of house shown in Figure 4.4 were probably destroyed when State Route 69 was constructed in 1954.

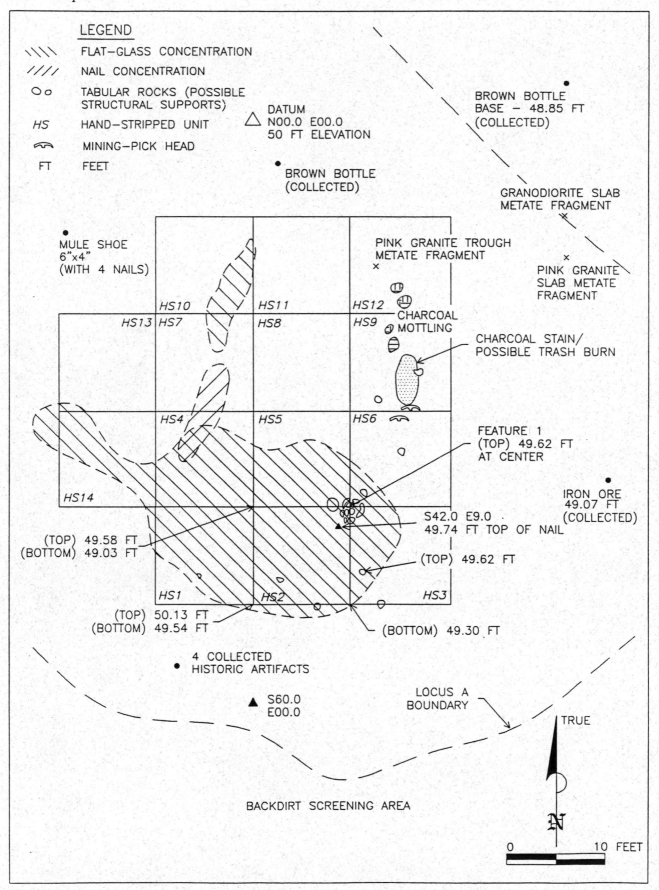

Figure 4.6. Site AZ N:11:19(ASM), area of Locus A excavated during data recovery.

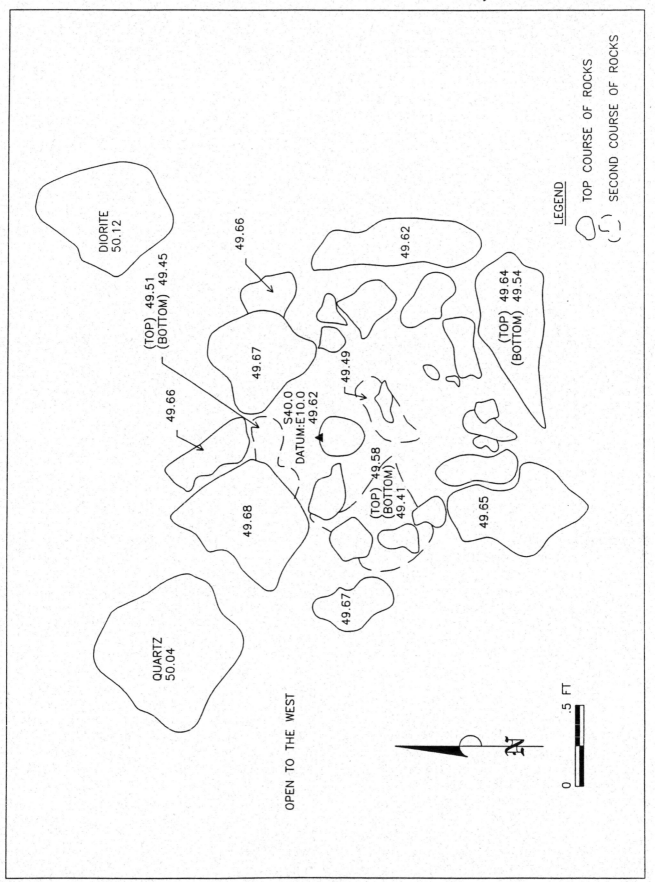

Figure 4.7. Site AZ N:11:19(ASM) Locus A, Feature 1, rock-lined hearth.

Other cans found were 1 sanitary food can and 3 rectangular external-friction can lids, as well as 194 unidentifiable can fragments.

This assemblage also included several can-related artifacts: 23 score-strip can-opener keys, 1 sardine-can-opener key, and 2 partial, unidentifiable can-opener keys. Many of the score-strip keys still had coiled strips attached. Other food-container-related items were a continuous-thread bottle cap and a round, 1-inch diameter, indented-center bottle cap.

Food Preparation and Consumption

Only two metal artifacts belonged in this category. They were the iron handle and top grinding portion of a coffee grinder.

Household Furnishings

Metal items in this functional category were fragments of a cast iron stove, three wall hooks/curtain-rod holders (each of a different type), two drapery hooks (Figure 4.8a), and two casters or rollers. One caster, of the type used on the bottom of a piece of furniture such as a chair, bed, or desk, had a missing wheel. The second caster-like object appeared to be a drawer roller, but it may also have been a furniture caster.

Architecture (Construction-Related)

The majority of the metal artifacts fell into this category. Wire nails alone were more numerous (1292) than any other type of artifact on the site; several other artifacts recovered were types commonly used in construction. Montgomery Ward and Company's Catalogue No. 57 shows an illustration of an elaborately decorated door butt (hinge) (Emmit 1969). The assemblage included several pieces of this type of hinge, as well as with two "acorn top" hinge pins that probably were also part of these hinges. Two keyhole escutcheons were of a style that dates to as early as 1885 (Herskovitz 1978:60–61). Three items were keys: an iron padlock key, a steel drawer key, and an iron door lock key (Emmit 1969:369, 372, 374). The door key (Figure 4.8b) fit into the keyhole escutcheons and most likely was the key to this lock. Other door-related items included a screen door spring and fragments of a barn-door hanger (illustrated in the 1894–1895 Montgomery Ward catalog [Emmit 1969:366]) with a 4-inch-diameter grooved iron wheel designed to roll across a track. The track would have been located above the doorway, allowing the door to be rolled open and shut.

Other metal items in this category included two iron pipe couplings (one galvanized), a segment of iron pipe, a round chrome-plated nut, 1/2-inch tacks, wood screws, U-shaped staples, iron washers, a cotter pin, and a galvanized wing nut. Several railroad spikes (of the common type known as "doghead" because of their profile) for both standard and narrow-gauge rails recovered from the site were likely scavenged from local railroads for use as fasteners in construction.

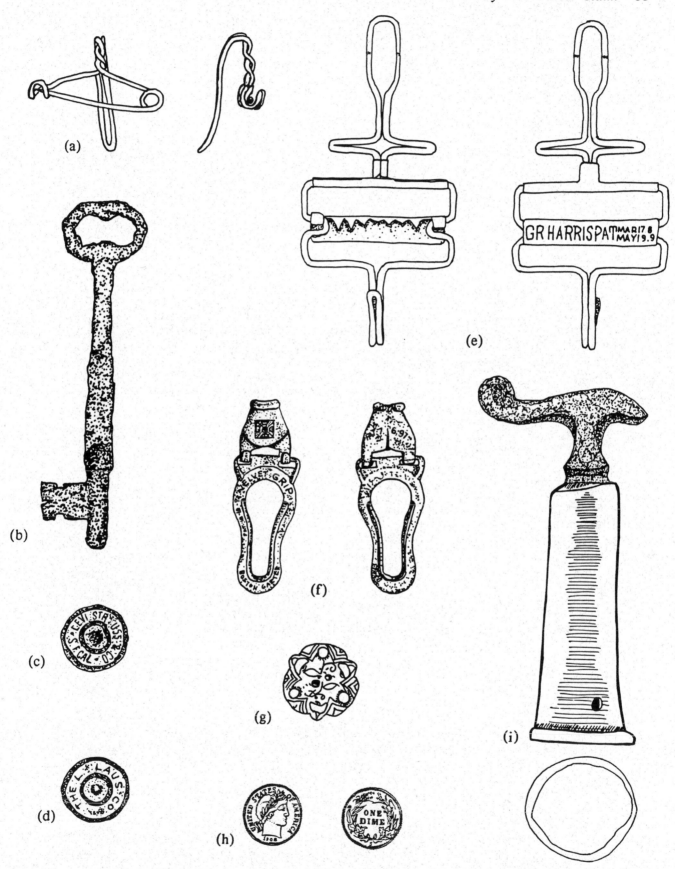

Figure 4.8. Selected metal artifacts recovered from Site AZ N:11:19(ASM). Drawn actual size.

Leisure and Recreation

Metal artifacts in this category were four hunting-related artifacts (pieces of ammunition), and a pocket tobacco tin. Two of the artifacts were rimfired cartridge cases, .22 Long or .22 Long Rifle caliber, with an "H" headstamp. The Winchester Repeating Arms Company used the "H" headstamp on .22 Long cartridges beginning in 1917 and on .22 Long Rifle cartridges beginning in 1945 and still manufactures both cartridges (Berge 1980:227). The third piece of ammunition was an unfired centerfire cartridge for a .45-caliber revolver. This cartridge had the "UMC .45 COLT" headstamp of the Union Metallic Cartridge Company, which first manufactured this type in 1873 (Barnes 1985). The "UMC" indicates that the cartridge was made prior to 1912, the year the Union Metallic Cartridge Company merged with E. Remington & Sons. The fourth piece of ammunition, a 16-gauge shotgun shell head stamped "1901 / NO. 16 / REPEATER," was also a Winchester Repeating Arms Company shell, produced in 1901.

Personal Items

This site yielded 102 personal items, nearly all from clothing. Thirty-two items were shoe or boot eyelets, of both the grommet "lace-through" and the hook "lace-over" type. Two shoe or boot nails were also present. These counts do not include eyelets and nails still attached to pieces of shoes or boots, which are discussed below under Leather. Thirty items were rivet buttons. Fifteen had raised lettering on the front reading "LEVI STRAUSS & CO. S.F., CAL" (Figure 4.8c), 1 had "THE L. ...LAUS CO" (Figure 4.8d), 3 had a cross-hatched pattern on the front, 1 had a stylized "M" stamped on the front and "PAT.'S APR. 21, 96 & SEPT. 1, 96" stamped on the back (a similar rivet button was recovered from Site AZ N:11:23(ASM); see Figure 6.11g), and 10 were plain or were too corroded to discern any lettering. Of 10 clothing rivets recovered, 7 had "L.S. & Co. S.F." (Levi Strauss & Company, San Francisco) stamped on the front and back, 2 were plain, and 1 had "S.F.U." stamped on the front. The Levi Strauss rivet buttons and clothing rivets have a wide date range, from 1850 to the present (Hull-Walski and Ayres 1989:157).

Clothing-related items also included a number of suspender and garter parts. Nine suspender slides and clasps were in the assemblage, four with lettering stamped on them. One had "...UG. 1900" stamped on the back, one had "...UG. 14 190...," one had "HARRIS PATENTS / TRADE MARK," and one was stamped "GR HARRIS PAT. MAR 17, 85 / MAY 19, 91" (Figure 4.8e). One of the four garter clasps had "VELVET GRIP / BOSTON GARTER / PAT. 12-13-92" stamped on the front and "PAT. 7. 6. 97" on the back (Figure 4.8f). A recovered copper garter button may correspond to this clasp. Also recovered were 6 other pieces of suspender or garter slides and clasps, in addition to 2 gilt trouser buckles, 2 shoulder brace and hose supporter buckles, 2 two-hole sew-through-type buttons (originally fabric covered), a corset fastener "eye," and a gold-plated collar button.

Two personal items recovered from the site were jewelry. One was a jewelry fragment or watch part, and the other was an ornately decorated gold-plated charm (Figure 4.8g).

Coins and Tokens

Only one item belonged in this category. It was a 1908 liberty head U.S. dime (Figure 4.8h).

Transportation

All of the metal transportation-related artifacts recovered from this site were either wagon parts or horse or mule tack. Thirteen iron wagon-bow staples of various sizes were identical to illustrations of similar staples in mail-order catalogs of the period (Emmit 1969:575; Israel 1968:62). Other wagon parts were 2 carriage bolts, 1 wagon axle clip, and an iron whiffletree tongue with a brass shaft tip (Figure 4.8i). Axle clips fastened the axle to the frame of the wagon (Herskovitz 1978:89–90); whiffletree tongues and shaft tips were parts of the rigging used to attach the draft animal to the wagon (Emmit 1969:574–575). Horse- or mule-related artifacts included four horseshoe or mule shoe nails and three iron buckles from a horse or mule harness or similar gear. One of the buckles was a bar buckle, another was a rectangular angled buckle, and the third was a barrel roller buckle. A similar barrel roller buckle is illustrated in the 1894–1895 Montgomery Ward catalog (Emmit 1969:322).

Tools and Hardware

Five recovered artifacts were tools or hardware. One was part of a wood-drill bit, one was an iron blade from a pair of scissors, one was an iron counter-sink punch (Emmit 1969:356), and two were remains of a pocket knife (specifically, the metal end piece and segments of its bolster lining).

Machinery

The field crew found no complete machines and identified only a few artifacts as machine parts. Three were small (approximately 1-inch diameter) toothed gears, one probably from the working mechanism of a clock. Two oblong items in the shape of five-pointed stars were adjoining pieces of an unidentified machine. One piece had rivets near each point of the star, a hole near the center, and a small gear attached just below the hole. The second star-shaped piece had a hole in the center and holes near each point of the star corresponding to the rivets on the first piece.

Mining and Quarrying

Functional items in this category were three "drifting"-type pickaxe heads (a short axe head, used in the narrow confines of a mine drift, or horizontal shaft). One had "WASHO..." stamped on one side.

Communication

Metal items in this category were all associated with writing. They included an ink pen stamped "ESTERBROOK / COLORADO / NO 2" (an illustration of a similar pen appears in the 1894–1895 Montgomery Ward catalog [Emmit 1969:109]), the metal tip of a pen holder, two possible pen holder parts, a wood pencil eraser ferrule (the metal cylinder that holds the eraser to the pencil), and two small cylinders that also appeared to be eraser ferrules of some sort.

Miscellaneous and Unidentified

Miscellaneous objects consisted of five barrel hoops, 10 pieces of small-to-medium-gauge wire, a wire bale tie, and part of a copper nameplate embossed "...AIO...." Among the artifacts with unidentified functions were two cut nails with the pointed ends deliberately curled back onto the shanks; a brass rod 1-3/8 inches long with round end pieces, one of them stamped "PAT. AUG. 85"; 14 small (3/4-inch wide) five-point tin stars; a cast-iron rod; and a cast-iron bar. Unidentified artifacts included 13 pieces of iron, 2 possible tool fragments, a small copper strip, and a combination brass screw or nut with an odd shape.

Glass

Glass was also abundant at AZ N:11:19(ASM), with 961 artifacts recovered, most of them fragments. The bulk of the assemblage consisted of window and bottle glass, although numerous fragments of jars, tableware, and lamp chimneys were also present.

Food

Items in this functional category included fragments from at least three food jars and a complete stopper from a condiment jar. The jar fragments were two rim shards from an SCA milk-glass jar with a friction finish, one rim shard from an SCA jar with a sheared finish, and one body shard from a white milk-glass jar. Although the original contents of these containers were unknown, they likely held fruits or vegetables. The club sauce–type glass bottle stopper did not match any bottles at the site. The stopper had a tapered shank and had "LEA & PERRINS" embossed along the top edge (Figure 4.9a).

Food Preparation and Consumption

Thirteen glass items represented two types of tableware. One artifact, a single shard with part of a starburst pattern, was an SCA press-molded sugar bowl lid. The other 12 shards were from a single SCA press-molded goblet decorated with a series of raised dots beneath the rim on the exterior of the cup. The stem of the goblet was faceted. The analyst could not identify the exact style, but similar pieces of stemware were sold in the late 1800s and early 1900s.

Household Furnishings

Forty glass fragments were from lamp chimneys. Eleven were clear and 29 were SCA glass. The two different colors suggested use of a minimum of two lamp chimneys at the site.

Architecture (Construction-Related)

All of the 453 glass shards in this category were classified as clear in color. However, tints ranging from aqua to green were visible when the fragments were viewed on edge, suggesting at least two or three different panes of glass.

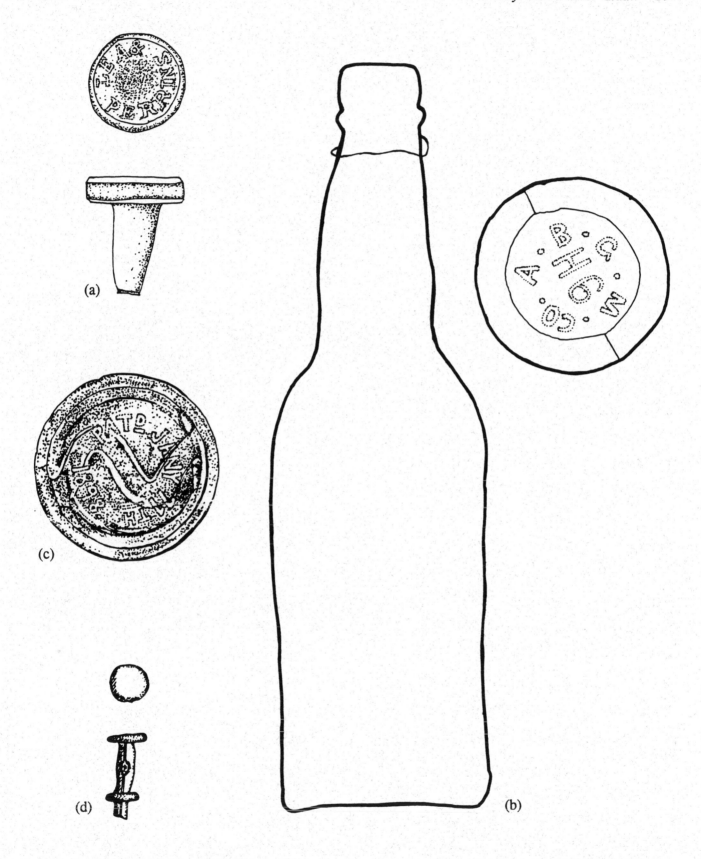

Figure 4.9. Selected glass artifacts recovered from Site AZ N:11:19(ASM). Bottle drawn 80% actual size, other artifacts drawn actual size.

Leisure and Recreation

Site AZ N:11:19(ASM) yielded one whole bottle and 276 bottle fragments. Analysis of the many base, finish, and embossed body shards recovered indicated that at least 25 glass containers were represented in the assemblage. At least 11 originally held alcoholic beverages.

Five of the bottles had held beer. The one complete bottle recovered was a brown beer bottle, 9-1/2 inches tall, with a hand-applied brandy finish, a bottle-stopper wire attached to its neck (Figure 4.9b), and the maker's mark "A.B.G.M. CO. / H6" embossed on the base. According to Toulouse (1971:26–27), the Adolphus Busch Glass Manufacturing Company used this mark between 1886 and 1928. The first fully automatic bottling machine, developed in 1903, came into wide-scale use over the next decade. The hand-applied finish on this bottle indicated manufacture before or during the switch-over to the fully automatic process. Fragments representing other beer bottles were two broken aqua bases, an aqua heel/base shard (embossed "... A.B. ... / Y1"), an aqua hand-applied crown finish and neck, 12 aqua body shards, 1 brown base 3 inches in diameter with no basemark, 1 brown heel/base shard, and 21 brown body shards. Several maker's marks contain these same letters, making positive identification difficult. The aqua crown finish dates between 1892, when this type of finish was introduced, and the introduction of fully automatic bottle making machines.

The six other alcohol bottles in the assemblage represented three different types of bottles. Four double ring/bead finishes, 29 body shards, and two base shards were from pumpkin-seed picnic flasks. Since all the finishes were hand applied and all the shards were SCA in color, manufacture of these bottles probably dated between the 1880s and circa 1917. A brown base embossed with a "B" was from an oval flask. Berge (1980:90–91) discusses a similar flask in his report on Simpson Springs Station, assigning a date between 1880 and 1913; he could not identify the maker's mark. One shard, part of a green hand-applied finish, was from a wine or champagne bottle.

Personal Items

Items in this category were 11 white milk-glass buttons, all with four holes. Eight of the buttons were 7/16 inch (18 ligne) in diameter, 1 was 1/2 inch (20 ligne) in diameter, and the other 2 were 5/8 inch (24 ligne) in diameter. Two of the 18-ligne buttons were decorated. Both had sunken panels, and one also had short, raised lines radiating out from the middle of the panel. All but the two largest buttons appeared to be from a shirt or blouse.

Medical and Health

Several bottle shards recovered from the site were from patent-medicine bottles. Five were rectangular-panel patent-medicine bottles of aqua glass. One was a bottle originally manufactured for H. E. Bucklen & Company, Chicago, Illinois, which operated between 1878 and the 1890s. This bottle may have contained Dr. King's New Discovery for Consumption (Berge 1980:111, 117–118). Two of the aqua medicine bottles were manufactured for Chamberlain & Company, Des Moines, Iowa, a company that started operations around 1879 and continued past 1900 (Berge 1980:94–95). One of these bottles had contained Chamberlain's Pain Balm, the company's first product, and the other had contained

Chamberlain's Cough Remedy, which they began producing in 1881. The remaining two aqua patent medicine bottles were for Hamlin's Wizard Oil, which was produced circa 1900 (Fike 1987:11).

Two other bottles had also held medicine. One was a large, brown, French square bottle represented by two shards that fit together to form a side of the bottle embossed "DR. T.W. GRAYDON.../...CINCINNATI, O.../...DISEASE...THE L...." The other medicine bottle, identified by an SCA base shard with a partial maker's mark on it, had an embossed "...x" that appeared to match the maker's mark "Rex." Peterson (1968:43) identified Rex as a trademark first used in 1896 by the Obear-Nester Glass Co. of St. Louis, Missouri, and East St. Louis, Illinois.

Fragments of a jar represented another health-related item. The embossed legend "...'VASELINE'.../...HESEBRO.../...NEW-YORK..." indicated that this was a pomade jar that had contained Vaseline petroleum jelly. Although Robert A. Chesebrough invented the jelly in 1859, it was not until 1878 that a trademark patent (No. 6,041) was granted for the name Vaseline (Herskovitz 1978:14). Originally Vaseline was sold only wholesale in large-volume containers; retail sales of the jelly in tin cans and jars began around 1887 (Wilson and Wilson 1971:110). While Vaseline is still manufactured, the embossing and color of this jar date it to between 1887 and circa 1917. The lid, which was also recovered, had "PATD JANY. 11TH 1898" embossed inside (Figure 4.9c) in such a way that the words had to be read through the top. Across the top of the lid was an impressed "sine wave" design.

Another item recovered was a fragment of a cobalt-blue syringe plunger (Figure 4.9d). Herskovitz (1978:32) reported recovery of similar syringe plungers from Fort Bowie, Arizona. Such syringes could have been for either human or animal use.

Ceramics

Most of the 320 ceramic artifacts recovered from AZ N:11:19(ASM) related to the serving and consumption of food. Other functional categories represented in the ceramic assemblage were household furnishings, architecture, leisure and recreation, and personal items.

Food Preparation and Consumption

Most of the ceramic sherds were originally part of tableware. Ten different designs appeared on these sherds (Table 4.1). Examination of the shape of the sherds and the decoration indicated a minimum of 2 bowls, 3 cups, and 7 plates or saucers (Table 4.2). All but 5 of the 312 sherds in this functional category were whiteware, a hard-paste earthenware covered with a white glaze. Two porcelain sherds were from the same cup, and three other porcelain sherds may have been part of this cup as well.

One sherd from an unidentified vessel bore a manufacturer's hallmark, "Homer Laughlin, East Liverpool, Ohio," in green over a white glaze. This hallmark was used between 1877 and 1900 (Gates and Ormerod 1982:132).

Table 4.1. Designs on Ceramics from Site AZ N:11:19(ASM)

Design	Description
1	Gold foliage over white glaze
2	Gold interlocking circles and flower heads along rim over white glaze
3	Design 2 over a molded relief pattern of a line of raised dots enclosed by two lines parallel to each other and the undulating edge of the vessel
4	Brown foliage over white glaze
5	Gold foliage over white glaze over a molded relief pattern of a line of raised dots enclosed by two parallel lines
6	Painted picture of house and scenery in green, blue, violet, red, and brown over white glaze
7	Painted picture of a house, red flowers with green leaves, blue sky, and other scenery; oriental in appearance
8	Green foliage with pink flowers over white glaze
9	Picture of a house in green, brown, blue, pink, and gray under clear glaze
10	Gold line along edge over white glaze

Household Furnishings

One sherd was part of a picture frame. This sherd was a hard paste earthenware with a white glaze and a molded relief decoration.

Architecture

One ceramic item, an earthenware doorknob with a white "porcelain" finish, fit into this functional category. Herskovitz (1978:116–117) reported recovery of similar doorknobs from Fort Bowie, Arizona.

Leisure and Recreation

One of the five recovered sherds in this category was from a gray crockery bottle that might have originally contained an alcoholic beverage. The other four sherds were parts of a porcelain doll or dolls. One of these sherds had black eyelashes painted over a pink slip.

Table 4.2. Vessels Represented by Sherds in the Ceramic Assemblage from Site AZ N:11:19(ASM)

Vessel Form	Number of Vessels Represented	Decoration	Number of Sherds
Whiteware			
Bowl	2	None	26
Cup	2	None	9
Plate	1	Design 1	2
Plate	1	Design 2	2
Plate	1	Design 3	8
Plate	1	Design 5	8
Plate	1	Design 6	4
Plate	1	Design 8	2
Plate	1	Design 9	1
Plate		None	14
Unidentified	*	Design 1	1
Unidentified	*	Design 4	1
Unidentified	*	Design 10	1
Unidentified	*	None	227
Unidentified	*	Hallmark	1
Total	**11**		**307**
Porcelain			
Cup	1	None	2
Unidentified	*	Design 7	3
Total	**1**		**5**

*Could be part of identified vessels or of other items

Personal Items

The only ceramic item in the personal category was a whole, plain, sunken-panel four-hole button. The button appeared to be unglazed porcelain but could have been highly fired earthenware.

Leather

Personal Items

The 13 pieces of leather were all parts of shoes or boots. One fragment of leather was a complete sole made of a single layer of leather, and another fragment was part of a multi-layered sole. Both pieces had numerous shoe or boot nails still embedded in them. Two other pieces of leather had copper eyelets, for both the grommet "lace-through" and the hook "lace-over" type.

Graphite

Unidentified

Eight pieces of graphite recovered from AZ N:11:19(ASM) were rectangular segments 7/32 inch wide by 3/32 inch thick and of various lengths under 2 inches. The function of these pieces was not clear, but they may have been pencil leads, like that found in rectangular carpenter's pencils produced today.

Shell

Personal Items

Nine four-hole shell buttons came from this site. Five of the buttons were 7/16 inch (18 ligne) in diameter, two were 9/16 inch (22 ligne) in diameter, and two were 1/2 inch (20 ligne) in diameter. Most of the buttons appeared to have exfoliated (lost some of their thickness due to deterioration).

SUMMARY AND DISCUSSION

The historic component of Site AZ N:11:19(ASM) appeared to be domestic trash marking the remains of the Bay View Placer Mining Claim, associated with Mary Van Patten and John Nelson. Census records listed Mrs. Van Patten's husband, Ezekiel, and Nelson as prospectors; the three pick-axe heads and a chunk of meteoritic iron recovered from the site supported an association with prospectors and miners.

On the basis of testing results, the SWCA archaeologists predicted that a building foundation would be found during data recovery. A historical photograph located at the beginning of data recovery indicated that a building had been in the site area around the turn of the century. However, comparison of the turn-of-the-century photo with the same view photographed today suggested that the building foundation might have been destroyed during work by the State Highway Department (now the Arizona Department of Transportation) on State Route 69 in 1954. Data recovery did not reveal a foundation, indicating that this feature had indeed been destroyed by highway construction. Archaeological remains recovered from the historic component of the site appeared to be domestic trash associated with this structure.

The majority of the artifacts on the site dated from the early 1900s and thus were consistent with the period when the known claimants were associated with the site (1900–1901 for the Van Pattens and 1901–1906 for Nelson). However, a few artifacts did not fit into this chronology. Five evaporated/condensed milk cans (manufactured between 1908 and 1914) and a 1908 coin were slightly later than Nelson's known association with the site, suggesting a slightly later occupation of the site than shown by the historical records. The items could also indicate the presence of a later visitor, perhaps someone who dismantled the superstructure of the house. The large quantity of nails and window glass recovered from AZ N:11:19(ASM) certainly suggested dismantling activity. Two pieces of ammunition found during data recovery postdated the site (one cartridge case was first manufactured in 1917, and the other was first made in 1945), and one piece of ammunition found in testing predated it (this was a military cartridge case issued ca. 1871–1873), but these items could easily have been deposited on the site by hunters before and after the recorded occupations.

The artifact assemblage provided some insight into the ages of the site's inhabitants. Only one toy was recovered, parts of a porcelain doll. This item could indicate the presence of a female child, or, equally likely, an adult female who had kept a cherished childhood memento. The latter appears the more tenable hypothesis in view of the fact that census records indicate that neither the Van Pattens nor John Nelson had children in residence with them at Huron. The lack of other toys or baby/infant items also suggested that children had not been present.

The assemblage also provided a little insight into the gender of the site's occupants. Although no items were clearly and exclusively associated with members of one sex (the possible exception being the aforementioned doll), several items *hinted* at the presence of males or females. The suspender parts recovered from the site were probably worn by a male. The fancy buttons and possible jewelry fragment were probably worn by a female. In the early twentieth century, the garters could have been part of the clothing of either sex. The pressed glass tableware, stemware, and assortment of decorative china probably lent an air of refinement to this mining site and hinted at a "woman's touch." Conspicuously absent from the assemblage were razors and razor blades, suggesting that if a male lived on the site, he did not shave.

The material recovered through testing and data recovery revealed other information about the quality of life on this early twentieth century placer mining site. Its inhabitants did not have electricity (no electrical components); they heated their residence and probably also cooked using a cast-iron stove (stove parts); and their light came from kerosene- or oil-burning lamps (lamp-chimney shards). They were literate, as evidenced by the items of writing paraphernalia recovered. They partook of coffee, alcoholic beverages (beer, whiskey, wine/champagne), and tobacco. They ate a variety of canned meat, fish, dairy, and vegetable products. There was no evidence that they grew any of their own food on-site, nor did they appear to have used home-canned (jar-preserved) food.

For transportation, the site's occupants relied on mule(s) and horse(s), as evidenced by the mule shoes, horseshoes, tack, and wagon parts found during testing and data recovery. Apparently the occupants did not have an automobile or other motorized vehicle. This finding is consistent with what is known from archival records about the dating of the site and the economic level/occupation of its inhabitants. Automobiles were present in Arizona in the early twentieth century but were essentially "rich-man's toys" until the 1910s (Rodda 1993). Automobile ownership would likely have been well out of the economic reach of the prospectors living on the Bay View Placer Mine site.

Medical and health items recovered during testing and data recovery suggested that the site's inhabitants were afflicted with a variety of aches, ailments, and other medical conditions consistent with a life of mining and prospecting. Skin chaffing, chapping, and other irritations were apparently treated with Vaseline, Mentholatum, and Hamlin's Wizard Oil. Aches were treated with Chamberlain's Pain Balm. For cold symptoms, the site's inhabitants used on at least one occasion Chamberlain's Cough Remedy. Respiratory disease of a far more serious nature is suggested by the presence of a bottle that may have contained Dr. King's New Discovery for Consumption (tuberculosis). The presence of a piece of medical syringe also suggests serious human illness, but this item could have been used for treating or inoculating mules or horses.

CHAPTER 5

AZ N:11:20(ASM)
THE PRINCES PLACER EROSION CONTROL DEVICE

Pat H. Stein

MANAGEMENT HISTORY

Site AZ N:11:20(ASM) is in the NW¼SW¼ of Section 33 in Township 13 North, Range 1 East on the USGS Poland Junction, Arizona, 7.5 minute quadrangle (Figure 5.1). The site is 3.1 miles southwest of Humboldt and 0.6 mile north of Poland Junction at an elevation of 4760 feet above mean sea level. The site lies entirely within the State Route 69 right-of-way and has been cleared of all vegetation except grasses. Chaparral forms the natural vegetation of most of the surrounding area and can be seen south and west of the site, which is on a hillside that declines to the east-northeast at a grade of approximately 3%. To the north and east, the land opens into a grassy valley. A small but deep gully cuts east-west through the site. At a point 0.1 mile east of the site, the gully joins a larger drainage, unnamed on the current USGS topographic quadrangle but historically known as Post Office Gulch. Post Office Gulch joins Galena Gulch 1.25 miles northeast of the site.

The present alignment of SR 69 bisects the site. A small artifact scatter lies west of the highway, and a larger artifact scatter, an erosion control device, and a small cluster of rocks lie east of it. The site measures 160 feet northeast-southwest by 150 feet northwest-southeast and encompasses 0.6 acre.

GPI Environmental, Inc., (GPI 1991) first recorded the resource during a preliminary survey of SR 69 from Cordes Junction to Prescott. Archaeological Research Services, Inc., revisited the site during an assessment of sites found during the preliminary survey (Hoffman 1991) and relocated it during the Class III survey of SR 69 from Mayer to Dewey (Hathaway 1992). Each study noted that most of the cultural material was within an area impacted by previous highway construction, that construction could have eroded the integrity of the site, and that the site appeared to be confined to the surface.

Design analysis by ADOT engineers determined that the entire site would be impacted by the proposed SR 69 project. The involved agencies concurred that the site should be considered potentially eligible for the National Register of Historic Places and that testing should be conducted to determine its extent, condition, and significance. During testing, SWCA project personnel conducted historical research, mapped and recorded the site, recorded all artifacts, and searched for possible subsurface remains. Based on the testing results, SWCA did not recommend or conduct additional work at the site during the data recovery phase.

HISTORICAL DATA

Archival research revealed that this archaeological site coincided with the location of the Princes Placer Mining Claim, a turn-of-the-century gold-mining property. Specifically, the location of this site exactly coresponded with the northern corner of the Princes Placer, as described and depicted in various historical records.

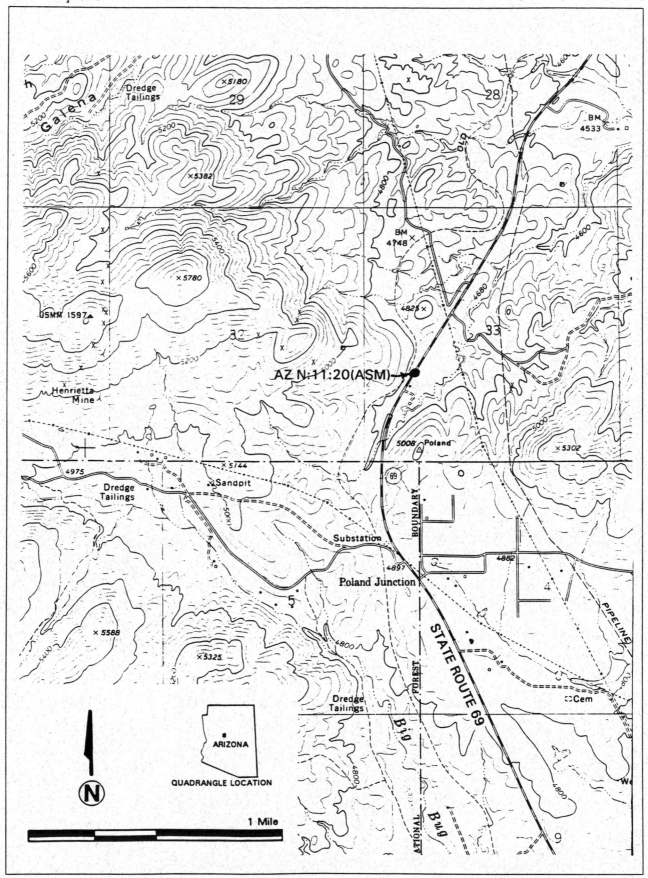

Figure 5.1. Location of Site AZ N:11:20(ASM), the Princes Placer erosion control device. Base map is Poland Junction, Arizona, USGS 7.5′ quadrangle, 1975.

Charles Ernest originally located the Princes Placer on May 20, 1898 (Yavapai County Recorder [YCR] Book of Mines [BM] 51:21). Ernest described his claim as

20 ac. of surface, placer ground. Commencing at a mon. of stone at center of S end of claim, and running 300 ft in a [sic] easterly direction to a mon of stone at SE corner of claim; thence in N direction 750 ft to a mon of stone at the center of E side of claim; thence N 750' to mon of stone at NE corner; thence W 600 ft to mon of stone at NW corner; thence S 750' to mon of stone at the center of the W side of claim; thence S 750' to SW corner, thence easterly 300' to mon. of stone to place of beginning. The claim may more generally be described as situated on Post-Office Gulch 1200 ft W of the Swindler Mine...in the Big Bug Mining District [YCR BM 51:21].

Little is known about Charles Ernest. The Book of Mines at the County Recorder's Office indicates that he had at least four other mining properties in the Big Bug Mining District around the turn of the century. He never patented his Princes Placer claim and sold his mineral rights in the claim to C. P. Wingfield on January 16, 1901 (YCR Book of Deeds [BD] 53:376). The deed for this transaction described the Princes Placer as "the placer bearing S & E of the Huron Station along east side of the Prescott & Eastern Railroad....Commencing at a point above the north end of the house of C. P. Wingfield and running south 500' to a monument of stone & 600' wide" (YCR BD 53:376).

Two items in this deed of transaction are noteworthy. First, Ernest (or General Land Office [GLO] officials) reduced the size of the claim between 1898 and 1901. Originally the claim measured 750 × 600 feet, but by 1901 it was only 600 × 500 feet. The second interesting point is that Wingfield was apparently already living on the claim when he purchased it.

One month after purchasing the Princes Placer, Wingfield had the claim professionally surveyed, as required under the Mining Law (see Chapter 1) to patent the claim. The Princes Placer survey, conducted by William H. Merritt in February of 1901, precisely mapped the boundaries of the claim and described all major improvements on it (Figure 5.2).

The plat and the surveyor's notes (Merritt 1901) provide some information about the property and its environs in early 1901. The claim was in the shape of a crude trapezoid that enclosed 7.76 acres. The northeast, southeast, southwest, and northwest sides of the trapezoid measured 575, 743.8, 580, and 460 feet, respectively. Merritt marked each corner with a mound of stones and set a 3.5-foot pine post in the center of each mound. The plat and surveyor's notes indicate that a wagon road hugged the shortest (northwest) side of the claim, that the Prescott & Eastern Railway (P&E) passed less than 0.1 mile west of the road, and that placer-bearing deposits were located along Post Office Gulch where it passed through the southeast side of the claim. Several improvements were also present on the claim. A 28 × 26–foot building labeled as "C. P. Wingfield's House" lay along the northeast side of the property, exactly 176 feet from the northern corner marker. A 20 × 18–foot building labeled a "house owned by the claimant [Wingfield]" was 217 feet east of the western corner marker. Other major improvements included "Shaft No. 1" (measuring 5 × 5 feet and 35 feet in depth) and "Shaft No. 2" (4 × 6 feet and 35 feet in depth), both on the western bank of Post Office Gulch.

Surveyor Merritt established a "Location Monument" near the eastern corner of the claim and then measured distances and directions from the monument to three nearby landmarks: the Huron Depot (N60°32′E at 759.5 feet), Wingfield's storehouse (N80°15′E at 507 feet), and Wingfield's store (S87°00′E

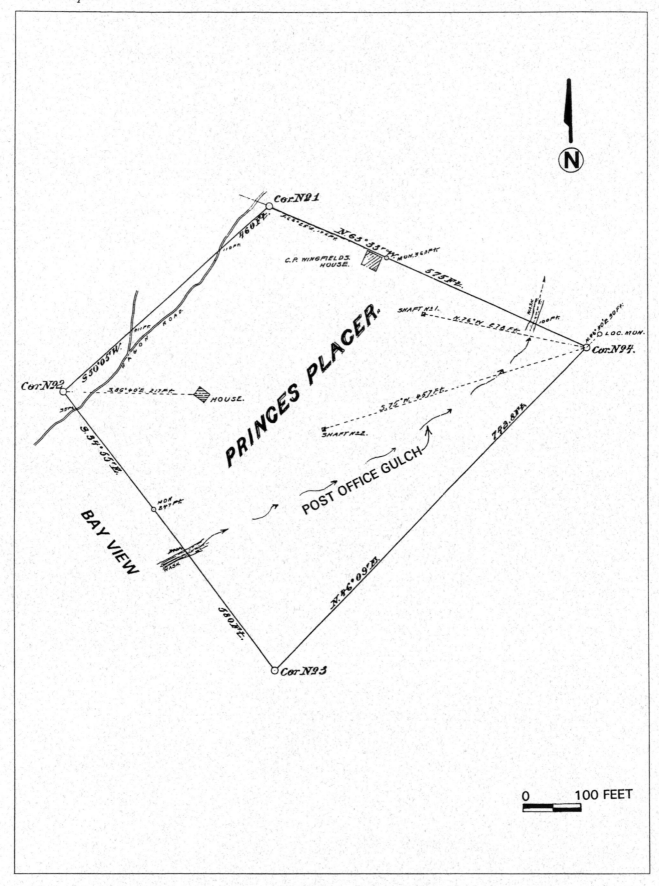

Figure 5.2. 1901 Mineral Entry Survey of the Princes Placer Mining Claim (Merritt 1901).

at 639.7 feet). The three landmarks indicate that Wingfield ran a commercial enterprise that had easy access to a shipping/receiving point along the P&E.

The mining and surveying records complement what is known about C. P. Wingfield from other sources. Charles Pleasants Wingfield was born in Cincinnati, Arkansas, on July 29, 1867, the eldest of eight children born to William Gilmore and Margrette Ann Pleasants Wingfield. When Charles was seven years old, his parents moved to Yavapai County and settled near the present town of Cottonwood, where they took up homesteading (Stephens 1955:129–130). In the mid 1890s Charles himself homesteaded 120 acres at Camp Verde, receiving his title patent in 1899. While in his early thirties Charles took a job on the building of the P&E. Working with "single men dry of throat and coarse of character" (Sayre 1985:50), Wingfield saw the opportunities afforded by his coworkers and established a saloon at Huron Station. The saloon opened in October of 1898 and enjoyed such immediate success that Wingfield made plans to establish a general store there. Assisted by his brother, Robert Wilson Wingfield, Charles expanded his commercial interests. The two Wingfield brothers soon supplied lumber, livestock, feed, mining supplies, general merchandise, and firewood to local mines; owned the Huron hotel; and employed many teamsters to transport supplies from Huron Station to outlying mining camps.

As the mines prospered, so did the Wingfields. Many of the mines had "played out" by 1910—particularly the McCabe Mine, which had been the Wingfield's largest customer—and the fortunes of the brothers declined until they could develop other successful ventures. Charles moved down the P&E tracks to the smelter town of Humboldt, where he rented a building from the railroad and operated a general store for several years (Sayre 1985:41). In 1909 Robert and William Gilmore Wingfield purchased the old sutler's store in Camp Verde; the store thrived and remained in Wingfield ownership for many decades. The Humboldt and Camp Verde stores earned for the Wingfields their reputation as the pre-eminent merchants of eastern Yavapai County (Wingfield 1954:203–206). Around 1943 Charles moved to Prescott, where he died in 1955 at the age of 88 (Sharlot Hall Museum [SHM] Obituary Book [OB]:967). Robert remained at Camp Verde until his death in 1964 at age 85 (Harvey and Harvey 1985:3).

Charles Wingfield received a title patent for the Princes Placer in July of 1903. It would appear that this claim never played a major role in his fortunes or reversals of fortune. According to the Arizona Department of Mines and Mineral Resources (ADMMR), the Princes Placer *may* have yielded gold, but the quantity is unknown (ADMMR Resources File [RF], Princes Placer). It appears that Charles Wingfield was primarily a merchant, not a miner, and that his commercial enterprises, not his mining ventures, led to his prosperity. Viewed within the context of Wingfield's other enterprises, the little 7.76-acre Princes Placer property served mainly as his place of residence in the early twentieth century.

In November of 1916 Wingfield sold his patented claim to Dora I. Lee of Humboldt for $1.00 (YCR BD 110:12). Lee retained most of the property through the rest of the historic period, selling only 0.22 acre of it, to Samuel B. Tenney, Jr., a local cattleman, in November of 1931 (YCR BD 151:582).

ARCHAEOLOGICAL DATA

On-site testing at AZ N:11:20(ASM) consisted of generating site plan and feature maps, recording (sketching and photographing) features, analyzing artifacts in the field, and excavating shovel tests in three features that appeared to have the potential for depth. The mapping confirmed that the site had been accurately plotted and delineated by previous investigators and that it lay entirely within the ROW. SWCA field personnel defined four features at the site (Figure 5.3). Since no designations had been assigned to the features during previous surveys, the testing crew called them Features A, B, C, and D. Definitions of terms describing historical artifacts appear in the Glossary.

Feature A was a wall of tabular metamorphic stones placed across a gully in courses with no mortar (Figure 5.4). The wall measured 50.0 feet northeast-southwest in length and a maximum of 12.5 feet northwest-southeast in width. Its top was level, with its maximum height (3.8 feet) in the central portion where it crossed the gully. The wall was free-standing in the center but was anchored at both ends in the banks of the drainage. Some of the uppermost stones were larger and flatter than the rest, giving the impression of capstones; a few of these stones had tumbled to the downhill (eastern) side of the wall. A shovel test indicated that the wall extended only 3 inches below the base of the drainage channel. The only artifact in direct association with the wall was a piece of wire mesh found on the western side of the feature near a packrat midden. The orientation of the wall across the gully, plus the fact that the wall was arresting arroyo cutting, indicated that the feature was an erosion control device.

Feature B was a mound of metamorphic rock measuring 7.5 feet northwest-southeast by 5.0 feet northeast-southwest and 0.5 foot in height (Figure 5.5). The testing crew examined the feature by carefully taking the rocks apart. The rocks were on the current ground surface, they bore no identifying marks or inscriptions, and no artifacts were within or beneath them.

This feature coincided exactly with the location of the northern corner of the Princes Placer claim; historically, this corner was marked by a mound of stones supporting a pine post inscribed with the claim name and corner number. Although no pine post was visible, the location and general appearance of this feature suggested that it was, in fact, the northern corner marker for the turn-of-the-century placer claim. The SWCA archaeologists devised a test to see if this was the case: using the 1901 Mineral Entry Survey plat (see Figure 5.2) as a guide, they attempted to locate on the ground the improvements shown on the plat. For example, the plat indicated that C. P. Wingfield's house was exactly 176 feet from the northern corner at a bearing of N63°33'W. A back azimuth shot from Feature B intersected a concentration of household artifacts and possible house remains approximately 175 feet from the mound of stone. This cultural material was outside the proposed ROW and continued eastward to Post Office Gulch.

Feature C was a sparse artifact scatter (5 ceramic sherds and 78 pieces of glass) measuring 75 feet northeast-southwest by 35 feet northwest-southeast and surrounding Feature B. The sherds were of hard-paste earthenware and likely came from one vessel, although its form could not be determined. The glass fragments appeared to represent eight bottles. The majority of the fragments were of sun-colored amethyst (SCA) (27 fragments), pale green (22), and brown (14) glass; however, pieces of amber (3), aqua (2), and clear (3) glass and white milk glass (3) were also present, as well as two complete bottle finishes and two partial bottle bases. An SCA brandy finish with a hand-applied lip suggested a date of manufacture prior to 1903. An SCA crown finish with a mold seam extending to the top of the lip suggested a date of manufacture between 1903 and 1917. One base fragment bore part of a maker's mark used by the Root Glass Company from 1901 to 1932. The other base also bore part of a maker's mark, but the fragment was too small to permit identification. Two shovel tests indicated that the artifacts were confined to the present ground surface.

Feature D was a sparse artifact scatter measuring 30 feet northeast-southwest by 20 feet northwest-southeast on the west side of SR 69. The scatter contained 2 pieces of a cobalt-blue serving dish, 5 pieces of an SCA glass container, 1 piece of pale green bottle glass, 1 clear glass bottle finish with a metal screw

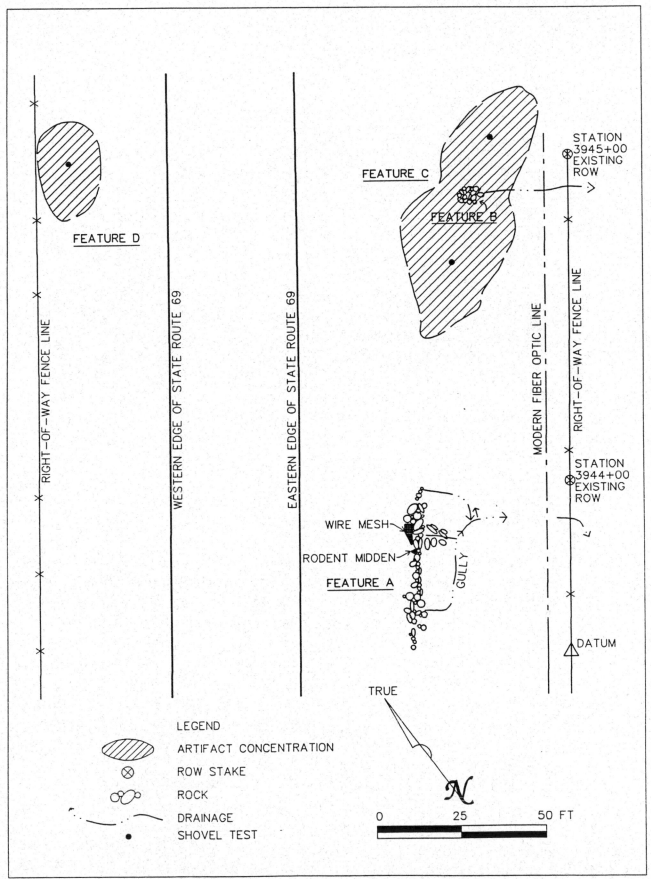

Figure 5.3. Site AZ N:11:20(ASM), the Princes Placer erosion control device.

Figure 5.4. Site AZ N:11:20(ASM), Feature A, wall of tabular stone; view west.

Figure 5.5. Site AZ N:11:20(ASM), Feature B, rock mound; view west.

cap, 1 20d wire nail, and fragments of a hole-in-cap can. The most closely datable objects were the SCA glass, which suggested an 1880–1917 date of manufacture, and the can fragments, which suggested a date in the late nineteenth or early twentieth centuries. A shovel test showed that the artifacts were confined to the present ground surface. An emerald-green wire insulator found 20 feet west of Feature D was of a type known as a "double petticoat" invented in 1883 by S. Oakley (Munsey 1970:295). This object likely came from electrical lines that were formerly strung along the railroad grade and road west of this site and should be considered an intrusive element.

The archival and archaeological data suggested that this site was indeed part of the Princes Placer Mining Claim. Feature B was probably the mound that marked the northern corner of the claim. Furthermore, the marker was likely built in February of 1901 when William Merritt surveyed the Princes Placer claim for Charles Wingfield and erected mounds of stones to demarcate its boundaries.

It is likely that Wingfield built Feature A, the soil erosion control device. In historic times this feature was upslope from Wingfield's house and downslope from a wagon road near the northwestern edge of the Princes Placer claim. Traffic along the wagon road may have destabilized the soil, resulting in the gullying seen at this feature. Wingfield probably sought to stabilize the soil and arrest the gullying so that his home would not be affected. The strategy appears to have worked; the wall is still largely intact, it is still retaining soil, and there are no signs of recent erosion. The hypothesis that Feature A was a soil erosion control device received further support from a rare photograph of Huron Station taken circa 1902. The photograph (see Figure 6.16) clearly depicts Charles Wingfield's house and shows a gully in an advanced state of erosion between the house and Huron Station.

It is difficult to determine precisely who deposited the artifacts found at Features C and D. The most tenable and logical hypothesis is that most of the artifacts were associated with the Wingfield household. The dating of the objects, and their domestic character, tend to support this hypothesis; at least, they do not refute it. An alternative hypothesis is that the objects were deposited by travelers along the wagon road that formerly ran along the northwestern side of the Princes Placer claim. A third hypothesis is that these artifacts were deposited by other residents of Huron, a dispersed community occupied circa 1898–1910s.

SUMMARY AND RECOMMENDATIONS

The features at Site AZ N:11:20(ASM), a compact and intriguing site, were on the northernmost part of the Princes Placer claim. Features A and B were likely associated with the Wingfield era of the site and represented, respectively, an erosion control device and a claim corner marker. Features C and D may also have represented Wingfield's activities on the property.

The mining claim was a gold placer. If it was ever more than modestly productive, that fact was not reflected in archival data. Wingfield earned his wealth not as a miner but as a merchant serving miners. The Princes Placer seems to have functioned mainly as Wingfield's place of residence from as early as 1898, when he worked for the railroad and opened a saloon at Huron Station, to as late as 1916, when he sold the claim.

A crucial point is that Site AZ N:11:20(ASM) represents only a small fraction of the 7.76-acre parcel that was once the Princes Placer claim. Wingfield's house was not part of this site but a short distance southeast of it, outside the present and proposed ROWs. The Wingfield house site will not be impacted by the proposed construction.

Testing identified Site AZ N:11:20(ASM), defined the historic context in which it functioned, and examined its archival and archaeological data sets. The investigation yielded a small but significant amount of information regarding historic Huron and C. P. Wingfield; for this reason, the site should be considered National Register-eligible under Criterion D. Testing also suggested that the site was unlikely to produce additional significant data. SWCA therefore did not recommend or conduct additional research at AZ N:11:20(ASM) during the data recovery phase of the SR 69 investigations.

CHAPTER 6

AZ N:11:23(ASM)
HURON STATION AND
THE MONTEZUMA AND EAGLE FRACTION LODE CLAIMS

Pat H. Stein
Elizabeth J. Skinner
Stewart Deats
John D. Goodman II

MANAGEMENT HISTORY

Site AZ N:11:23(ASM) is in the NE¼NW¼SW¼ of Section 33 in Township 13 North, Range 1 East on the USGS Poland Junction, Arizona, 7.5 minute quadrangle (Figure 6.1). The site is approximately 3 miles southwest of Humboldt and 0.7 mile north of Poland Junction on the west side of State Route 69. It lies near the base of a northeast-facing hillslope in open grassland and chaparral at an elevation ranging from 4760 feet to 4800 feet above sea level. The nearest drainage, 0.2 mile east of the site, is unnamed on current topographic maps but was known historically as Post Office Gulch. Post Office Gulch joins Galena Gulch 1.1 miles north-northeast of the site. The site measures 420 feet north-south by 420 feet east-west, encompasses 4 acres, and lies on private land and an Arizona Department of Transportation (ADOT) easement.

Historian John Sayre (1985:50–55) first identified this site, today marked mainly by an earthen platform along an abandoned railroad grade, as Huron Station. Huron Station was a stop along the Prescott & Eastern (P&E) Railway, built in 1898 by Frank Murphy (see Chapter 1). Archaeologists did not inventory the site until Archaeological Research Services, Inc., (ARS) conducted a Class III cultural resource survey for the Mayer to Dewey segment of the proposed SR 69 project (Hathaway 1992). The survey recorded the resource as a historic artifact area of moderate to high density associated with four features: a railroad grade with a leveled earthen platform, a cobble retaining wall, a depression resulting from ore extraction, and a mound containing fragments of possible copper ore. The study concluded that the site was potentially eligible for the National Register of Historic Places (NRHP) under Criterion D because of its potential to yield important information pertaining to transportation history, mining history, and the historic occupation of this region of central Arizona.

ADOT's engineering and design analysis determined that complete avoidance of this large site would not be feasible. ADOT staff proposed a new right-of-way (ROW) that would avoid the retaining wall, mining depression, and ore mound, but would impact an artifact concentration and part of the railroad grade and earthen platform. SWCA's testing program included archival research, brushing the ROW to better define the extent and condition of remains, mapping the entire site, photodocumentation of all features, excavating test units and trenches in features suspected of having depth, gridding the portion of the site within the ROW and collecting all diagnostic artifacts within the grids, and making additional observations about portions of the site outside the ROW.

Archival research during the testing phase of the investigations confirmed that the site marked the remains of Huron Station and revealed that it also represented the remains of two lode mining claims.

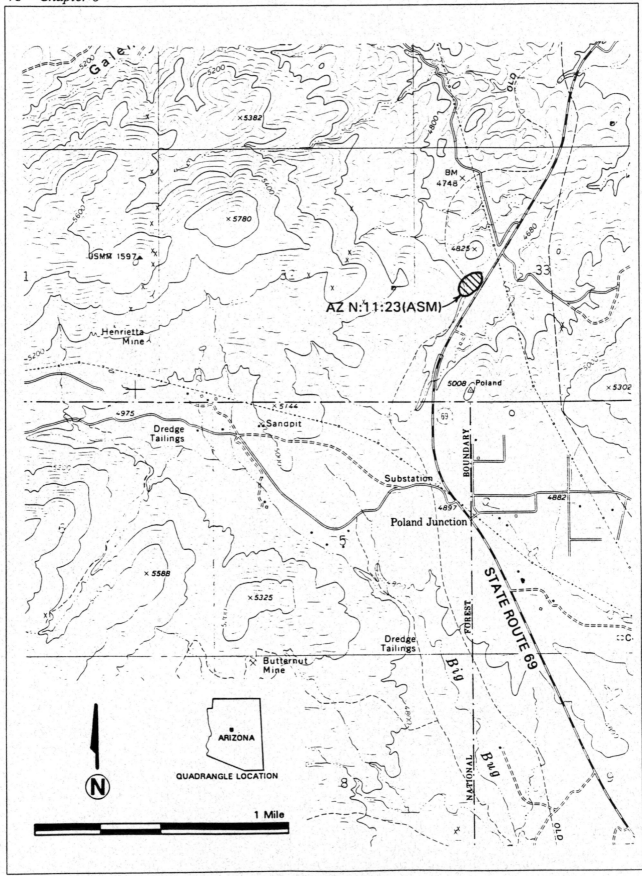

Figure 6.1.   Location of Site AZ N:11:23(ASM), Huron Station and the Montezuma and Eagle Fraction lode claims. Base map is Poland Junction, Arizona, USGS 7.5′ quadrangle, 1975.

Archaeological test data indicated that the site contained a moderate density of historical material, the dates of which were generally consistent with the dating of the site through archival records. During testing, the site yielded important information concerning mining, transportation, and the early twentieth century occupation of central Arizona and appeared capable of yielding further information on these issues. SWCA therefore deemed the site eligible for the NRHP under Criterion D and recommended data recovery at the portion of the site within the ROW.

HISTORICAL DATA

Archival research revealed that Site AZ N:11:23(ASM) had a rich and complex history associated with both mining and railroading. The site represented not only Huron Station, but also two patented mines known as the Eagle Fraction and Montezuma lode mining claims. [*Please note*: the mining claims at this site differ in location and history from those of the *same names* described in Chapter 7.]

Sayre (1985:50) wrote that Frank Murphy and his associates carefully orchestrated the route of their Prescott & Eastern Railway to cross several mining properties in which they held a financial interest. Sayre further maintained that the railroad crossed one of Murphy's mines at Huron, the location of AZ N:11:23(ASM). SWCA's investigations found no evidence that Murphy ever *owned* mines at Huron Station; at least, Murphy's name did not appear as the claimant or owner of record for any mines there. Instead, Murphy and his associate E. B. Gage financially backed (that is, *bonded*) some of the individuals who located claims at Huron Station around the beginning of the twentieth century, and that appears to have been the extent of Murphy's involvement in mining activity there.

The earliest recorded mining activity at Huron took place in May of 1896 when John F. Brinley located the Swindler Claim, a 16-acre property on what would now be the eastern side of SR 69. Brinley's action triggered additional mining claims in the locality: Brushy Flat (located by F. E. Wager and Theo H. Wade in July of 1897); Montezuma (located by Teofilo Montain, Guadalupe Trujillo, Murseano Rivera, John Brinley, Lulu Krackenberger, and Adam Krackenberger in July of 1898); Victor (located by Adam Krackenberger and Joe Banes in January of 1900); Huron No. 1 and Huron No. 2 (both located by George Hull's Huron Gold Company in January of 1903); and Eagle Fraction (located by Frank Nester in January of 1909) (General Land Office [GLO] 1915). These seven lode claims formed a cluster of contiguous properties, ranging in size from 15.6 acres to 20.6 acres (Figure 6.2), that exploited a single vein bearing copper, gold, and silver (Dunning 1951).

GLO Mineral Entry Survey records show that these early miners made modest improvements to their claims by excavating discovery cuts, shafts, and tunnels. Such improvements were necessary to keep their claims active and valid. While it is not known if their efforts bore fruit and were profitable, their discoveries apparently piqued the interest of George Hull, who consolidated the seven claims into one property during the period between 1901 and 1915–1916. Collectively, the seven claims became known as the "Hull-Huron Mining Property" (ADMMR Resources File [RF], Hull-Huron Mining Property). In most cases, Hull acquired mineral rights to the claims by purchasing them from their locators for prices ranging from $50 to $200. However, he acquired the Montezuma claim in 1920 by "jumping" it: proving to the Government Land Office that he, and not its original locators, had made necessary improvements to the property during a five-year period.

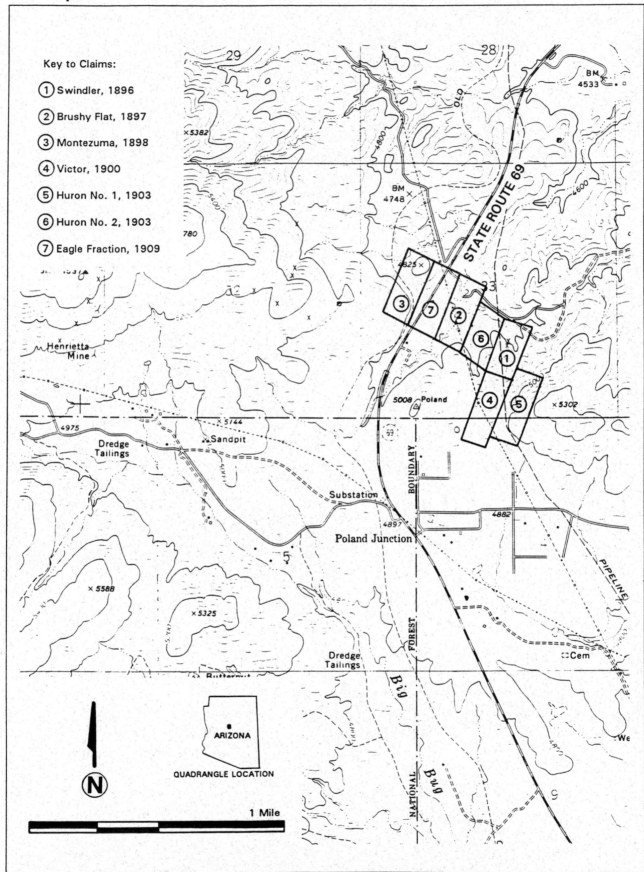

Key to Claims:

1 Swindler, 1896

2 Brushy Flat, 1897

3 Montezuma, 1898

4 Victor, 1900

5 Huron No. 1, 1903

6 Huron No. 2, 1903

7 Eagle Fraction, 1909

Figure 6.2. Lode claims at Huron. These seven claims became the "Hull-Huron Mining Property." Base map is Poland Junction, Arizona, USGS 7.5′ quadrangle, 1975.

George W. Hull was an entrepreneur who attempted many activities and achieved success in several of them. Born in Massachusetts in 1839, he moved to Nevada at the age of 19 and built a toll road into the booming mining town of Hamilton. From Nevada he found his way to Arizona Territory, where he first operated a store and freighting business in Flagstaff. When the transcontinental railroad reached Flagstaff in 1882, he relocated to the Verde Valley, where he established a freighting business between Camp Verde and Jerome, bought a ranch in the Middle Verde, and established a store at the junction of the Camp Verde and Cherry Creek roads. In the 1880s he proposed and may have been responsible for building toll roads from Camp Verde to Grief Canyon and Beaver Creek (Young 1974:79–80).

The ambitious entrepreneur quickly earned the nickname of "Make-a-Million Hull," for he vowed to continue his wheelings and dealings until he became wealthy (Young 1974:79). A turning point in his quest came in 1883 when he began to acquire property in Jerome. He displayed a great faculty for this activity and soon owned much of the ground on which the town was built. He sold lots in Jerome—carefully retaining mineral rights beneath the surface—and used the proceeds to launch his own mining company. Organized in 1899, the United Verde Extension Gold, Silver & Copper Mining Company later evolved into the bonanza United Verde Extension Mining Company (UVX). By the turn of the century, the fame of Jerome's deposits had spread far and wide, and Hull had no trouble attracting investors from England, Scotland, and France as well as the United States. He established a permanent residence in Jerome and eventually became its mayor, a territorial representative, and a city councilman (Young 1972:180–182, 1974:79–83). George Hull was particularly adept at bringing mineral claims to patent, a milestone he achieved with his Huron properties in 1916.

Hull owned the mineral properties in Jerome and the seven claims at Huron at approximately the same time. To some extent the Huron claims took a back seat because they were less lucrative. Dunning (1951) reported that Hull was developing the Huron property when his Jerome property began to pay off and that he ceased operations at Huron to concentrate on Jerome. Dunning also stated that Hull intended to focus on Huron once his affairs in Jerome were settled, but that he died before this goal could be realized.

Although he was more actively engaged in developing his Jerome mines, Hull did manage to exploit his Huron claims to some extent. He sank approximately 1500 feet of shafts, tunnels, and drifts and extracted rich ores. Around 1906 he extracted from the Swindler claim alone a total of seven rail carloads of ore (approximately 300 tons) that assayed per ton at 7.5% copper, $4.00 in gold, and several ounces of silver [2]. Hull shipped all ore taken from these workings to a smelter at Swansea, Arizona, in the Buckskin Mountains south of the Bill Williams River (Dunning 1951; Dunning and Peplow 1959).

In an effort to further develop the Huron property, Hull tried to attract investors to capitalize the venture. Through advertisements placed in *Yavapai Magazine* (*YM*) in 1914 and 1915, he reported that he had already invested $25,000 in the workings, had dug 1500 feet of shafts, tunnels, and drifts, and had

---

[2]In assaying, most metals, including copper, are expressed in percentages. However, precious metals (such as gold, silver, and platinum) are expressed in troy ounces per short ton. During the historical period of these assay figures (indeed, until the 1930s), gold had a government-fixed price of $20.67 per troy ounce. Therefore, in the 1906 assay figures for the Huron property, copper was expressed as a percentage and silver was expressed in troy ounces per short ton, but gold was expressed by converting it from its troy-ounces-per-short-ton figure to its market equivalent ($4.00) at the government-fixed rate.

exposed veins varying from 4 feet to 10 feet in width and assaying at $4 to $20 per ton in gold (*YM* July 1914 13:3, September 1915 9:1).

While trying to attract financial backers for Huron, Hull became embroiled in lawsuits that had disastrous consequences. In the spring of 1916 he optioned all of the stock in his Jerome mining company (then called the Hull Copper Company) to a competitor, Will L. Clark of the United Verde Copper Company. This action prompted the filing of a lawsuit against Hull by his minority stockholders, who charged that Hull's dealings with United Verde had effectively squeezed out their interests. In May of 1916 the court appointed an accountant to audit the books of the company and investigate the allegations (*YM* March 1917 9:2). Hull soon brought a suit of his own against United Verde, charging that the company had failed to pay him $142,722 from the stock-option deal. Following a grueling session on the witness stand in October 1916, George Hull collapsed while leaving court and died a short time later.

Upon Hull's death, his Huron property (along with four other mining claims in the Big Bug Mining District) passed to his heirs, George B. and Mary A. Hull. Mary outlived George and retained ownership of the Huron property through the end of the historic period. The Hull family still owned the Huron property in 1985–1986 when Long Lac Minerals Exploration Ltd. conducted exploratory drilling on the Swindler claim (ADMMR RF, Hull-Huron Mining Property). This was the last recorded instance of mining activity on the property.

The preceding paragraphs have provided a wide-angle view of historical events surrounding Site AZ N:11:23(ASM). The points to be emphasized are that mining activity at the site was closely related to mining activity on adjacent claims and that these seven claims were managed as a group for most of the historic period. The rest of this section focuses more tightly on the site itself.

The ARS archaeologists who conducted the Class III archaeological survey recognized that Site AZ N:11:23(ASM) marked the location of historic Huron Station (Hathaway 1992:42–43). SWCA's investigations found that the site represented not one but three historic properties. In chronological order, these were Huron Station, the Montezuma Claim, and the Eagle Fraction Claim.

Maps housed at the Sharlot Hall Museum verified that Huron Station was at the location of site AZ N:11:23(ASM), as did Sayre (1985). The P&E established the station in the spring of 1898 when the railroad was being constructed (Sayre 1985:9, 50). Railway records (cited in Sayre 1990:219) indicate that the station eventually included a bunkhouse, a cistern, a depot, a section house, and a warehouse (Table 6.1). The most substantial structure was the depot, measuring 64 × 20 feet. According to a newspaper account, it was built in the fall of 1898 (*Arizona* Journal-Miner [*AJM*] 18 October 1998 1:4).

Huron Station became the nucleus of a small, dispersed community of miners, prospectors, and entrepreneurs and provided essential services and goods to outlying mines and camps. The first entrepreneur to establish a business was Charles Pleasants Wingfield (see Chapter 5), who opened a saloon at Huron Station in October of 1898. Although the saloon thrived, Wingfield soon sold it to Franklin Nester (spelled Nest*or* in some records). Frank Nester, a bachelor originally from Michigan, was 30 years of age when he acquired the Huron saloon in 1900. According to census records, Nester continued to operate the business until at least 1910.

After selling the saloon, C. P. Wingfield, with his brother Robert W. Wingfield, opened a general store at Huron. Soon the Wingfield brothers were involved in many aspects of the local economy, supplying

Table 6.1. Structures Formerly Present at Huron Station

Structure	Size	Material	Year Built	Cost	Remarks
Depot	20 × 64 feet	wood	1898	unknown	Retired 1923
Bunkhouse	unknown	wood	1898	unknown	
Section House	unknown	wood	unknown	unknown	Retired 1929
Warehouse	25 × 25 feet	wood	unknown	unknown	
Cistern	12,000 gallons	concrete	1916	$537.00	

Adapted from Sayre 1990:219

lumber, livestock, feed, mining supplies, general merchandise, and firewood to local mines; operating a hotel; and employing many teamsters to transport the supplies being sold. C. P. Wingfield became the community's most outspoken (and usually only) booster and by 1901 was regarded as "a sort of mayor over Huron" (*AJM* 29 May 1901 3:4).

Huron soon gained other refinements. Shortly after the P&E Railway began to operate, the Western Union Telegraph Company and Wells Fargo opened offices in the depot; in fact, the same agent served all three companies (Sayre 1985:53) Wells Fargo was an especially important and lucrative business for Huron because the stage company carried virtually all ore shipments from outlying mines (Sayre 1979:53). A post office was established at Huron in April of 1901, with Harvey Stamp as its first postmaster (Theobald and Theobald 1961:107). Other amenities at Huron included telephone service, provided by the Prescott Electric Company, and electricity, utilized mainly by mining companies rather than the general population. Yavapai County created a Huron School District in 1902 but disbanded it in 1904 because of its small enrollment (Sayre 1985:53).

Huron's peak years were 1900 to 1907, when it supplied services and materials to McCabe, a mining camp of four to six hundred people approximately two miles northwest of the station. However, as McCabe's fortunes declined, so did Huron's, its population dropping from 50 in 1900 to just 22 in 1910 (Spude and Paher 1978:33; U.S. Census Bureau 1910). Although Huron enjoyed some resurgence during World War I when the Big Ledge Copper Company and the Big Ledge Extension Mining Company reopened mines near the town, the new life was short. The end of the war brought the end to Huron. The railroad retired the depot from service in 1923, and the post office struggled to remain open until 1928 (Sayre 1985:54).

In 1925, when the railway and station were shadows of their former selves, surveyors for the Atchison, Topeka and Santa Fe Railway (AT&SF) (then the owner of the P&E) mapped the railbed and station. The resulting plat (Figure 6.3), discovered by SWCA researchers in the files of the AT&SF branch office in Winslow, appears to be the only historic-era map of Huron Station that has survived to the present day. As the map indicates, by 1925 all that remained of the station were the depot and a warehouse. Today archaeological Site AZ N:11:23(ASM) marks all that is left of Huron Station.

AZ N:11:23(ASM) was also the location of the Montezuma and Eagle Fraction claims. Detailed Mineral Entry Survey plats of these mining parcels have survived to the present day (Merritt 1915) (Figure 6.4). As mentioned previously, the Montezuma claim was located in July of 1898 by a group of six Hispanic and Euroamerican miners, then was successfully "jumped" in August of 1910 by George Hull. Frank Nester located the Eagle Fraction claim in January of 1909 and sold it to Hull in October of 1911. By the time the claims were platted in 1915, they contained several improvements: the Montezuma Claim included a discovery cut, three shafts, and two tunnels, and the Eagle Fraction contained a discovery shaft, one tunnel, and two houses. Surveyor's notes accompanying the plats (Merritt 1915) indicate that the houses on the latter claim measured 30 × 16 feet and 26 × 20 feet. They may have belonged to Frank Nester. Editions of the *Arizona Business Directory* indicate that Nester resided at Huron and maintained his saloon there circa 1900 to 1912.

Using the Mineral Entry Survey plats and surveyor's notes (Merritt 1915), SWCA's field personnel were able to tentatively identify various features at Site AZ N:11:23(ASM) (see Testing, below). The only shortcoming of the otherwise excellent plats is that they do not depict railroad-related structures other than the grade; that is, they do not depict the depot, bunkhouse, and so forth. Mining plats in general did not depict improvements that were owned by entities other than mining claimants.

ARCHAEOLOGICAL DATA

Testing

The testing crew began field work by removing brush. The northern end of the site had a dense vegetative cover, the removal of which helped to define the site's extent, condition, and nature. Brushing and mapping revealed two features that had not been detected during the survey, but otherwise did not significantly alter previous impressions of the site. The site contained a total of five features, two trash concentrations, a railroad grade, and a possible dirt road or trail.

Feature designations assigned during the survey were retained during the testing, with the following exceptions. Feature 3, downhill of and adjacent to Feature 2, a depression, was simply the backdirt from that excavation and thus was included with Feature 2 rather than given separate feature status. A feature discovered as the result of brushing became Feature 3, and a feature discovered as the result of mapping became Feature 5. Two areas with dense artifact concentrations were designated as Trash Areas A and B. Figure 6.5 is the site map generated during the testing investigations.

The proposed construction would impact the eastern half of the site, an area containing part of Feature 1, all of Features 3 and 5, most of Trash Area A, the possible dirt road or trail, and a portion of the railroad grade. Features 2 and 4, Trash Area B, and most of the railroad grade would not be impacted.

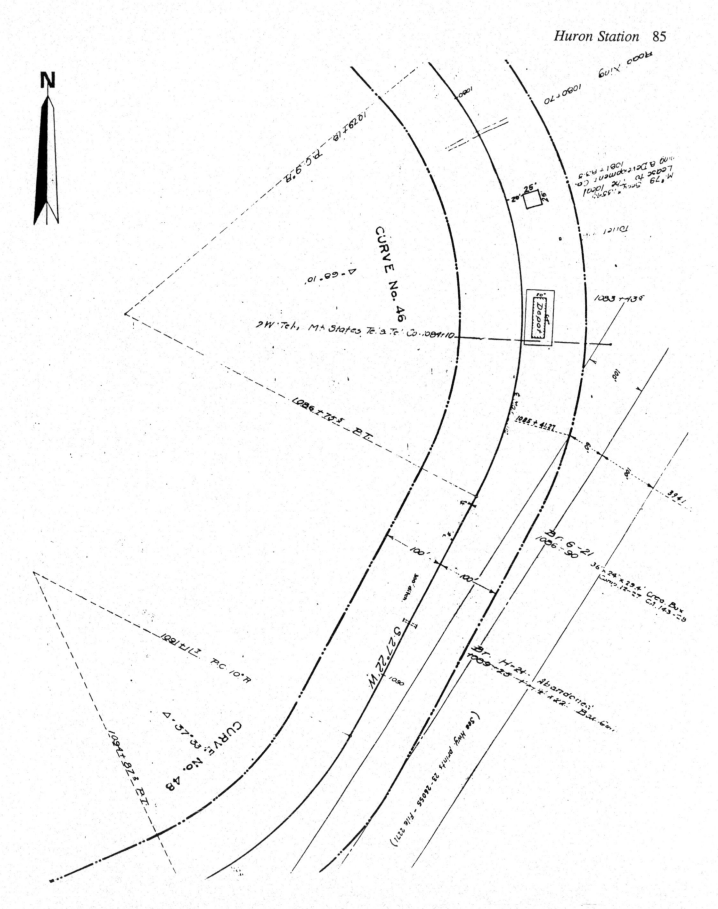

Figure 6.3. 1925 railway map of Huron Station (Atchison, Topeka and Santa Fe Railway 1925).

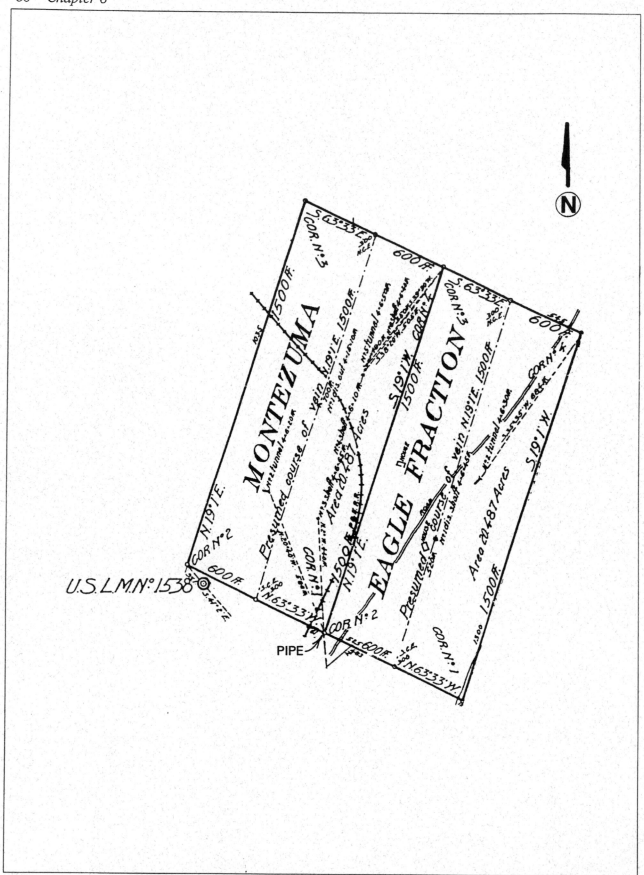

Figure 6.4. 1915 Mineral Entry Survey plat of Montezuma and Eagle Fraction lode claims (from Merritt 1915).

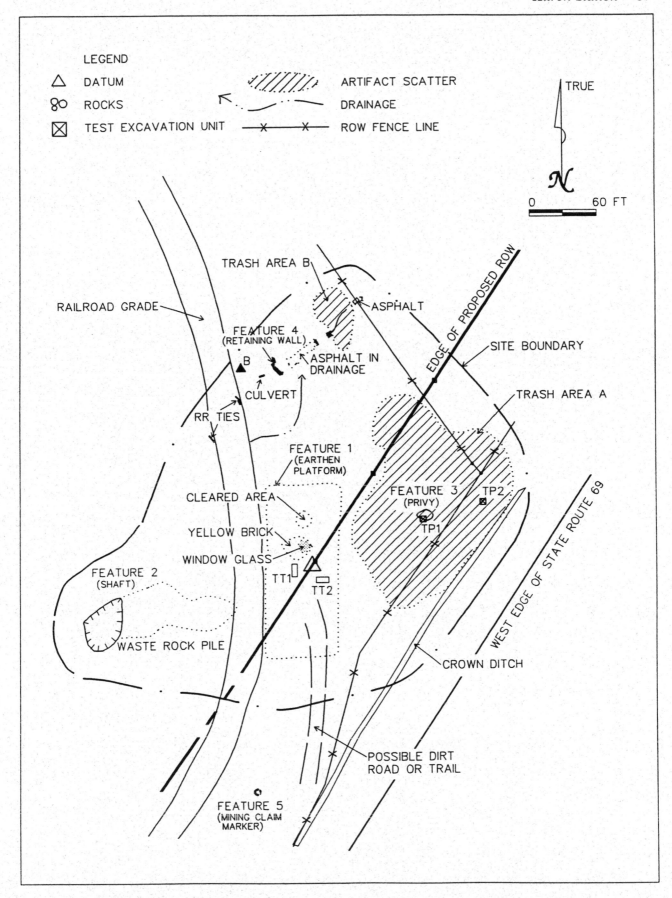

Figure 6.5. Site AZ N:11:23(ASM), Huron Station and the Montezuma and Eagle Fraction lode claims.

During testing SWCA's archaeologists mapped the entire site, placed test units and trenches in Features 1 and 3 and Trash Area A, gridded the portion of the site within the ROW, collected all diagnostic artifacts in the grid, recorded nondiagnostic artifacts in the grid, and made additional observations about portions of the site outside the ROW. Descriptions of each element of the site follow. Definitions of terms used in describing and measuring historical artifacts are in the Glossary at the end of this report.

Feature 1 was an earthen platform along the eastern side of the Prescott & Eastern Railway grade (Figure 6.6). The platform was roughly rectangular in shape, measuring 240 feet north-south by 60 feet east-west, with a level top. It was on a northeast-facing hillside and stood a maximum of 2 feet above the surrounding hillslope. A faint dirt trail appeared to extend from the eastern side of the feature in a southerly direction. Artifacts atop the platform were of moderate density and included a burned ceramic doorknob, bolts, railroad spikes, hole-in-cap can fragments, pieces of strap iron, fragments of crockery and hard-paste earthenware (representing one jar, three bowls, and a plate), an electrical insulator, a rubber heel, wire nails, and pale green, amber, dark green, and sun-colored amethyst (SCA) glass.

Figure 6.6. Site AZ N:11:23(ASM), Feature 1, earthen platform; view southwest.

In the approximate center of the earthen platform was a concentration of window glass, yellow brick, and wire nails, all burned. The bricks were 4 inches wide by 2-1/4 inches thick; they were so fragmentary that their length could not be determined. A groove extended along one face of each brick. None bore a manufacturer's mark. North of the concentration of burned material was a perfectly circular clearing 15 feet in diameter. The clearing was obvious, as surface rocks had been pushed aside and the center was completely devoid of artifacts and vegetation. The clearing appeared to mark the spot where a large, circular object, perhaps the cistern for Huron Station (see Table 6.1), once stood.

Two test trenches in the earthen platform exposed some subsurface materials. Test Trench 1, through the center of the feature, measured 15 × 2 feet. Five inches below the present ground surface the excavators encountered burned horizontal boards anchored with wire nails. Atop the boards were a variety of artifacts: a can rim, an iron bar, a garter belt clasp, a crown bottle cap, a hinge fragment, a piece of sheet metal, a bolt, and numerous wire nails. These materials appeared to mark a wooden floor or platform within Huron Station, perhaps the platform that supported the train depot building. Test Trench 2, placed near the eastern edge of the earthen platform, measured 10 × 2 feet. Excavation to a depth of 1 foot exposed no cultural material.

Feature 2 was a depression and an associated backdirt or spoils pile on the western side of the railroad grade. The depression was of irregular shape, measured 60 feet north-south by 40 feet east-west, and had a maximum depth of 4 feet. The backdirt pile, downslope from the depression, measured 90 feet east-west by 40 feet north-south and had a maximum height of 2 feet. As previously noted by Hathaway (1992:40), the backdirt pile contained fragments of copper ore and a low density of historic artifacts, including amber and SCA glass fragments, baling wire, strap metal, and fragments of hole-in-cap cans.

The location of this feature exactly matched the location of the "No. 3 shaft" indicated on the 1915 Mineral Entry Survey plat for the Montezuma Claim (Figure 6.4). As surveyed in 1915, the shaft was 4 feet wide by 6 feet tall by 65 feet long and had a value of $650.00 (Merritt 1915). Feature 2 likely marked the collapsed remains of the No. 3 shaft and its associated backdirt/ore pile.

Feature 3 was a small, leveled area measuring 8 × 6 feet discovered during vegetation removal. The feature was in the middle of Trash Area A and was slightly depressed in the center. Its location approximately matched the location of a "House" indicated on the 1915 Mineral Entry Survey map of the Eagle Fraction Claim (Figure 6.4), a mining property located by Frank Nester in 1909, purchased by George Hull in 1911, and patented by Hull in 1916.

The small size and slightly depressed center of the feature suggested that it might have been a privy associated with the Eagle Fraction house. Shovel-scraping the surface to see if a horizontal privy stain might be present exposed a dark charcoal stain and soft earth beginning approximately 2 inches below the present ground surface. Test Pit 1, a 5 × 5–foot unit placed in the center of the feature to test its depth, seemed to indicate that it was not a privy. The western half of the pit contained compact, sterile soil and decomposing rock. The eastern half consisted of a soft, charcoal-flecked soil containing numerous objects: many tiny fragments of cans, a pocket tobacco tin, sheet-metal fragments, pieces of hog and baling wire, a bucket handle, wire nails, a railroad spike, a metal bowl fragment, a Remington 410-12–gauge shotgun shell, a harness buckle, a wagon-bolt nut, a conveyor belt idler, hard-paste earthenware fragments from at least two vessels, milled lumber fragments (burned), leather boot lacings, a piece of a leather glove, and pieces of amber, pale green, green, SCA, aqua, and clear glass. The most closely datable objects were the shotgun shell (ca. 1911) and a bottle fragment bearing an American Bottle Company basemark (ca. 1905–1929).

Within the test unit, the feature continued to a depth of 1.3 feet below the present ground surface. However, the feature appeared to be deeper beyond the northern wall of the unit. No soil laminations or discolorations were present such as one would likely encounter in a privy, nor was the edge of the feature burned, as would be expected on a fire pit. Test Unit 1 appeared to have struck the southern corner of a large trash pit, continuing to the north, associated with the Eagle Fraction house or with Huron Station.

Feature 4 was a cobble wall north of Feature 1 and outside of the proposed ROW (Figure 6.7). The wall was L-shaped, with one arm measuring 15 feet and the other measuring 2.5 feet. The dry-laid wall was a maximum of eight courses high. Situated along the outer curve of the railroad grade, the wall appeared to have successfully arrested the headcutting of a drainage that threatened to erode the grade. Below the wall, the drainage had already taken a severe toll on the landscape. Although badly eroded, the wall appeared to mark the remains of the foundation of the warehouse depicted on the 1925 map of Huron Station (Figure 6.3). The warehouse, constructed at an undetermined date, originally measured 25 × 25 feet and had a wood-frame superstructure (Table 6.1). Trash Area B (see below) was approximately 60 feet downslope from Feature 4.

Figure 6.7. Site AZ N:11:23(ASM), Feature 4, cobble wall; view north.

Feature 5 was a 3-inch metal pipe projecting 1 foot from the ground. This object was given feature status because it marked an element of critical importance in interpreting the site: it marked the southeastern corner of the Montezuma Claim and the southwestern corner of the Eagle Fraction Claim (noted by an arrow on Figure 6.4). This corner point was firmly established during the Mineral Entry Survey of 1915 (Merritt 1915). The Mineral Entry Survey plat depicted improvements (such as shafts and houses) in relation to claim corners, providing bearings and distances to the improvements from the corners. Using the pipe as a corner and the 1915 plat as a guide, SWCA personnel were able to positively identify Features 2 and 3 of the archaeological site as elements of the Montezuma and Eagle Fraction claims.

Trash Area A was of moderate to high density and measured 190 feet north-south by 150 feet east-west in the eastern portion of the site. This trash area surrounded Feature 3 (see above) and was likely associated with a house depicted on the 1915 Mineral Entry Survey plat. The house was probably the residence of Frank Nester, the individual who maintained a saloon at Huron circa 1900–1912 and held the Eagle Fraction claim from 1909 to 1911. Artifacts, which supported a domestic/household association, consisted of items related to food consumption/preparation (hole-in-cap cans, bottle glass, frying pans, a spoon), architecture (wire nails, wire, window glass), and personal use (overall snaps, clothing snaps, tobacco tins, shoe buckles). Of particular interest were many liquor bottles from the Los Angeles Brewing Company and the Arizona Brewing Company, suggesting an association with saloon keeper Nester.

The most closely datable objects were bottle basemarks, ceramic hallmarks, and Bernardin bottle closures. Bottle basemarks included those of the Adolphus Busch Glass Manufacturing Company (1886–1928), the American Bottle Company (1905–1916), Cannington, Shaw & Co. (1875–1913), Nuttall & Co. (1872–1913), F. E. Reed Glass Co. (1881–1927), R & Co. (circa 1880–1900), Streator Bottle & Glass Co. (1881–1905), and William Franzen & Son (1900–1929). Ceramic maker's marks included those of Knowles, Taylor, and Knowles (1905–1929), Homer Laughlin China (circa 1901–1915), and C. C. Thompson Pottery (1889–1938). Metal Bernardin closures on liquor bottles dated from 1897 to 1920 (see Artifact Analyses, below).

Test Unit 2, a 5 × 5-foot pit placed near the eastern edge of the site in an area with particularly abundant material, revealed a dense quantity of bottle glass (pale green, aqua, SCA, and amber) within 2 inches of the present ground surface. Below that, the soil was culturally sterile. The test suggested that the material had eroded downslope from the main part of Trash Area A, which surrounded Feature 3.

Trash Area B was of low to moderate density, measured 55 feet north-south by 40 feet east-west, and was 60 feet downslope from Feature 4, the retaining wall. Like Feature 4, this trash area was outside the proposed ROW and would not be impacted by construction. The area contained lumber, wire nails, pieces of asphalt, fragments of hole-in-cap cans, a Log Cabin syrup can, a Los Angeles Brewing Company Bernardin closure, hard-paste earthenware fragments, and a 30-mm rifle cartridge case.

In summary, the testing results indicated that Site AZ N:11:23(ASM) represented the remains of two mining claims (the Montezuma and the Eagle Fraction) and a train station (Huron Station). The proposed highway construction would impact Features 3 and 5, most of Feature 1, and nearly all of Trash Area A, but not Features 2 and 4 or Trash Area B. The investigations indicated that the portion within the ROW contained significant subsurface material that was not exhausted through testing. Testing of Feature 1 revealed the probable in situ burned remains of a floor or platform associated with Huron Station. Testing of Feature 3 and Trash Area A revealed remains likely associated with Frank Nester, an early miner and saloon keeper of Huron. SWCA recommended data recovery within the ROW, specifically, horizontal stripping and excavation of areas of Features 1 and 3 and Trash Area A. The investigators expected this procedure to yield significant data relating to the railway and mining histories of the site.

Data Recovery

SWCA field personnel began data recovery at this site by re-establishing the grid from testing and setting up 10 × 10–foot squares for manual stripping (hand-stripped, or HS, units). They then excavated within the three proposed areas: the remains of the train platform (Feature 1), the terrace containing a depression (Feature 3), and the trash concentration (Trash Area A). During the data recovery fieldwork, the excavators found five additional features, four in the ROW and one outside the ROW, and added them to the site map (Figure 6.8). One new feature was substantial and therefore was assigned a number (Feature 6) and excavated. The investigations included 13 HS squares, all but one measuring 10 × 10 feet; the exception, HS 7, followed the outline of Feature 3. The excavators screened all soil from these units through 1/4-inch mesh, collected all diagnostic artifacts from the screen, and counted and described nondiagnostic artifacts. Diagnostic artifacts were collected from three additional areas outside the HS units: (1) in Trash Area A just southwest of Feature 3 to the north, west, and east of HS 8 and 9; (2) on the west side of SR 69 east of the fence and the eastern extent of Trash Area A; and (3) in the vicinity of Feature 6 on the east side of the fence line.

The additional features found during data recovery were a rock alignment, a rock ring, a rock pile, and a rock retaining wall with a leveled area (Feature 6), all within the ROW, and four partially exposed railroad ties outside the ROW. The rock alignment was a linear, single-course, single-row alignment oriented roughly north to south. The alignment of 30+ weathered schistose and phyllite boulders and cobbles was approximately 18 feet long; the rocks ranged in size from 6 inches in diameter to 1.5 feet square. The larger boulders had slumped downslope to the east. The excavators interpreted this alignment as the berm of the wagon road that once connected Huron with the McCabe Mine (as depicted by Sayre 1985:55). South of the alignment was a small (4-foot-diameter), shallow (0.5-foot-deep) depression flanked on the east and south by medium-sized cobbles that formed a semicircle around the depression. The cobbles averaged 1.5 × 1.25 feet. Shovel tests in the feature indicated that it did not extend beneath the surface; the nature and function of this small feature could not be determined. The third feature in the group, south of Feature 1, consisted of a pile of rocks with a broken wooden stake near the center. The feature measured 2.5 × 2.6 feet overall, and the rocks ranged from about 4 inches to 8 inches in diameter. This feature appeared to be an old highway survey marker. Feature 6 was a low, U-shaped cobble retaining wall around a small earthen terrace. The feature outside the ROW consisted of four partially exposed railroad ties on the grade of the former P&E Railway.

At the center of Feature 1, the earthen platform, the excavators reopened Trench 1, where during the testing phase possible remains of the train depot's wooden platform were uncovered. They then worked laterally (HS 1, 2, and 3) to try to expose as much of the platform as possible, and quickly discovered that the test trench had apparently encountered the only remaining in situ portion of the train depot. A few ephemeral carbon stains could be traced in an area measuring approximately 30 × 10 feet, likely marking the locations where depot floor joists had once rested. Artifacts found associated with Feature 1 included over 700 wire nails of various sizes, globules of melted glass, fragments of SCA bottles, flat (window) glass, and milk glass, whiteware and stoneware sherds, bone fragments, and a few miscellaneous metal items. The results of the excavation of the wooden platform area within Feature 1 suggested that the depot had been of wood-frame construction, had included several windows, had been cleaned out upon retirement from service, and had burned (or been burned) following its retirement.

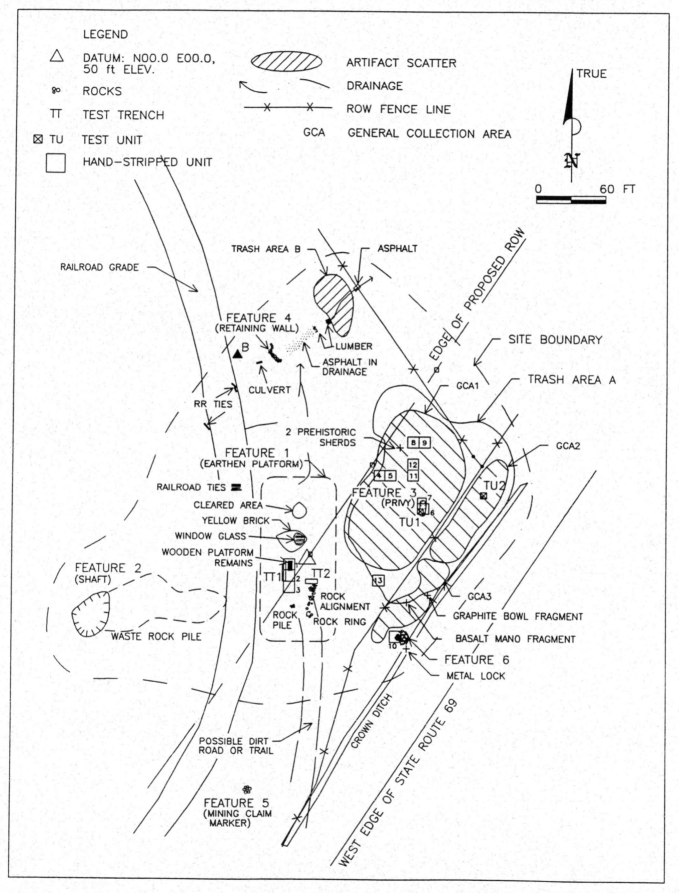

Figure 6.8. Site AZ N:11:23(ASM) plan map, as amended during data recovery phase.

The southwest corner of HS 6, placed over the depression, Feature 3, had been excavated as Test Unit 1 during the testing phase. Excavation of HS 7, opened north of HS 6 to further expose the dark soil concentration found in HS 6, was by five cultural strata. The field crew cleared HS 6 of surface artifacts, stripped the first three strata with a shovel, and screened the soil with 1/4-inch mesh. They removed Strata IV and V with a trowel and screened that fill with 1/4-inch mesh as well. Feature 3 was approximately 2.5 feet deep and had been built into a matrix of decomposing metamorphic slate. All five strata identified contained some cultural material, although most artifacts from Stratum I were on the present ground surface, and a bottle was the only artifact found in Stratum V. Lenses of sterile soil separated Strata II and III, Strata III and IV, and Strata IV and V (Figure 6.9). Stratum II contained numerous artifacts, including flat glass, bottle glass, metal, ceramics, and faunal remains. This stratum also contained many pieces of partially burned wood. Artifacts were most abundant and most diverse in Stratum IV; this assemblage included an 1891 dime, complete bottles, many bottle caps, shot-glass and stemware fragments, bottle corks, wire nails, ammunition, clothing fasteners, earthenware and porcelain fragments, other glass, metal, and faunal remains. Although the testing results had suggested that Feature 3 was part of a larger trash concentration, data recovery results indicated that it was, after all, a privy, which had been periodically sanitized during use by tossing in layers of sterile soil. The privy measured 13 feet long by 4 feet wide and was 2.5 feet deep. The most numerous items were 551 metal bottle caps, most of them embossed "Los Angeles Brewing Company." The contents of the privy and the general dating of its artifacts suggested that this feature (and the adjacent Trash Area A) were associated with the Huron saloon started by Charles Wingfield in 1898 and sold to Frank Nester by 1900.

The field crew placed HS 10 in Feature 6, which appeared to be a platform partially outlined by a rock retaining wall. The excavators extended HS 10 beyond its original 10 × 10-foot dimensions another 3 feet to the north, south, and east to follow the feature out. They first removed the overburden to a depth of approximately 3 inches below modern ground surface (bmgs), using a shovel and trowel and screening all soil through 1/4-inch screen. The majority of the artifacts from the overburden were metal and included many blanks (pieces of unworked and partially worked bar iron), horseshoe nails, horseshoe fragments, and other nails, cans, and bolts. A few pieces of bottle glass and earthenware sherds were present as well. Removing the overburden exposed two possible subfeatures and a large stain (Figure 6.10).

Subfeature 6-1, a circular, rock-lined pit, was excavated by bisecting it, excavating the south half with a trowel, and screening the soil through 1/4-inch mesh. Bedrock formed the sides and bottom of the feature, and the burned fill contained chunks of rock, bedrock, and artifacts. Subfeature 6-1 appeared to be the foundation for a barrel or stove. Subfeature 6-2, a circular, ashy pit containing cut and burned metal fragments, was excavated in full with a trowel and all soil was screened through 1/4-inch mesh. The pit was roughly circular in plan view, with straight sides. As with Subfeature 6-1, the sides and bottom of the pit were defined by bedrock. The unburned fill contained a number of burned artifacts. Field personnel could not determine the function of this subfeature. Subfeature 6-3 was a charcoal stain measuring 10 × 6 feet. The stain was bisected, and the eastern half was excavated by removing the fill with a trowel and screening it through 1/4-inch mesh. The western half was then excavated in the same manner. The pattern of the stain was very irregular in plan view, extending to the west, northeast, and southwest into Subfeatures 6-1 and 6-2 and to the east under the rock retaining wall. The field personnel explored the stain under the retaining wall by excavating and removing a portion of the wall. After excavating approximately 3 feet east into the rubble, they determined that the stain was not structurally related to the

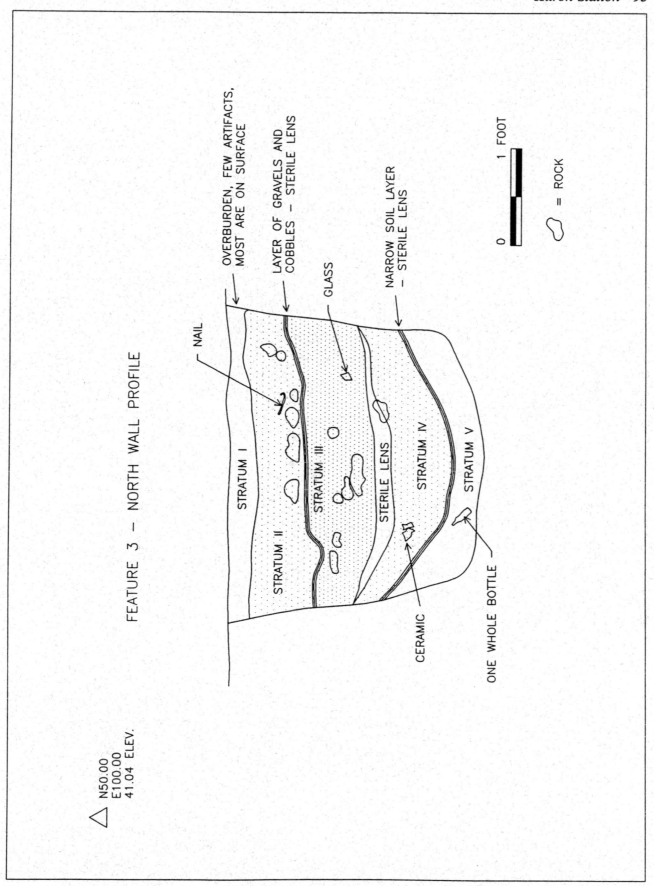

Figure 6.9. Site AZ N:11:23(ASM), profile of Feature 3, privy.

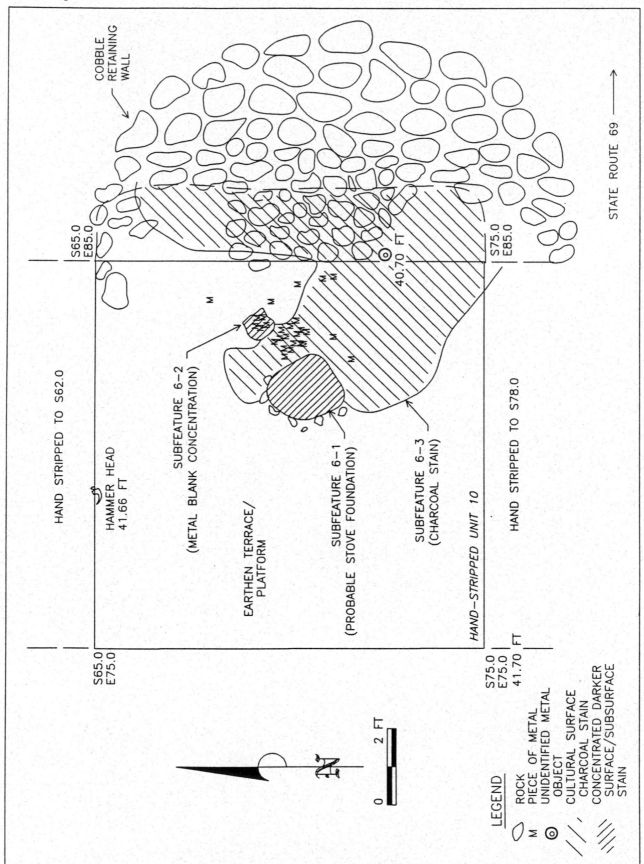

COBBLE RETAINING WALL

S65.0 E85.0

40.70 FT

S75.0 E85.0

STATE ROUTE 69 ⟶

HAND STRIPPED TO S62.0

HAMMER HEAD 41.66 FT

SUBFEATURE 6-2 (METAL BLANK CONCENTRATION)

EARTHEN TERRACE/ PLATFORM

SUBFEATURE 6-1 (PROBABLE STOVE FOUNDATION)

SUBFEATURE 6-3 (CHARCOAL STAIN)

HAND-STRIPPED UNIT 10

HAND STRIPPED TO S78.0

S65.0 E75.0

S75.0 E75.0 41.70 FT

0   2 FT

LEGEND

⬭ ROCK
M PIECE OF METAL
◎ UNIDENTIFIED METAL OBJECT
⟋⟍ CULTURAL SURFACE
⟋ CHARCOAL STAIN
⟍ CONCENTRATED DARKER SURFACE/SUBSURFACE STAIN

Figure 6.10. Site AZ N:11:23(ASM), Feature 6, blacksmith's temporary work area.

rock rubble. Most artifacts from Subfeature 6-3 were metal and included nails, bolts, and horseshoes and horseshoe fragments. A few pieces of glass and the fragments of an earthenware jug were the only nonmetal artifacts. On the basis of the metal blanks, horseshoe fragments, horseshoe nails, and extensive burning, the excavators interpreted Feature 6 as a blacksmith's temporary work area that at one time may have been partially enclosed by a rock wall that later collapsed onto the work area.

The field crew excavated HS 4 and HS 5 in a portion of Trash Area A thought to contain a building foundation, suggested by a very slightly elevated mound showing a moderate amount of rock. Excavating the northern half of the unit to approximately 5 inches bmgs and the southern half to approximately 2 inches bmgs revealed that the suspected rock foundation was, in fact, cobbles weathering from a rock outcrop. However, these units contained a large quantity of artifacts, primarily bottle glass, with only a few fragments of window glass, bottle caps embossed with "LOS ANGELES BREWING CO, LOS ANGELES, CAL," shell cartridges, a possible thermometer, a few pieces of leather, a few cans, burned bone, two ceramic sherds, many nails, and miscellaneous metal pieces.

Although the field personnel excavated HS 8 and HS 9 to approximately 3-1/2 inches bmgs to further examine the depth and content of Trash Area A, most artifacts were on the surface or in the overburden. Artifacts in these units included bottle glass, a few pieces of earthenware and porcelain, a few cans, nails, Los Angeles Brewing Company bottle caps, miscellaneous metal, and a piece of possible flaked glass. The purpose of HS 11 and HS 12 was also to obtain additional general information about Trash Area A. HS 11 was placed over an ephemeral rock ring with a diameter of approximately 8 feet that formed a rise with a very slight central depression. Excavation revealed this "rock ring" to be shale from the decomposing bedrock approximately 3-1/2 inches below the surface. Artifacts were abundant in HS 11 and HS 12 and included bottle glass, earthenware, metal cans, Los Angeles Brewing Company bottle caps, clothing fasteners, various nails, cartridges, and miscellaneous metal. HS 13, also placed in Trash Area A, was over a slightly mounded area south of the main concentration and west of the fence. This unit encountered culturally sterile soil approximately 5 inches bmgs. The artifact inventory in this unit differed from the assemblages from the other units in Trash Area A; although bottle glass, nails, earthenware, cans, and cartridges were abundant, Los Angeles Brewing Company bottle caps were not.

Artifacts collected from the surface in the central portion of Trash Area A consisted of a baking powder can, a safety pin, a possible harmonica part, a shotgun shell, bottle finishes and bases of green, brown, aqua, SCA, and clear glass, earthenware plate, cup, and crockery sherds, and a battery core. The small number of artifacts collected from the surface in the eastern area of Trash Area A included pieces of metal, bottle bases and finishes of brown glass, and earthenware plate and bowl sherds. The area north and west of Feature 6 also contained only a few artifacts: one rivet, a few bottle and jar fragments (SCA, aqua, brown, and clear glass), and one earthenware sherd. Other diagnostic artifacts point-provenienced from Trash Area A included a 1906 penny and nine Los Angeles Brewing Company bottle caps.

ARTIFACT ANALYSES

Metal

Metal was the most abundant material type at Site AZ N:11:23(ASM). Nearly half (4116) of the 8291 artifact fragments recovered from the site were made of some type of metal. The state of preservation of the metal artifacts varied greatly; iron artifacts generally were much more corroded and oxidized than were nonferrous items. When necessary, the analyst brushed artifacts clean to help in their identification. In some cases neither form nor function could be identified, because of either poor preservation or fragmentary condition.

Food

Almost all of the approximately 930 can fragments recovered from the site were crushed, heavily corroded, and incomplete. The few well-preserved specimens represented a variety of food-can types: round hole-in-cap fruit or vegetable cans (9 recovered specimens), sardine cans (1), condensed or evaporated milk cans (4), oval sardine cans (5), round sanitary food cans (5), round external-friction can lids (2), rectangular meat cans (6), and lard pails (1 specimen, with extruded ears and a wire handle). One of the round hole-in-cap cans was 2-5/8 inches in diameter and was embossed "10 OZ NET." The condensed/evaporated milk cans were crushed and could not be accurately measured. One of these cans had been opened using an ice pick or punch to make holes opposite each other on the top of the can. Rock (1992) states that the Sanitary Can Company, founded in 1904, first produced sanitary cans in that year. The external-friction can lids were from baking powder cans, one of which was embossed "CALU.../...6 OZ.../...BAKING P..." (Calumet Baking Powder).

Twenty-five can-opener keys were also in the assemblage. Thirteen were sardine-can keys (Figure 6.11a), eight were score-strip type keys, and four were fragments that could not be identified by type. Several of the score-strip keys in the assemblage still had the coiled metal strips attached.

Food Preparation and Consumption

The three metal artifacts in this functional category were handles of forks, knives, or spoons. No hallmarks or patterns were detectable because of the poor state of preservation of these artifacts.

Household Furnishings

Artifacts in this category included a segment of a curtain rod and an iron wire coat or hat hook. A similar hook appears in the 1897 Sears, Roebuck catalog (Israel 1968:89). The only other items in this category were four small, toothed, nonferrous gears, 1 inch or less in diameter, probably from a clock.

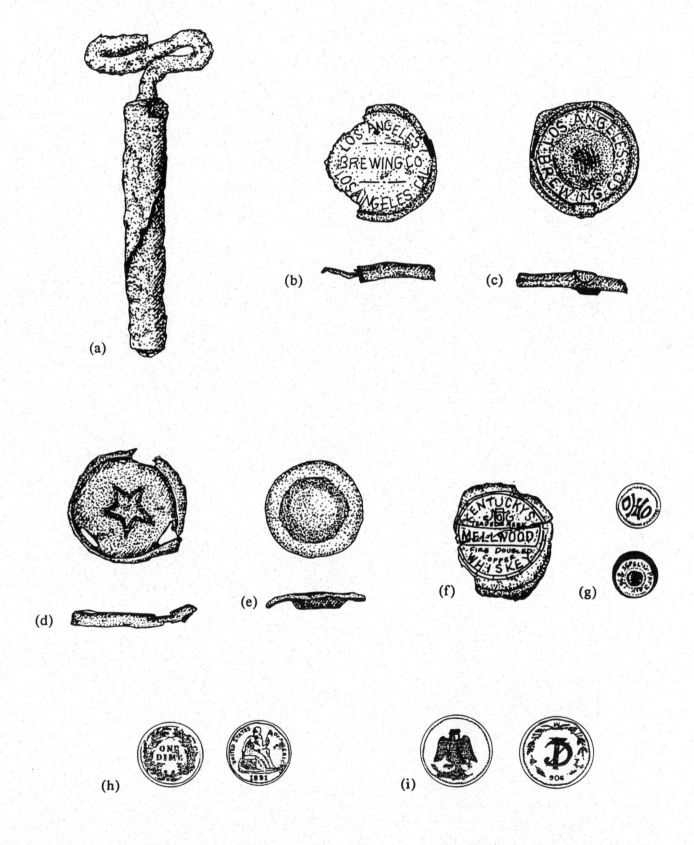

Figure 6.11. Selected metal artifacts recovered from Site AZ N:11:23(ASM). Drawn actual size.

Architecture (Construction-Related)

Many of the recovered artifacts were common in the construction of buildings. Wire nails were the most numerous (1493). Other construction-related artifacts included a window-spring pin, 12 wood screws, 3 U-shaped staples, 2 square-cut nails, 7 washers, 22 nuts, 94 bolts, and 4 iron brackets. Several items were door hardware: an "acorn-top" door-hinge pin, a rectangular doorknob rod, two pieces of a door lock, a segment of a door-bolt chain, a fragment of an elaborately decorated door-hinge plate, and an eclipse door-check cap. These last two items are illustrated in the 1895 Montgomery Ward catalog (Emmit 1969).

Leisure and Recreation

A large number of metal items recovered from the site related to leisure and recreation: 698 were bottle closures, 72 were pieces of ammunition, 40 represented tobacco tins, and 2 were miscellaneous items. Most (534) of the bottle closures were of a general type known as the "Bernardin Metal Cap with Neckband," designed by Alfred L. Bernardin of Evansville, Indiana, and patented in 1885 (Herskovitz 1978:74). This closure consisted of a metal cap with a neckband that buckled into a slot. The assemblage included two variations of the Bernardin closure: one with a flat cap and the other with the center of the cap indented. Most of the flat caps had "LOS ANGELES BREWING CO., LOS ANGELES, CAL" stamped on the top (Figure 6.11b); "LOS ANGELES BREWING CO." was stamped on the top of the indented caps (Figure 6.11c), and two caps of the flat variety bore a five-pointed star (Figure 6.11d).

In addition to his patent for beer-bottle *caps*, Bernardin also held patents on beer-bottle cap *disks* made of tin (Herskovitz 1978:74). The site assemblage included 79 of these discs, which were 15/16 inch in diameter and had an indented center (Figure 6.11e). The disks covered the bottle cork, with the indentation resting in the bottle mouth, and were held in place by a securing wire. The result was tighter corkage, and the disk prevented the wire from cutting into the cork (Herskovitz 1978:73; Lief 1965:15).

Sixty-one crown-cap bottle closures were in the assemblage. Since their introduction in 1892 (Lief 1965), crown caps have continued to be commonly used on beer and soda bottles.

The remaining bottle closures recovered from the site were 11 complete lead-foil bottle covers and fragments of 12 more. One of the covers was stamped "KENTUCKY'S WHISKEY / TRADE MARK / MELLWOOD / FIRE DOUBLED / COPPER," with a crest stamped over the words "TRADE MARK" (Figure 6.11f). A partial cover was stamped "TAYLOR & WILLIAMS / WHISKEY / LOUISVILLE." Nine foil bottle covers bore five-pointed stars. On two of these covers, short radiating lines surrounded the star; on seven others the star was in the center of a shield enclosed by a circle with a row of dots along the outside of the circle. Dates for such bottle covers have not been determined.

Seventy-two pieces of ammunition were in this category: 6 shotgun shells and 66 cartridges. Five of the shotgun shells were for 12-gauge guns; each had a different headstamp. One "CLIMAX" and one "CONICAL CLIMAX" shell were produced by the United States Cartridge Company. Steward (1969:69) dated the manufacture of these shells to between 1872 and 1929. According to Herskovitz (1978:51), the single "NO. 12 / NITRO CLUB" shell found was first produced in 1899. However, the shell bore the headstamp of the Remington and Union Metallic Cartridge Company (REM-UMC) and therefore was post-1912, the year the two companies merged. A "U.M.C. CO. / NO. 12 / MAGIC" shell was a type produced beginning in 1874 (Herskovitz 1978:51; Steward 1969:62), predating the merger with Remington. A shotgun shell manufactured by E. Remington & Sons had the headstamp "410 - 12 m/m." Remington produced this shell between 1871 and 1912 (Steward 1969:45).

The 66 cartridges ranged in size from .22 caliber to .44-40 caliber. The 48 cases from .22-caliber ammunition represented three different types. The most common of these was the .22 Long or Long Rifle, with 32 specimens recovered. The .22 Long was introduced in 1871 as a black powder revolver load, while the .22 Long Rifle was not developed until 1887 (Herskovitz 1978:47). Both rounds used cases with the same dimensions and thus can be distinguished only by examining unfired rounds. Two unfired specimens found were the Long (not Long Rifle) variety. Another 15 specimens were .22 Short cartridge cases. Herskovitz (1978:47) stated that this type is the oldest commercially manufactured, self-contained metallic cartridge. It is still commonly used.

One .30-caliber cartridge case was present, a Winchester Centerfire. This cartridge was manufactured by the Winchester Repeating Arms Company (WRA) from 1895 to 1936 (Barnes 1985:49). Three cartridges represented two different types of .32-caliber ammunition. Two were .32-caliber automatic cartridges produced by WRA between 1903 and 1936 (Barnes 1985:177). The other cartridge had a "U.M.C. 32 CFW" headstamp and was manufactured by the Union Metallic Cartridge Company (UMC) from 1882 to 1912 (Barnes 1985:62).

Each of five examples of .38-caliber cartridge cases had a different headstamp. Two were manufactured by UMC prior to its merger with E. Remington & Sons. The production of one of these rounds, the .38 Long Solid Head, ceased in 1900 (Barnes 1985:103). Two other cartridges, the .38 Smith & Wesson Special and the .38-55, were made by the merged company after 1912 (Barnes 1985:78, 103). A .38-caliber cartridge with the headstamp "WRA. CO. / 38 S&W" was produced by WRA between 1887 and 1936 (Barnes 1985:190).

Three different types of cartridge case were represented among the eight .41-caliber cases found. Six were of the .41 Long Colt type, produced by U.M.C. from 1877 to 1912 (Barnes 1985:192). The other two were a .41 Long Colt Double Action cartridge and a .41 Short Colt Double Action cartridge, both made by WRA between 1877 and 1936.

A .44-caliber cartridge with the headstamp "U.S. / .44 W.C.F" was manufactured by the United States Cartridge company from 1873 to 1929 (Barnes 1985:81; Steward 1969:69). Originally the .44-40 Winchester Centerfire was made for use with the 1873 model of the Winchester rifle and the Colt single-action revolver. Since that time, however, the number of arms using this type of ammunition has greatly increased (Herskovitz 1978:49). The assemblage also included one fragment of a center-fired cartridge with no headstamp. This cartridge had a .441-caliber rim.

Other metal artifacts in the Leisure and Recreation category were 5 upright pocket tobacco cans, 35 upright tobacco can lid fragments, a harmonica plate, and a zinc alloy pour spout. According to Rock

(1992), the upright pocket tobacco can was introduced around 1906. The spout was of the type used by bartenders to attach to liquor bottles; it was 1-3/4 inches tall, 1 inch wide, and internally threaded.

Personal Items

The excavators recovered 16 clothing-related metal artifacts. Three were rivet buttons. One had the stylized word "OHIO" stamped on the front and "PAT. APR. 21 '96 & SEPT. 1 '96" stamped on the backing piece (Figure 6.11g). (A rivet button with the same patent dates but with a different design on the front came from AZ N:11:19[ASM].) The references consulted did not identify the manufacturer of these buttons. The second rivet button was embossed with a circle of dots and "SCOVILL MFG. CO" on the front and an "S" inside a diamond on the back. The third rivet button was plain and had no lettering on it. One other metal clothing item, a suspender clasp, was stamped "PRESIDENT" on the front and "SHIRLEY MAKE" over two parallel horizontal lines on the back. Other clothing-related metal artifacts were one two-piece four-hole button, two overall suspender clasps, a fragment of a suspender clasp, a suspender buckle or belt/garter clasp, the male half of a snap fastener, and five shoe or boot eyelets (four of the grommet "lace-through" type and one of the hook "lace-over" type). One safety pin was also found.

Coins and Tokens

The two coins collected from AZ N:11:23(ASM) were an 1891 U.S. dime (Figure 6.11h) and a very worn 1906 U.S. one-cent piece (Figure 6.11i). It is interesting that the excavators found no "C. P. Wingfield" trade tokens. According to Michael (1986:48), Wingfield issued such tokens for use at his Huron store early in the twentieth century.

Transportation

Numerous metal artifacts recovered from the site related to animal-powered transportation, most of them either wagon parts or horse or mule tack and accoutrements. Twenty-seven carriage bolts and eight carriage-bolt nuts of various sizes were of types commonly used in wagons. Other wagon-related artifacts were one wagon-box strap, one singletree or doubletree clip, one segment of a wagon brake rod, and two wagon axle clips. Singletree and doubletree clips connected the harness of the draft animal to the wagon tongue. An illustration of such clips can be found in the 1895 Montgomery Ward catalog (Emmit 1969). The axle clips fastened the axle to the frame of the wagon (Herskovitz 1978:89–90).

Horse or mule accoutrements included 124 horseshoe nails, 2 complete horseshoes, and 6 horseshoe fragments. Nearly all of these items came from Feature 6, interpreted as a blacksmith's work area. One of the horseshoes was for a left front hoof and the other was for a left rear hoof. Front shoes are a U shape with a nearly closed top, almost circular at the toe and quarters and wider at the heels. Rear shoes are more acorn shaped, more pointed at the top and quarters, and usually narrower at the heels (Berge

1966:17; Herskovitz 1978:82). Usually the outside arm of a horseshoe is slightly longer than the inside arm, making side identification possible.

The two pieces of horse or mule tack recovered were a D-shaped iron ring and a square-angled buckle from a horse or mule harness. The first object may have been from a saddle-girth strap. A buckle nearly identical to the one found was advertised in the 1897 Sears, Roebuck catalog (Israel 1968:764).

Since the grade of the former Prescott & Eastern Railway extends through the site, it is not surprising that the site also yielded railroad-associated artifacts: eleven railroad spikes. Nine were standard size, and two were the smaller 2-1/2-inch size used on light-weight rails. Two of the standard-size spikes were headstamped with either a "6" or a "9."

Tools and Hardware

Two iron hammer heads, one broken iron padlock, and a piece of a scissors handle were in this category. One of the hammer heads was from a cobbler's hammer, while the other was a standard claw-hammer head.

Machinery

An iron crank handle attached to a large gear was the only item in this category. The analyst could not determine its function.

Communication

The only items that clearly fell in this category were three pencil eraser ferrules and one ink pen. Several electrode-tipped wires and a segment of insulated copper wire may have been parts of electrical devices such as radios, telephones, or telegraphs, but they could not be positively assigned to this functional category.

Miscellaneous

Miscellaneous artifacts consisted of 254 metal blanks recovered from Feature 6. These fragments were pieces "dubbed" (pinched) off of bar/rod stock. Stock shapes identified from examining the dubbing fragments were square rods, round rods, and flat, rectangular bars. The metal blanks appeared to have provided the raw materials for a blacksmithing operation.

Unidentified

The function of 46 wire segments (23 small gauge, 17 medium gauge, and 6 large gauge) was not known. Several homemade wrought-iron items included two rings, two C-shaped objects, three eyebolt-shaped rods, one eye-shaped rod, and an oval handle. Over 160 metal artifacts were in such poor condition, were such small fragments, or were so unusual that the analyst could not determine their function.

Glass

Glass was also abundant, with 3723 fragments recovered. Alcoholic beverage bottle shards comprised most of the assemblage. Many fragments of flat (window) glass, jars, tableware, and lamp chimneys were also present.

Food

Most items representing this functional category were from food containers: fragments of 3 clear glass condiment bottles, each with a machine-applied club sauce finish; pieces of 1 SCA fruit or vegetable jar with a hand-applied, continuous thread finish; and one body shard from a clear Kerr "self-sealing" mason jar. The style of lettering on the Kerr's jar indicated that it could have been manufactured from 1904 until the 1950s (Peterson 1968:42; Toulouse 1971:306–308). A round SCA jar base had a "BISHOP / & / COMPANY" basemark. This food processing company, based in San Diego, California, operated from 1890 to 1920 (Toulouse 1971:86). Other food-related glass items included fragments of a white milk-glass canning jar lid liner and 2 plain club sauce–type bottle stoppers with tapered shanks, one brown and one aqua.

Food Preparation and Consumption

Forty-seven glass fragments represented at least 21 different glasses or tumblers. A number were bases: 4 clear shot-glass bases 1-7/16 inches in diameter, 4 clear shot-glass bases 1-3/8 inches in diameter, 3 broken SCA tumbler bases with fluted heels 1-1/2 inches in diameter, 2 clear round tumbler bases, and 3 SCA round tumbler bases. Other items were 6 fragments representing a minimum of 3 pieces of clear stemware (either wine glasses or goblets), 6 fragments from an SCA press-molded tumbler, and a fragment of a clear beer-mug handle.

Household Furnishings

Twenty-five pieces of plate glass were from a mirror, although the silver backing had eroded. Also in this category were 10 fragments of an SCA press-molded vase and 138 lamp-chimney fragments. Two of the chimney fragments were SCA; the rest were clear. The two colors of glass and examination of the rim fragments indicated that the assemblage represented a minimum of three lamp chimneys.

Architecture (Construction-Related)

All of the 251 window glass fragments recovered were classified as clear glass. However, tints ranging from aqua to green were visible when viewing the fragments on edge, implying a number of different panes of window glass.

Leisure and Recreation

Most artifacts in this functional category were fragments from alcoholic beverage bottles; some were from soda or mineral-water bottles. Table 6.2 indicates that most (50 of 72) of the bottle finishes recovered were hand applied, suggesting that most of the bottles were made before or shortly after the introduction of the Owens fully automatic bottle-making machine in 1903 (Lorrain 1968). One of the bottle finishes still had its cork and metal closure (Figure 6.12a).

Basemarks from several such containers were present. Three examples exhibited the "A.B.G.M. CO." mark used from 1886 to 1928 by the Adolphus Busch Glass Manufacturing Company; 4 examples had the "C.S. & C.L." mark used from 1875 to 1913 by Cannington, Shaw & Company; 3 examples bore the "R & Co." mark used from 1866 to 1892 by Ripley & Company, or from 1879 to 1888 by Roth & Company; and 1 example had the "W F & S Mil" mark used from 1900 to 1921 or 1929 by William Franzen & Sons (Herskovitz 1978; Toulouse 1971). A mineral-water bottle base had a raised figure of a devil and the word "PLUTO" (Figure 6.12b). Hull-Walski and Ayres (1989:84) reported a similar basemark from dam construction camps in central Arizona but were unable to discover a date.

Feature 3 (the privy) yielded two whole beer bottles. One was 11-1/2 inches tall, with a hand-applied beer finish and "M. B. & G. CO. / 17" on the base (Figure 6.13a). According to Toulouse (1971:348), this maker's mark was used by the Massillon Bottle and Glass Company from 1900 to 1904. The other whole beer bottle was 12 inches tall, with a hand-applied brandy finish and "A.B.G.M. CO. / B22" on the base (Figure 6.13b). The Adolphus Busch Glass Manufacturing Company used this mark between 1886 and 1928 (Toulouse 1971:26–27); however, the hand-applied finish suggests that the latest possible date of manufacture for this bottle was circa 1903.

Only one glass Leisure and Recreation artifact recovered from this site did *not* relate to drinking. It was an opaque blue and white machine-made marble. Randall and Webb (1988) and other standard sources offered no other information on this specimen.

Table 6.2. Leisure and Recreation Category Bottle Finishes from Site AZ N:11:23(ASM)

Finish	Application Method	Color	Contents	Count
Beer	Hand	Aqua	Beer	2
Beer	Unidentified	Aqua	Beer	2
Beer	Hand	Brown	Beer	3
Beer	Unidentified	Brown	Beer	7
Beer with single bead	Hand	Brown	Beer	1
Brandy	Hand	Aqua	Liquor or beer	2*
Brandy	Hand	Brown	Liquor or beer	3
Brandy	Unidentified	Brown	Liquor or beer	2
Brandy	Hand	Green	Liquor or beer	1
Brandy with single bead	Hand	Aqua	Liquor or beer	1
Brandy with single bead	Hand	Brown	Liquor or beer	4
Brandy with single bead	Unidentified	Brown	Liquor or beer	1
Brandy with single bead	Hand	Clear	Liquor	1
Brandy with single bead	Hand	Green	Liquor or beer	2
Brandy with single bead	Unidentified	SCA	Liquor or beer	1
Brandy with double bead	Hand	SCA	Liquor	1
Champagne	Hand	Green	Champagne or wine	7
Crown	Hand	Aqua	Beer or soda	2
Crown	Machine	Aqua	Beer or soda	1
Crown	Unidentified	Aqua	Beer or soda	1
Crown	Hand	Brown	Beer	2
Crown	Unidentified	Clear	Mineral water or soda	1
Crown	Hand	SCA	Mineral water or soda?	1
Double ring	Hand	SCA	Liquor	3
Oil	Hand	Aqua	Liquor?	4
Oil	Hand	Brown	Liquor?	2
Oil	Unidentified	SCA	Liquor?	1
Packer	Hand	Clear	Various	5
Packer	Hand	SCA	Wine	1
Soda	Unidentified	Aqua	Soda or mineral water	1
Soda	Hand	Brown	Soda or mineral water	3
Soda	Hand	Green	Soda or mineral water	1

*One finish retained its cork and metal closure.

SCA = sun-colored amethyst

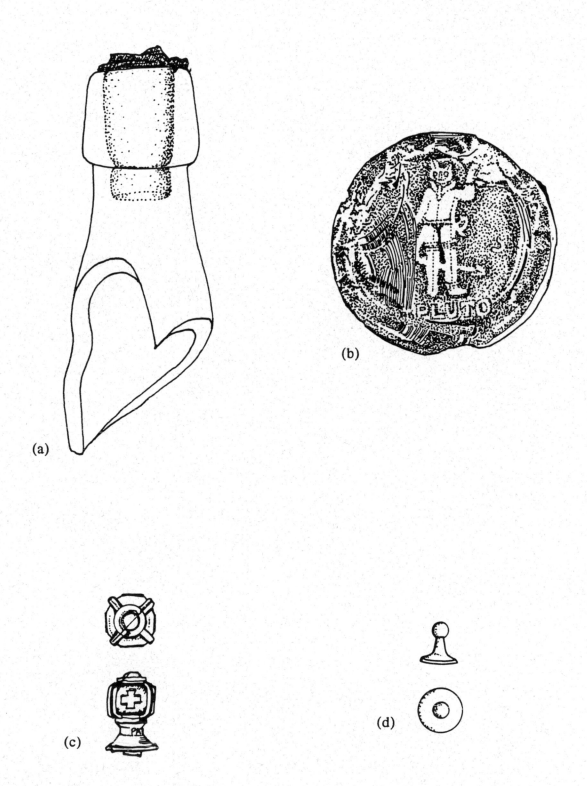

Figure 6.12. Selected glass artifacts recovered from Site AZ N:11:23(ASM). Drawn actual size.

Figure 6.13. Two whole aqua glass beer bottles recovered from Feature 3 (privy) at Site AZ N:11:23(ASM). Drawn 65% actual size.

Medical and Health

Several glass artifacts recovered were in this functional category. Fragments of at least two milk-glass cold cream or Mentholatum jars were present. One had "...CO / PACKERS / CHICAGO" on its base, suggesting an association with the Packer Manufacturing Company, formed in 1869 and continuing through the early twentieth century (Periodical Publishers Association 1934). Rim shards indicated that one of these jars had a friction finish and another had a continuous thread screw-top finish.

Bottle body shards collected were from at least two square brown bitters bottles. Seven shards that fit together read "J. HOSTETTER'S / STOMACH BITTERS." Hostetter's was a popular brand that was manufactured from 1869 to 1954 (Hull-Walski and Ayres 1989:94; Wilson 1981). At least two other fragments were from an H. E. Bucklen & Company bitters bottle. This Chicago company produced bitters and patent medicines from 1878 into the 1890s (Berge 1980:117–118; Hull-Walski and Ayres 1989:101). Over a dozen other brown bitters bottle fragments in the assemblage bore embossing but were too small for identification.

One whole patent-medicine bottle came from Feature 3 (Figure 6.14). This aqua panel bottle, manufactured for Chamberlain & Company, Des Moines, Iowa, originally contained Chamberlain's Colic and Diarrhea Remedy, first produced in 1882 (Berge 1980:94–95). The company started operations around 1879 and continued into the early 1900s.

The only other artifacts related to the Medical and Health category were a segment of a 1/8-inch diameter clear syringe plunger, a bottle stopper, and two segments of a 3/16-inch diameter tube. The bottle stopper had a cube-shaped grasp with medical crosses on each side and "PAT 636821" embossed around the neck (Figure 6.12c). A painted white stripe ran the length of one side of the tube; although no markings were visible on the stripe, the tube appeared to have originally been part of a medical thermometer.

Personal Items

Four whole glass buttons belonged in this category. Two were milk-glass shirt or blouse buttons, one white and one pink, both with four holes in a sunken panel. The other two buttons were white milk-glass collar buttons (Figure 6.12d), identical to a collar button illustrated in the 1895 Montgomery Ward spring and summer catalog (Emmit 1969:168).

Communication

Two aqua glass fragments were from a wire insulator. One was embossed "NEW Y...," probably signifying New York. The insulator likely came from a telegraph or telephone line; Huron Station is known to have provided both types of communication services in the early twentieth century.

Figure 6.14.   Complete aqua glass medicine bottle recovered from Feature 3 (privy) at Site AZ N:11:23(ASM).   Drawn actual size.

Miscellaneous and Unidentified

Nineteen pieces of melted glass recovered from Feature 1, the depot area, were probably pieces of window glass that melted when the depot burned. An SCA disk approximately 1-1/4 inches in diameter appeared to have been flaked from the base of a bottle or jar. The analyst could not determine the purpose of this artifact. Twelve other fragments, all from brown beer bottles, may also have been flaked.

Ceramics

The majority of the 253 ceramic fragments from this site were tableware. Other items in the ceramic assemblage represented a variety of functional classes.

Food Preparation and Consumption

Most of the ceramic artifacts recovered from AZ N:11:23(ASM) fell into this functional category. The 210 sherds were from tableware, such as bowls, cups, plates, and saucers, with eight different designs represented (Table 6.3). Although the analyst could not identify or date any of the designs using standard sources such as Cunningham (1982), examination of the shapes and decoration of the sherds indicated that the assemblage represented a minimum of three bowls, three cups, seven plates, and two saucers (Table 6.4). All but 7 of the ceramic sherds were whiteware, a hard-paste earthenware covered with a white glaze. All of the identified vessel forms were whiteware, except for one porcelain plate.

Table 6.3. Designs on Ceramics from Site AZ N:11:23(ASM)

Design	Description
1	Hand-painted Japanese scene of a woman, an umbrella, and foliage in red, green, and black paint over clear glaze
2	Thin band of gold along rim over white glaze
3	Pink roses and geometric designs of green, orange, and blue over white glaze
4	Pink flowers and green vines over white glaze
5	Red flower buds with green foliage over clear glaze
6	Grayish-blue flower buds, flowers, and foliage over white glaze
7	Gold flowers, stems, and leaves arranged in a circle over clear glaze
8	Green foliage with pink flowers over white glaze

Table 6.4. Vessels Represented by Sherds in the Ceramic Assemblage from Site AZ N:11:23(ASM)

Vessel Form	Number of Vessels Represented	Decoration/Marks	Number of Sherds
Whiteware			
Bowl	2	None	4
Cup	2	None	4
Plate		None	69
Saucer	1	None	1
Plate	1	Design 2	5
Saucer	1	Design 2	2
Bowl	1	Design 3	5
Plate	1	Design 3	3
Plate	1	Design 4	2
Plate	1	Design 6	1
Plate	1	Design 7	6
Cup	1	Molded relief	1
Plate	1	Molded relief	1
Unidentified	*	None	93
Unidentified	*	"Lion and Unicorn" crest hallmarks	2
Unidentified	*	John Edwards hallmark	1
Unidentified	*	Knowles, Taylor & Knowles hallmark	1
Unidentified	*	East End Pottery Co. or Wheeling Pottery Co. hallmark	1
Unidentified	1	Design 5	1
Total	**15**		**203**
Porcelain			
Plate	1	Design 1 and "JAPAN" hallmark	1
Unidentified	*	Design 1	2
Unidentified	*	None	4
Total	**1**		**7**

*Could be part of identified vessels or of other items.

Six sherds had a manufacturer's hallmark or other marks. Two had portions of hallmarks with the "Lion & Unicorn" crest, and one had the words "ROYAL IRONSTONE" as well (Figure 6.15a). Not enough of either hallmark was present to positively identify the manufacturer. One sherd bore a portion of a "John Edwards, England" hallmark. According to Thorn (1947:56), this hallmark was first used in 1891. Another sherd bore the "Knowles, Taylor & Knowles, E. Liverpool, Ohio" hallmark dating between approximately 1890 and 1907 (Gates and Ormerod 1982:119). A partial hallmark was one used by either the East End Pottery Company, East Liverpool, Ohio, between 1903 and 1907, or the Wheeling Pottery company, Wheeling, West Virginia, from 1894 to 1901 (Gates and Ormerod 1982:41; Thorn 1947:155). The porcelain plate bore the word "JAPAN" on its base, indicating a date after 1890; before 1891 the United States did not require identification of the country of origin on imported ceramics.

Architecture (Construction-Related)

The ceramic items in this category were three fragments of one earthenware doorknob with a white "porcelain" finish, identical to doorknobs recovered from AZ N:11:19(ASM) and Fort Bowie (Herskovitz 1978:116–117). This type was common in the late nineteenth and early twentieth centuries.

Leisure and Recreation

Three ceramic artifacts clearly belonged to this functional category. A complete porcelain bottle cap (Figure 6.15b) bore a shield design with the words "THE OLD / GOVERNMENT / WHISKEY" on its top. Whiskey had also been the contents of a shattered crockery jug recovered from Subfeature 6-3, a large charcoal stain near the blacksmithing area. The one-handled, one-gallon jug had a brown glazed interior and a white glazed exterior with a blue transfer design and "MYER..Y, / FUL...N / WIS...KY / COVINGTON, KY." (Figure 6.15c). The third artifact was a leg from a porcelain doll (Figure 6.15d). The white leg was solid, molded in one piece with a sock and shoe, and had thin blue line painted around the top of the sock. A hole in the interior surface of the thigh would have been used to attach the leg to the doll's torso.

Personal Items

Three porcelain sunken-panel buttons were the only ceramic personal items discovered. One was black with two holes, one was white with two holes, and one was white with four holes. The size of the buttons suggested they were from shirts or blouses.

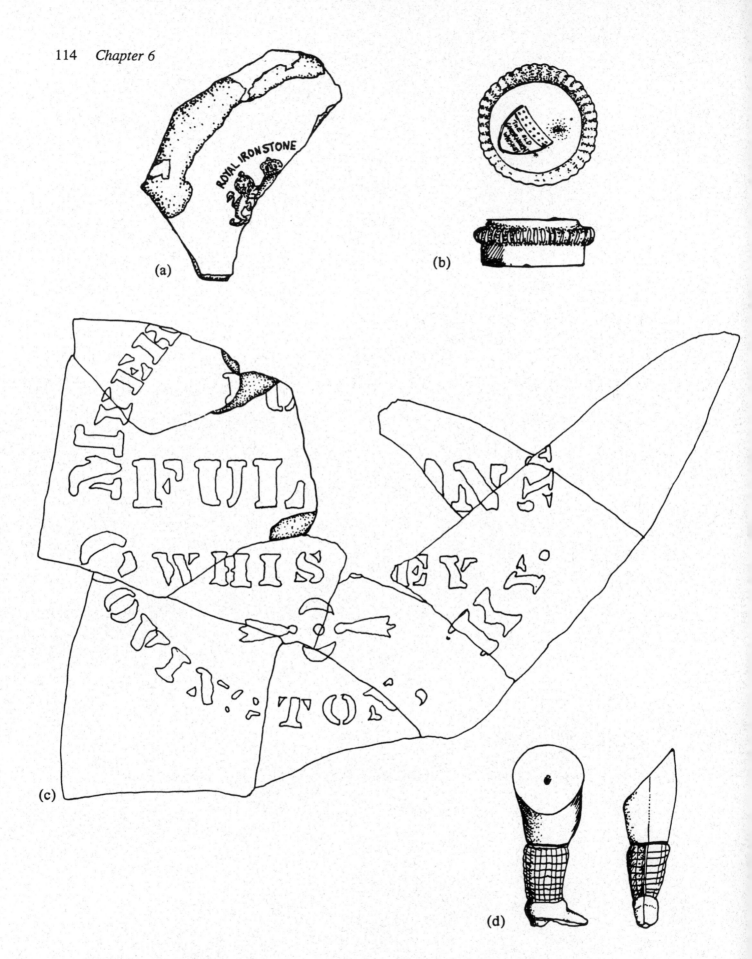

Figure 6.15. Selected ceramic artifacts recovered from Site AZ N:11:23(ASM). Drawn actual size.

Mining and Quarrying

One ceramic artifact belonged in this functional category. It was the base and lower body of an assay crucible, measuring 5 inches in diameter.

Miscellaneous and Unidentified

The analyst could not identify the function or contents of 35 remaining sherds, although 33 apparently represented vessels. Twenty-seven sherds were fragments of five crockery containers. One sherd represented a crockery bottle with a mottled brown and tan glaze. Four sherds from another crockery container of unidentified form had a grayish-white glaze on both the interior and exterior. Another 15 sherds represented two other ceramic containers. An earthenware hard-paste sherd with a white glaze represented a jar. Another six hard-paste earthenware sherds with a white glaze represented two containers of unidentified shape.

The analyst could not identify two ceramic artifacts. One was a hard-paste earthenware sherd with mottled red and yellow glazes on one side and mottled red and brown glazes on the other side. The other unidentified sherd was a soft-paste earthenware with a brown glaze on both sides.

Leather

Personal Items

One whole boot and seven small pieces of shoes or boots came from Feature 3, the privy. The boot was for the right foot, had a red polish, and had 18 eyelets. The lower 10 eyelets were the "lace-through" grommet type and the upper 8 were the "lace-over" hook type.

Unidentified

Nineteen fragments of leather were in the form of small sheets and knotted and twisted strips. The function of these fragments was not apparent.

Graphite

Miscellaneous

Two pieces of graphite recovered from AZ N:11:23(ASM) were cylindrical battery cores. One was 5/16 inch in diameter and 2-1/4 inches long, and the other was 27/32 inch in diameter and 2 inches long. These artifacts might have been part of a *car* battery.

Shell

Personal Items

The only shell artifacts found were seven buttons, three with four holes and four with two holes. They ranged in size from 1/2 inch (20 ligne) to 19/32 inch (26 ligne) in diameter.

Rubber

Miscellaneous and Unidentified

Two of the rubber artifacts collected were black bottle stoppers, 1-1/2 inches long and shaped like truncated cones. They likely came from medicinal vessels of some sort. Five fragments of rubber were of unknown function. One was a small (less than 1 inch square) rectangle of black rubber with a flat head wood screw drilled through it.

Cork

Leisure and Recreation

Recovered artifacts in this category were one whole cylindrical bottle cork and one fragment of a cylindrical bottle cork. Both appeared to be the size of a modern wine bottle cork.

Miscellaneous

A cork disk of unknown function measured 1/8 inch in thickness and 15/16 inch in diameter. The disk may have been part of some type of bottle closure.

Bone

Personal Items

AZ N:11:23(ASM) yielded one bone button with four holes. It was 21/32 inch (32 ligne) in diameter and 3/32 inch thick.

Pigment

Leisure and Recreation

A fragment of a disk of blue pigment was approximately 1/8 inch thick. The size and shape of the disk suggested that it had come from a set of watercolor paints.

Synthetic Materials

Personal Items

The single artifact in this category was of celluloid. The item was part of a woman's hair sidecomb made to resemble tortoise shell.

Unidentified

A segment of a cylinder 1/8 inch in diameter was made of plastic. The function of this item was not apparent.

Faunal Remains

Of the 50 faunal specimens recovered from the site, 45 were from the privy, Feature 3. The 10 taxonomically identifiable specimens were 4 beef bones (*Bos taurus*), 3 mutton bones (*Ovis aries*), 1 chicken bone (*Gallus gallus*), and 2 cottontail bones (*Sylvilagus audubonii*). Most of the 40 unidentifiable fragments probably were beef bone.

The four identified beef fragments were from secondary retail meat cuts with hand-sawed ends. Two of the specimens were "O-bone" fragments, probably from large round steaks. Round steaks are cut from the central section of beef thighs, and individual steaks may or may not be prepared with the small O-shaped femur bone left in place. The O bones found in round steaks usually have a width of approximately

1/2. inch. One beef femur fragment with hand-sawed ends had a length of 2-1/2 inches; this bone probably was from a small round roast. One sawed lumbar vertebra probably was from a high-quality T-bone steak.

Identified sheep elements included one ulna fragment, one metatarsal, and one proximal phalanx. These elements were from very low value parts of the animal, and none exhibited butchering. The ulna fragment may have been from a foreshank cut. Sheep metapodials and phalanges from a formally butchered carcass generally are thrown away because of their low meat-to-bone ratio. The chicken bone was a femur. Two cottontail elements were in the assemblage: one proximal scapula fragment obtained from the privy and one calcaneus from HS 11. The analyst could not ascertain whether the cottontail elements had been deposited naturally or culturally.

The identified beef elements were from relatively high quality meat cuts, indicating that the site occupants had access to a variety of superior steaks and roasts. The mutton elements and the single chicken bone suggested the availability of a variety of meat types. Rectangular meat-tin fragments and associated score-strip keys recovered at this site indicated consumption of canned meat.

It is noteworthy that nearly all of the specimens were recovered from the privy fill. Perhaps bone deposited in the privy was protected from the scavengers, animal trampling, and weathering that would have impacted bone deposited at other areas of the site. It is also possible that exposed bone would have quickly decomposed in the shallow soil of the site.

SUMMARY AND DISCUSSION

Results of archaeological testing and data recovery investigations at Site AZ N:11:23(ASM) confirmed that the site marked the remains of Huron Station, a Prescott & Eastern Railway facility founded in 1898, and the Montezuma and Eagle Fraction lode claims, located in 1898 and 1909, respectively. Feature 1, Feature 4, and the railroad grade corresponded to the locations of the depot, warehouse, and grade depicted on a 1925 map of Huron Station (see Figure 6.3). Features 2 and 5 matched the locations of a Mineral Entry Survey corner point for the Montezuma and Eagle Fraction claims and the No. 3 shaft of the Montezuma claim as depicted on a 1915 Mineral Entry Survey plat (see Figure 6.4).

Archival evidence indicated that Huron Station existed mainly to provide goods and services to outlying mines and mining camps, especially the McCabe Mine, and that the station prospered as long as its satellites did. As the mines' fortunes declined after 1907, Huron's future dimmed. Despite a brief resurgence during World War I, the community witnessed a period of depopulation in the 1910s from which it never recovered. Its voting precinct was discontinued in 1912, its depot was retired from service in 1923, and its post office was closed in 1928. Only its railroad grade saw continued, occasional service through 1958. In that year, the Atchison, Topeka & Santa Fe Railway legally abandoned its line through Huron and pulled the rails.

Archival evidence also indicated that the Montezuma and Eagle Fraction lode claims were two of a group of seven claims at Huron that became consolidated into George "Make-a-Million" Hull's mining empire during a period beginning in 1901 and ending in 1915-1916. Hull's Huron properties, as well as his more extensive holdings in Jerome, were primarily copper claims. Hull was just beginning to develop his Huron claims when his Jerome claims became big producers, and he died before fully developing the Huron properties. However, before his death, Hull *did* manage to patent his Huron claims (in 1916), to excavate approximately 1500 feet of shafts, tunnels, and drifts, to invest about $25,000 in the properties, and to extract more than seven rail carloads of ore. The only mining activity on the Huron claims following Hull's death in October of 1916 was exploratory drilling by Long Lac Minerals Exploration on the Swindler claim in 1985–1986.

Artifact data accorded well with this chronology. The vast majority of the artifacts recovered from the site dated to the late nineteenth and early twentieth centuries, when Huron was at its peak. A few artifacts postdated 1910, when Huron was still occupied but in decline. Virtually no artifacts were of the modern period, after Huron was abandoned.

Archival data indicated that a saloon had been present at Huron; artifact evidence in the form of abundant alcoholic beverage bottles, brewing company bottle caps, and shot-glass fragments eloquently confirmed that such was indeed the case. Records indicated that the saloon had been founded in 1898 by Charles Wingfield, sold in 1900 to Frank Nester, and operated by Nester until at least 1910. But where, exactly, was the saloon? It did not appear on any of the historic-period maps discovered during the course of the project. The privy, which yielded so many brewing company bottle caps, clearly appeared to be a "two-holer" that served patrons of the saloon; the saloon must have been nearby. Yet the only areas of the site that appeared to have been occupied by any buildings were Feature 1 (the depot), Feature 4 (the warehouse), and possibly Trash Area A (which was very slightly elevated, contained a greater density of surface trash than the rest of the site, and had rocks—a possible building foundation—eroding at the surface). Feature 4 was outside the ROW and so was not tested or excavated. Archival and archaeological evidence from testing and excavation at Feature 1 confirmed that this spot had indeed been occupied by the depot and that the depot had thoroughly burned (or *been* burned) sometime following its retirement in 1923. Excavation revealed that Trash Area A was simply a shallow trash concentration; its tantalizing rocks were from shallow bedrock, not a building foundation.

The question "where was the saloon?" continued to haunt SWCA's researchers well past the fieldwork stage of the investigations. A thorough search of repositories listed in Chapter 2 had failed to find even a single historical photograph of Huron Station or to shed light on the issue. Serendipity finally provided the answer. As the artifact analysis and synthesis drew to a close, the Principal Investigator happened to be working on a project in the Verde Valley that was unrelated to the SR 69 investigations. In a small file folder in the bottom drawer of a dusty filing cabinet at the Camp Verde Historical Society, she unexpectedly came across a 1902 photograph of Huron Station. It was a momentous discovery because the photograph appeared to be the only one taken of the station during its heyday. Moreover, the photograph had been taken at relatively close range and was both interpretable and "readable," given the topography of the area and what SWCA researchers by then knew about that area from their investigations.

The 1902 photographer had been standing uphill from (west of) Huron Station and had taken a view eastward, showing the railroad grade and depot in the foreground, a light-colored trail crossing the grade and leading from the depot past a house in the midground, and Post Office Gulch in the background. Comparison of the 1902 photo with a 1901 Mineral Entry Survey plat of the Princes Placer Mining Claim (see Figure 5.2) suggested that the house in the midground was that of C. P. Wingfield. Moreover, the photo showed Huron's saloon, labeled as such (Figure 6.16): the saloon was in the depot building.

This was indeed a startling discovery. Historical photographs and records for other historical depots along the Prescott & Eastern Railway and its close relative, the Bradshaw Mountain Railway (Sayre 1985), indicated that the other depots did not allow saloons to operate within the building. The Huron depot thus appears to have been an interesting, and perhaps unique, exception.

Artifact data suggested that the main supplier of the Huron saloon was the Los Angeles Brewing Company. SWCA investigators therefore undertook special archival research to learn about this company. Through historical newspapers, SWCA learned that the California firm opened a special branch brewery in Prescott in June of 1901 and operated it for several years. The brewery, located along the Santa Fe, Prescott & Phoenix Railway line (*AJM* 10 June 1901:2[3]), could readily and cheaply ship its product to Huron via the Prescott & Eastern Railway. Therefore, much of the Los Angeles Brewing Company beer consumed in the Huron saloon was likely brewed in Prescott, not Los Angeles. This finding provides a cautionary tale for historical archaeologists concerning the limitations of archaeological data and the value of supplementing them with archival research. An archaeologist working at Huron Station who looked no further than its large number (530) of Bernardin caps bearing the Los Angeles Brewing Company name might conclude that the saloon was highly dependent upon (economically tied to) a distant (California) supplier. However, newspaper research indicated that, in this case, the supplier was local, thanks to its branch brewery in Prescott.

An intriguing observation concerning the Huron saloon is that the metal caps from its beer bottles far outnumbered the bottles themselves. This suggests that the bottles, and perhaps other trash as well, were routinely hauled away from the site and disposed of elsewhere. An alternative and perhaps more tenable hypothesis is that the caps (which necessarily broke during the process of opening) were discarded on-site, whereas the bottles (which tended to remain intact after opening) were repeatedly shipped back to the Prescott brewery for refilling. Recycling may have been a familiar concept to the proprietor of Huron's saloon.

The SWCA investigations revealed other information concerning daily life and how work space was organized at Huron. Although archival sources made no mention of it, archaeological data strongly suggested blacksmithing at the site (Feature 6), at least on a limited scale. From the types of metal blanks recovered, this activity most likely included shoeing horses and mules and making small repairs to wagons. Blacksmithing would have been a valuable and necessary service for the freighters who operated between Huron Station and outlying mines such as McCabe.

Figure 6.16. 1902 photo of Huron Station; view east. Shows depot/saloon (lower left), railroad grade (foreground) (note railroad ties), C. P. Wingfield's house (right midground), trail across tracks leading from depot toward Wingfield's house (light-colored track in foreground), and Post Office Gulch (background). From *Prescott Prospect*, 1902; courtesy *Sharlot Hall Museum*.

CHAPTER 7

AZ N:11:25(ASM)

Pat H. Stein

MANAGEMENT SUMMARY

Site AZ N:11:25(ASM) is in the SE¼NW¼SE¼ of Section 28 in Township 13 North, Range 1 East on the USGS Poland Junction, Arizona, 7.5 minute quadrangle (Figure 7.1). The site is on the east side of State Route 69, 2.2 miles southwest of Humboldt and 1.75 miles northeast of Poland Junction, at elevations ranging from 4560 feet to 4600 feet above mean sea level. The property is along an unnamed drainage that joins Galena Gulch 0.3 mile east of the site; Galena Gulch joins the Agua Fria River approximately 1.3 miles east of the site. Vegetation in the area ranges from dense riparian woodland along drainage bottoms to grasslands above the washes. The site measures 450 feet northeast-southwest by 180 feet northwest-southeast, encompassing a total of 1.9 acres on land administered by the Bureau of Land Management (BLM) and on an Arizona Department of Transportation (ADOT) easement across BLM land.

The site was first recorded by Archaeological Research Services, Inc., (ARS) (Hathaway 1992) during the Class III cultural resource survey of the SR 69 Mayer to Dewey segment. The ARS surveyors encountered a total of eight features (designated numerically) and three trash areas (designated alphabetically). Features included a mine shaft, cobble retaining walls, leveled areas, a rock structure, a road segment, and a possible ore processing area. Artifacts suggested a mid-twentieth-century association for the site, perhaps a mining operation. The property was considered potentially eligible for the National Register of Historic Places (NRHP), and ARS recommended avoidance or testing/data recovery.

At first, avoidance of the resource did not appear feasible; ADOT engineers estimated that construction would impact nearly all of the site. However, subsequent engineering and staking by ADOT indicated that only the western portion of the site—an area including Features 1 through 4—would be affected. The testing program conducted by SWCA included archival research, mapping of the entire site, photodocumenting each feature, testing features within the ROW for subsurface remains, and analyzing cultural material. The researchers made general observations about artifacts on the site as a whole, and more detailed observations and controlled collections for artifacts within the proposed ROW. SWCA did not recommend or conduct additional work at the site during the data recovery phase.

HISTORICAL DATA

A thorough search of archives (see Chapter 2) revealed little about the possible function and dating of Site AZ N:11:25(ASM). According to the archives, the site area was never patented, claimed, or leased. Historically, the properties nearest this location were the Montezuma and Huron lode mining claims [*Please note*: the mining claims discussed in this section differ in location and history from those of the same names described in Chapter 6.] The northwestern corner of the Montezuma claim was only 0.1 mile southeast of the site, and the Huron claim lay directly south of the Montezuma claim; each claim included 20.662 acres (Figure 7.2). Because these mining properties were so close to the site and may, therefore, have been related to it, the following section summarizes their history.

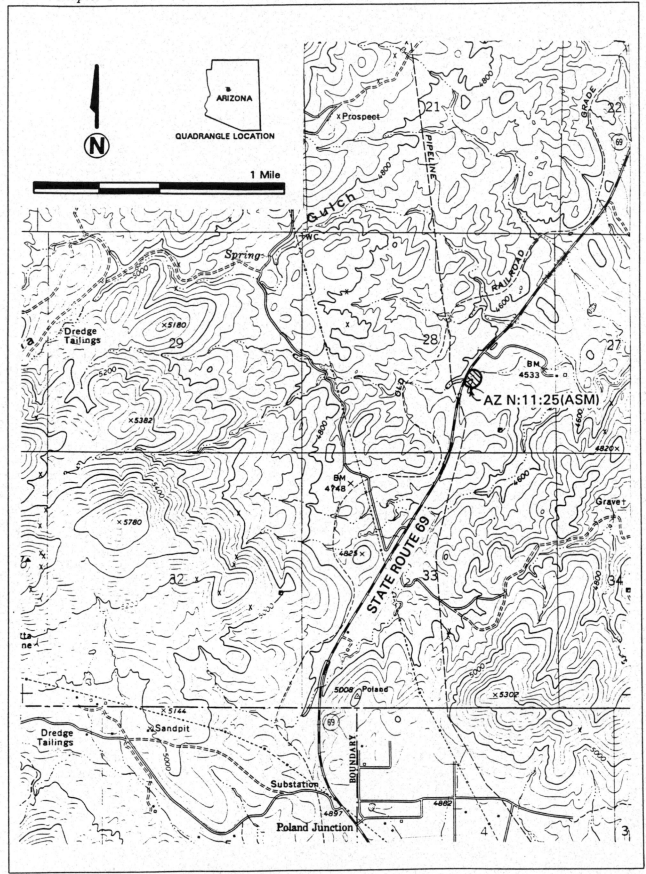

Figure 7.1. Location of Site AZ N:11:25(ASM). Base map is Poland Junction, Arizona, USGS 7.5′ quadrangle, 1975.

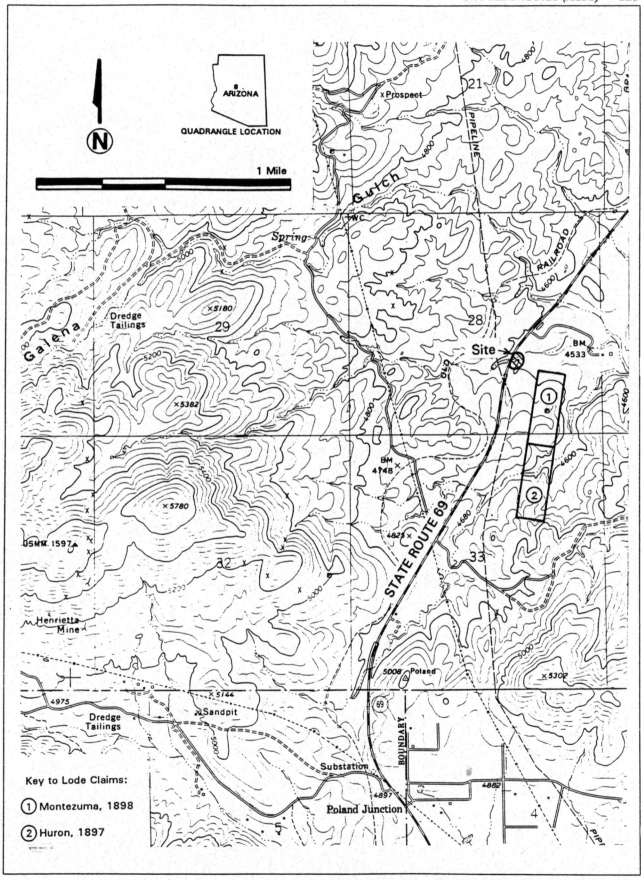

Figure 7.2. Location of Montezuma and Huron mining claims in relation to Site AZ N:11:25(ASM). Base map is Poland Junction, Arizona, USGS 7.5′ quadrangle, 1975.

J. H. Hicklin first located the Montezuma Lode Claim in January of 1898. When Hicklin filed his record of claim with the Yavapai County Recorder, he had sunk a discovery shaft on the property but had made no other improvements (Yavapai County Recorder [YCR] Book of Mines [BM] 50:64). In August of the same year, Hicklin, then a resident of McCabe in the Big Bug Mining District, sold an undivided half-interest in his Montezuma claim to A. Cushman of Delta, Colorado, for $500 (YCR Book of Deeds [BD] 45:258). In December of 1900, Hicklin sold the remaining half of his claim to Henry Murray Lee and Charles Frederick Reed of Arapahoe County, Colorado, for only $250 (YCR BD 52:511). At the time of sale, the only improvement to the property was the aforementioned discovery shaft. Two months after the sale, Lee and Reed bought out Cushman's share of the property for $250 (YCR BD 54:21).

The history of the Huron Lode Claim paralleled and eventually merged with that of the Montezuma claim. Charles Kingsley, a resident of Big Bug, Yavapai County, first located the Huron property in January of 1897 (YCR BM 45:490–491). When Kingsley filed his record of claim with the County Recorder, he noted that he had sunk a discovery shaft on the property but had made no other improvements, nor had any been made when he sold the claim to Lee and Reed in July of 1901 for $500 (YCR BD 55:180).

Lee and Reed promptly began to develop their Huron and Montezuma properties. They made improvements to the claims, sinking a total of five shafts on the two properties, as a necessary step toward patenting them. A surveyor for the General Land Office (GLO) (Fisher 1902) produced a plat that precisely defined the limits of the claims and showed the locations of the five shafts (Figure 7.3). The surveyor noted that the claims were bounded on all sides by government land. According to BLM records, Lee and Reed received their patent to the two claims in June of 1904 (GLO 1902). Files at the Arizona Department of Mines and Mineral Resources indicate that the lode claims were valuable mainly for their gold and silver content (Arizona Department of Mines and Mineral Resources Resources File, Montezuma & Huron MES 1673).

In January of 1910 Reed sold his half-interest in the patented claims to his partner for $1.00 (YCR BD 85:588). No further mention of the Huron and Montezuma properties appeared in archival records until 1926. In February of that year, Lee filed a form with the Yavapai County Chamber of Commerce stating that he was actively seeking investors to further develop his properties (Sparkes 1926). The form indicated that Lee had extended his main shaft to a depth of 200 feet and had excavated a drift extending 20 feet east of the main shaft at a depth of 160 feet. Lee noted that he hoped to excavate drifts 100 feet west, 100 feet east, and at least 300 feet north from the bottom of the main shaft. He estimated that the work would require a capital investment of $10,000. Lee also noted that he was willing to lease or bond the property to another miner, who would do the excavating, and to split any profits that resulted. To promote his claims and thus attract investors, Lee added that the Montezuma and Huron were likely to yield high-grade gold and copper ores (Sparkes 1926). Lee realized and duly noted that the Huron was an underground extension of George Hull's Swindler Lode Claim, a relatively well known and profitable deposit approximately 0.5 mile to the south/southwest (see Chapter 6).

Whether Lee ever secured the assistance he sought is not known. It *is* known that in May of 1937, he sold the Huron and Montezuma properties to Henry A. Dameron, a Prescott resident, for $1.00. The Yavapai County Recorder Book of Deeds indicates that Dameron owned a great deal of real estate in the Prescott area in the 1930s and 1940s. He developed a subdivision in Prescott that bears his name, as does a street. Dameron retained the Huron and Montezuma claims through the rest of the historic period.

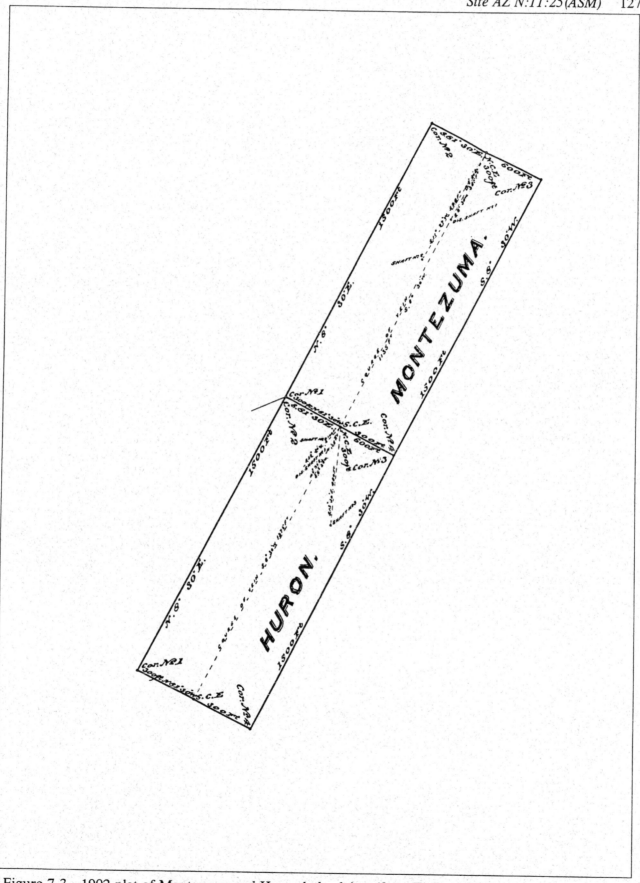

Figure 7.3. 1902 plat of Montezuma and Huron lode claims (from Fisher 1902).

The only other archival information regarding the area of AZ N:11:25(ASM) came from a 1954 set of construction plans for SR 69. The plans for this portion of the highway (ADOT Project S-38 [9]:Sheet 8) indicated that an "abandoned mine shaft" was less than 100 feet east of a proposed concrete box culvert to be built along the highway. The plans also noted that the mine shaft would be fenced during construction. Hathaway (1992:48–49) duly noted that the location of Feature 1 at AZ N:11:25(ASM) coincided with that of the old mine shaft. Unfortunately, neither the 1992 survey nor subsequent archaeological investigations yielded additional historical information about the mine shaft.

ARCHAEOLOGICAL DATA

The focus of testing was on mapping the entire site, photodocumenting each feature, testing features within the right-of-way (ROW) for any subsurface remains, and analyzing cultural material. SWCA archaeologists recorded general observations about artifacts on the site as a whole and made more detailed observations and controlled collections within the ROW. The mapping effort relocated the features reported by Hathaway (1992) (Figure 7.4); the present investigations retained the designations assigned during that survey (Features 1 through 8 and Trash Areas A, B, and C). The testing crew discovered three additional features and assigned to them numbers 9, 10, and 11. Subsurface testing included a 5 × 5-foot test pit in Features 1 and 2, a shovel test in Feature 3, and a 2 × 8-foot trench in Feature 4.

In the following feature descriptions, elements that will be impacted by construction (Features 1, 2, 3, 4, 9, and 11) are described in much greater detail than those that will not be impacted. Terms used in describing and measuring historical artifacts are defined in the Glossary.

The Class III survey recorded Feature 1 as a 10-foot-square mine shaft, located in a drainage bottom and enclosed by a collapsed barbed wire fence. Removal of dense brush during testing revealed that this feature was neither a shaft nor square but a platform measuring 19 feet north-south by 10.5 feet east-west. The northern and eastern walls of the platform were of uncoursed schist rubble; the southern and western sides were built into the surrounding drainage slope. The platform was relatively flat on top and had a maximum height of 40 inches. Remnants of the collapsed fence consisted of barbed wire attached to two metal posts and one 4 × 4-inch wooden post. The fence was so collapsed and uprooted that the archaeologists could not ascertain its original location relative to the platform. Aside from the fence posts and barbed wire, no associated surface artifacts were present.

A 5 × 5-foot test pit placed inside the northern corner of the platform revealed rubble and earth fill. The only artifacts encountered were a modern Coca Cola can and a few tiny scraps of metal, all in the top 6 inches of fill. Excavators extended the test pit to a depth of 3 feet and then discontinued it when no more cultural material was encountered.

Feature 2 was a masonry building measuring 14.5 feet north-south by 8 feet east-west (Figure 7.5). The building had full-height walls (maximum extant height, 4.9 feet) of unmortared schist and conglomerate cobbles. The average wall width was 1.6 feet, but the base of the rear (western) wall was as much as 2.5 feet thick in places because this part of the building had been built into bedrock. An opening at the southeastern corner marked what had likely been an entryway. The rest of the walls had no openings, suggesting that the building had lacked windows. The roof was gone, and the structure lacked direct evidence to suggest what the original roofing material had been. Corrugated metal sheets noted 50 feet east of the structure may have been part of the roof.

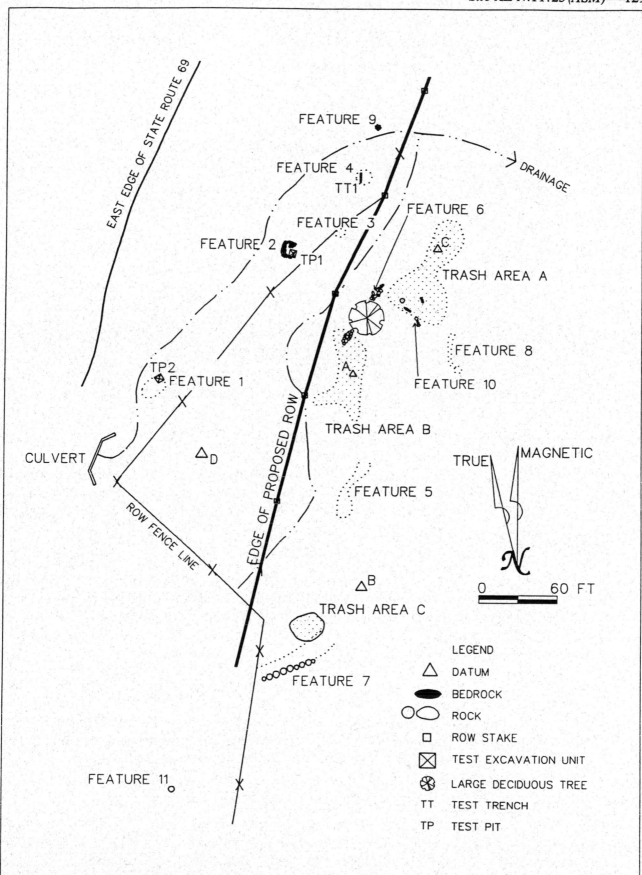

Figure 7.4. Site AZ N:11:25(ASM).

Figure 7.5. Size AZ N:11:25(ASM), Feature 2, masonry structure; view northwest.

Surface artifacts in association with Feature 2 were metal and glass items. Metal objects consisted of a water valve, a shovel head, a cast-iron handle, several tin-can scraps, a tobacco-can lid, 12 wire nails, a piece of 1/2-inch galvanized wire mesh, two pieces of strap iron, three evaporated milk cans, a sanitary can containing ashes, a key-strip-opened coffee can, a pry-type reclosable lid, a screw lid, and a spool from wire fencing material. The shovel head bore the lettering "CONNEAUT / MINING BEND," indicating that the tool had been manufactured by the Conneaut Shovel Company of Conneaut, Ohio. This manufacturing plant opened in 1905, was absorbed by the American Fork & Hoe Co. in 1931, and discontinued operations circa 1957 (*Conneaut News-Herald* 1946; Conneaut Telephone Directory 1957). The most closely datable metal items were two relatively intact evaporated milk cans; their method of manufacture and dimensions suggested a date of 1917–1929 or 1950 to the present. Glass items consisted of two whole, clear bottles and numerous fragments, from an amber beer bottle with a hand-tooled finish, a sun-colored amethyst (SCA) bottle with a semiautomatic finish, an aqua panel bottle, a pale green panel bottle, two clear bottles, a clear, embossed bowl or cup, and a clear vase or tumbler. One of the whole bottles bore a basemark used by the Owens-Illinois Glass Company circa 1929–1954. The aqua panel bottle fragment was embossed with "THE CELEBRATED H.H.H. HORSE MEDICINE." Fike (1987:147) states that this type of bottle dates circa 1868. The presence of this early artifact on what is essentially a twentieth-century site suggests that the bottle was a collected or curated item.

The field crew excavated a test unit measuring 5 × 5 feet by 1 foot deep in the entryway of the structure to determine the depth of the walls, ascertain if the building had a floor, and look for subsurface material. The test unit revealed that the walls of the building extended to a depth of only 5 inches below the present ground surface. Only slight charcoal flecking 2–3 inches below the present ground surface suggested a "floor," and the only artifacts encountered (within 3 inches of the surface) were a chisel head, a piece of wire, 8 wire nails, and 12 tiny fragments of a pale yellow/honey-colored canning jar. The color of the glass suggested a 1914–1930s date of manufacture.

Feature 3 was a depression measuring 8 feet north-south by 6.7 feet east-west filled with loose trash (Figure 7.6). When excavated, the depression was concave in profile, with a maximum depth of 3 feet. Artifacts in the feature included sanitary cans, galvanized metal stovepipe, numerous pieces of corrugated sheet metal, an insecticide sprayer (marked "STANDARD OIL COMPANY OF CALIFORNIA"), a cone-top beer or soda can, a skillet (stamped "MADE IN U.S.A. / NATIONAL"), pocket tobacco cans, paint and lard pails, coffee cans, a small propane tank, a rectangular fuel can fashioned into a dollhouse by cutting out a door, oil cans, baling wire, an oval fish can, two pieces of a rubber shoe sole or tire tread, and brown and clear glass bottles. The most closely datable objects were the cone-top can (manufactured from 1935 through the 1950s) and an oil can bearing a patent date of 1898. Artifacts from the very base of the feature consisted of a bottle base, five evaporated/condensed milk cans, the key from a score-strip-opened meat can, the wire handle from a pail or bucket, a crushed sanitary can, and a crushed lard bucket. The most closely datable of these items were the bottle base (no basemark but of clear glass, suggesting a date from 1930 to the present) and the milk cans (a type and size manufactured from 1931 to 1945).

Figure 7.6. Site AZ N:11:25(ASM), Feature 3, depression with trash; view northeast.

After removing and analyzing the trash from the feature, SWCA archaeologists excavated a shovel test in the central base of the depression. They immediately encountered rocky, culturally sterile soil. No evidence of soil discoloration or other stratigraphy such as one might encounter in a privy was present.

Feature 4, a circular leveled area on a slope, measured 8 feet in diameter. The feature had been created by excavating the upslope part of the hill to a depth of 2–4 feet and placing the backdirt downhill to form a small terrace. Clearing away vegetation revealed no artifacts in direct association with the feature. Artifacts in closest proximity were two pocket tobacco cans 25 feet to the south and a small piece of sheet metal 10 feet to the east. A 2 × 8–foot test trench excavated across the feature exposed only a sterile, sandy clay loam without cultural material. The excavators discontinued the test unit at a depth of 13 inches below the present ground surface.

Feature 5 was a leveled area measuring 50 feet north-south by 10 feet east-west that appeared to represent the remains of a poorly defined trail or unpaved road beginning and ending within the site. Feature 6 was a cobble retaining wall constructed along the top of a drainage embankment. The wall measured 60 feet long by 6 feet wide and was of unmortared schist and conglomerate cobbles. Feature 7 was a dirt road segment, approximately 80 feet long by 10 feet wide, trending east-west across the southern edge of the site. A rock alignment 60 feet long ran along the southern edge of the road. Feature 8 was a concentration of gravel and steel cable in an area measuring 35 feet north-south by 8 feet east-west, on the eastern edge of the site.

Feature 9 was a cobble cluster within the drainage at the northern end of the site. The cluster was roughly circular, approximately 4 feet in diameter, and 6–8 inches high. The feature appeared to be cultural rather than natural but had no artifacts associated with it.

Feature 10, a stone and concrete foundation at the southern edge of Trash Area A, measured at least 15 × 10 feet. The configuration of the stones and their proximity to trash containing predominantly domestic/household items suggested that the feature marked the foundation of a house.

Feature 11 was a rock cairn 3.4 feet in diameter on the southwestern edge of the site. In the center of the cairn was an upright schist slab measuring 20 × 9 × 7 inches and sunk 3 inches into the ground. The testing crew carefully examined the rocks in the cairn but found no inscriptions or other identifying marks. The location of the feature did not correspond to the location of any corner marker indicated on plats for the Huron and Montezuma Lode Claims (see Figure 7.3), the properties historically closest to Site AZ N:11:25(ASM). Feature 11 was only 100 feet from the edge of current SR 69 and probably represented a temporary survey marker associated with the highway.

Trash Area A, in the northeastern portion of the site, measured 80 feet northeast-southwest by 50 feet northwest-southeast. As noted above, this trash area was associated with a possible house foundation (Feature 10). Within Trash Area A was an ash and charcoal concentration measuring 10 feet in diameter and cultural material of moderate to high density. Artifacts included hole-in-cap and sanitary cans, hole-in-cap rectangular meat tins, pocket tobacco tins, baking powder cans, lids from coffee canisters, pieces of lumber, wire nails, galvanized stove pipe, yellow brick (some stamped "USA CO"), red brick, 1-1/2-inch coaxial cable, a car-seat spring, a typewriter carriage base, an enamelware bowl, fragments of a green-glazed hard-paste earthenware bowl, white ironstone fragments, porcelain fragments, and many bottle and jar fragments (mostly clear and brown in color, with a few pieces of cobalt, rose, and SCA glass). The most closely datable artifacts were a Kerr Glass Manufacturing Company bottle base bearing a patent date of 1915, a French's bottle base bearing a patent date of 1938, an Owens-Illinois Glass Company basemark dating from 1929 to 1954, and numerous sanitary/evaporated milk cans suggesting a 1917–1929 or 1950 to present date of manufacture.

Trash Area B, measuring 80 feet north-south by 40 feet east-west, was in the central portion of the site approximately 40 feet west of Trash Area A. Feature 6, the rock retaining wall, extended into this trash area. Cultural material was of moderate density and included evaporated/condensed milk cans, several sanitary cans, a spice-can lid, coffee-canister lids, yellow brick (stamped "L.A.S. CO"), cast-iron stove parts, a fancy, butterfly-shaped door hinge, fragments of worked sheet and tubular aluminum or pot metal, a belt buckle, the rubber wheel of a toy, the metal frame from a change purse or small pouch, a small copper or brass two-photo picture frame, porcelain tableware sherds, an aluminum screw cap, and fragments of clear and brown glass containers. The most closely datable items were a can bearing a patent date of 1910, a Hazel-Atlas bottle basemark dating from 1920 to 1964, an Owens-Illinois Glass Co. basemark dating from 1929 to 1954, and a Clorox container dating from 1929 to 1962.

Trash Area C measured 28 × 25 feet and was near the southern edge of the site immediately north of Feature 7. Cultural material was of low to medium density and included 20 sanitary cans, a baking powder can lid, a coffee can lid, fragments of a clear glass container, 3/4-inch steel cable, several pieces of strap metal, electrical wire encased in 5/8-inch rubber tubing, and baling wire. The only closely datable item was a KC Baking Powder can lid embossed "SAME PRICE TODAY / AS 43 YEARS AGO," indicating a 1943 date of manufacture.

SUMMARY AND RECOMMENDATIONS

Testing results indicated that Site AZ N:11:25(ASM) was a habitation site probably occupied between the 1920s and the early 1950s. Feature 10, a stone and concrete foundation associated with household trash (Trash Area A), most strongly suggested the habitation function. Feature 2 was likely an outbuilding associated with the house, a hypothesis supported by the feature's small size, absence of windows, low density of trash, and lack of a well-defined floor.

Testing neither confirmed nor refuted the earlier hypothesis that the site was associated with mining (Hathaway 1992:49). Historical data provided little insight regarding the age and function of the site. BLM and county records did indicate that mining occurred a short distance southeast of the site, at the Huron and Montezuma lode claims, from the late nineteenth century through at least 1926; it would not be unreasonable to assume that Site AZ N:11:25(ASM) was associated with the later phases of development at one or both of those properties. A 1954 highway construction map depicting an "abandoned mine shaft" at or near Feature 1 provided the only direct historical evidence for mining at the site. However, when cleared of brush and tested, Feature 1 appeared to be a rock and earthen platform rather than a mine shaft.

Despite the fact that SWCA archaeologists could not precisely define the site's historic context, AZ N:11:25(ASM) appears to be eligible for the National Register of Historic Places. This habitation site appears capable of yielding significant data regarding the occupation of central Arizona in the mid-twentieth century and is therefore eligible for the NRHP under Criterion D. The artifacts and features of the site could provide important insights concerning material culture and lifestyles in eastern Yavapai County from circa 1920 through the early 1950s.

The proposed construction will impact Features 1, 2, 3, 4, 9, and 11 in the western portion of the site and will avoid Features 5, 6, 7, 8, and 10 and Trash Areas A, B, and C. During testing field personnel recorded in detail the features and artifacts to be impacted by construction. The ROW portion of the site is unlikely to yield additional important information because its surface manifestations have now been thoroughly studied and because this portion of the site lacks depth. Therefore, SWCA did not recommend or conduct additional work at the site during the data recovery phase of the investigations.

CHAPTER 8

AZ N:12:29(ASM)

Pat H. Stein

MANAGEMENT HISTORY

Site AZ N:12:29(ASM) is in the SE¼NW¼NW¼SW¼ of Section 15 in Township 12 North, Range 1 East on the USGS Poland Junction and Mayer, Arizona, 7.5 minute quadrangles (Figure 8.1). This area is 6 miles south of Humboldt and 2 miles northwest of Mayer at an elevation of 4590 feet above mean sea level. The site is on a low bedrock outcrop with thin soil, approximately 20 feet above and to the west of existing State Route 69. Dense chaparral vegetation covers the site and its environs. The nearest drainage is Big Bug Creek, 350 feet west of the site. As originally recorded, the dimensions of the site were 145 feet northwest-southeast by 85 feet northeast-southwest, a total of 0.28 acre. Vegetation removal during the present investigations revealed that the site was somewhat smaller, measuring 72 feet north-south by 31 feet east-west, encompassing only 0.05 acre. The site is on Bureau of Land Management (BLM) land and an Arizona Department of Transportation (ADOT) easement across BLM land.

GPI Environmental, Inc., (GPI 1991) first recorded AZ N:12:29(ASM) during preliminary investigations for the SR 69 project. During the Class III archaeological survey of SR 69 from Mayer to Dewey, Archaeological Research Services, Inc., (ARS) recorded the site in more detail (Hathaway 1992). Hathaway tentatively interpreted the site as an informal trash dump representing several depositional (dumping) episodes. The trash consisted mostly of household refuse, and no features were noted in association with the material. The majority of items at the site appeared to have been manufactured between 1915 and 1930. The Class III survey report also noted that the site was approximately 200 feet southwest of an abandoned pre-1954 road segment and would have been easily accessible from that road. ARS recommended testing to assess the eligibility of the site for the National Register of Historic Places.

Engineering analysis by ADOT staff calculated that the proposed construction would impact virtually the entire site. In consultation with other agencies, ADOT recommended that testing be conducted to formally evaluate the site's National Register eligibility, as well as its extent and condition. SWCA's testing program consisted of archival research, site resurvey and mapping, in-field analysis of a sample of artifacts, collection of diagnostic artifacts, and excavation of shovel-test units. SWCA did not recommend or conduct additional work at the site during the data recovery phase.

HISTORICAL DATA

Thorough research at federal, state, county, and private repositories found no record of any attempt to claim, patent, or otherwise work the land at Site AZ N:12:29(ASM). With the exception of the ADOT easement across this land, the parcel in historic and modern times had always been federal (BLM) land with no record of settlement, or attempted settlement, by private parties.

Archival maps provided some insight regarding land use patterns of the site's environs during historic times. The General Land Office (GLO) surveyed the township containing the site in 1911–1912 and again

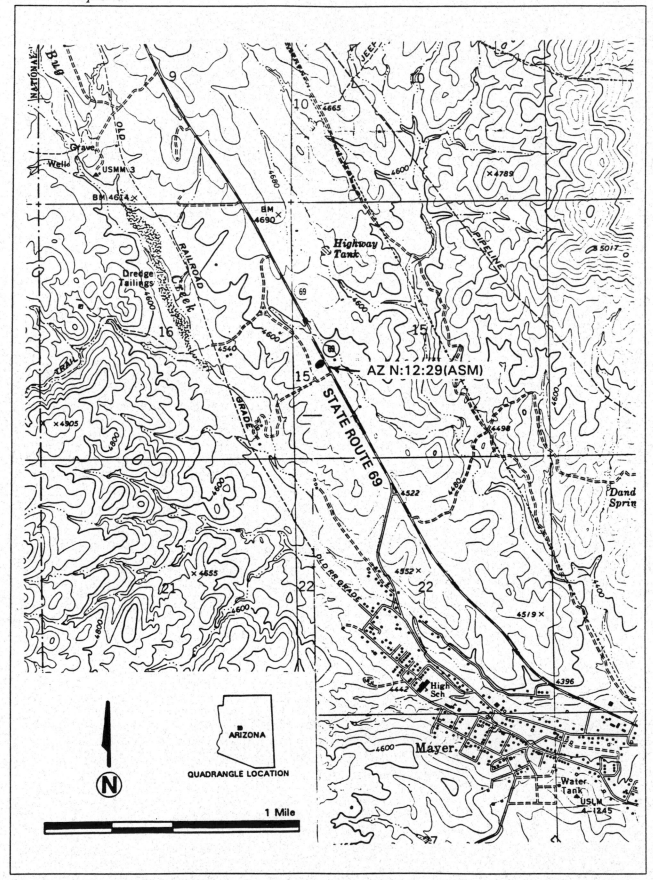

Figure 8.1. Location of Site AZ N:11:29(ASM). Base map is Poland Junction, Arizona, USGS 7.5′ quadrangle, 1975.

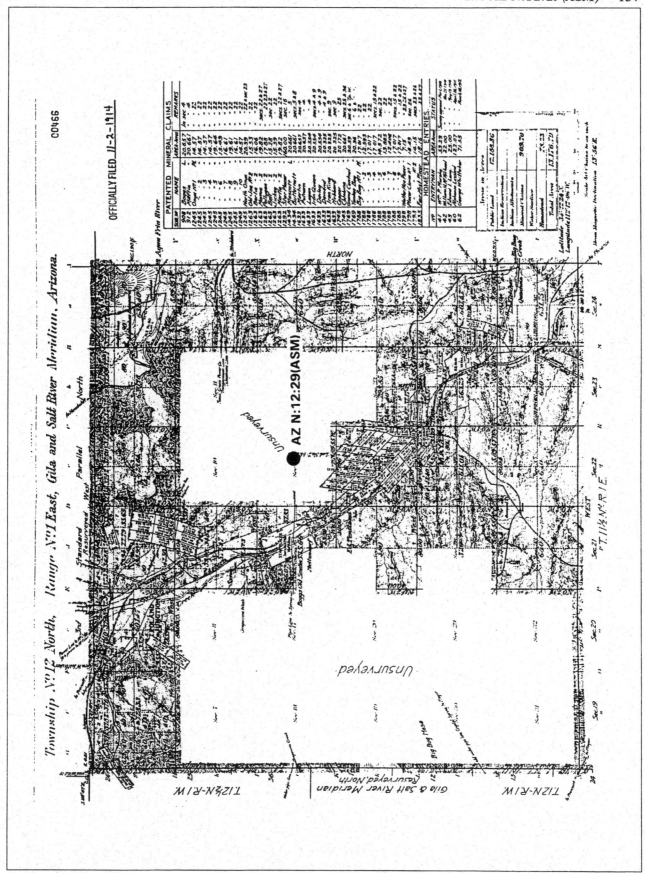

Figure 8.2. 1914 General Land Office map of Township 12 North, Range 1 East.

in 1933 (GLO 1914, 1935). The map generated by the earlier survey (Figure 8.2) indicated 48 patented mining claims and only five homestead within the township. Two major transportation arteries ran through the township at that time. The Prescott-Phoenix wagon road ran generally north-northwest to south-southeast through the township, closely following the east bank of Big Bug Creek in the general site area. The second major transportation artery in the 1910s was the Prescott & Eastern Railway, which generally paralleled and ran close to the wagon road; in the general site area, the railroad followed the west bank of Big Bug Creek. During the 1911–1912 GLO survey, no development whatsoever (no mines, homesteads, roads, or railroads) existed at the location of Site AZ N:12:29(ASM).

The situation had changed by the date of the 1933 GLO survey (Figure 8.3). Although the site still was not the scene of any mining, homesteading, or other activity, it now lay near the junction of two roads. The Prescott-Phoenix wagon road platted during the 1911–1912 survey had now been replaced by a highway—an early alignment of SR 69—that ran farther east of Big Bug Creek and passed within 215 feet of the site. The second road branched off the highway immediately south of the site and led to a series of private claims to the west. Closest to the site (1/4 mile west) was the Star Placer, a 160-acre gold placer that had been located in 1890 by a partnership of eight individuals, had been extensively and productively worked in the 1890s by the Commercial Mining Company, and had played out by the early twentieth century (Arizona Department of Mines and Mineral Resources File, Star Patented MES 1292). In its heyday, the Star Placer had been a well-developed property with three houses, a store, a barn, a smelter, an ore roaster, a mill, placer diggings, and a pipeline for bringing water from the Bradshaw Mountains to the diggings (Fisher 1898). Immediately north of the Star Placer (1/2 mile northwest) was the William H. McMichael property, a homestead filed in 1908 and patented by the claimant in 1913 (USDI Bureau of Land Management Homestead Entry Survey HES 42). Farther west, the road led to the Hackberry mining claim (*Note:* not to be confused with the mine of the same name in Mohave County) (1-1/2 miles west) and eventually terminated at the Carbine and South Carbine mining claims (2 miles west). The Hackberry, Carbine, and South Carbine properties were gold lode claims worked in the early twentieth century.

SWCA researchers discovered only the above archival information regarding Site AZ N:12:29(ASM) and its environs and could not establish the precise historic context of the site or associate the site with any particular historical event, process, or individual. Since the site is at the junction of two historic-era roads, the trash at the site could have been deposited by anyone using those roads in historic times. The investigators hoped that on-site investigations (described below) would provide greater insight into the resource and its historic context.

ARCHAEOLOGICAL DATA

Removal of the dense vegetation that covered and obscured the site revealed that it was somewhat smaller than previously recorded and that it contained three distinct loci of trash, designated Trash Areas A, B, and C (Figure 8.4). The investigators focused on characterizing the artifact assemblage as a whole, ascertaining if differences existed among the loci in terms of age or function, and determining if any of the loci contained subsurface material. Testing methods consisted of mapping and photographing the site and its trash areas, analyzing all artifacts within controlled study transects, collecting all temporally diagnostic artifacts from each locus, and excavating a shovel test in the center of each locus. To establish the controlled study units, the field crews randomly selected a compass bearing for each trash area and used this bearing to set up a 2-foot-wide transect across and through the center of each trash area. Please see the Glossary for definitions of terms used in describing historical artifacts.

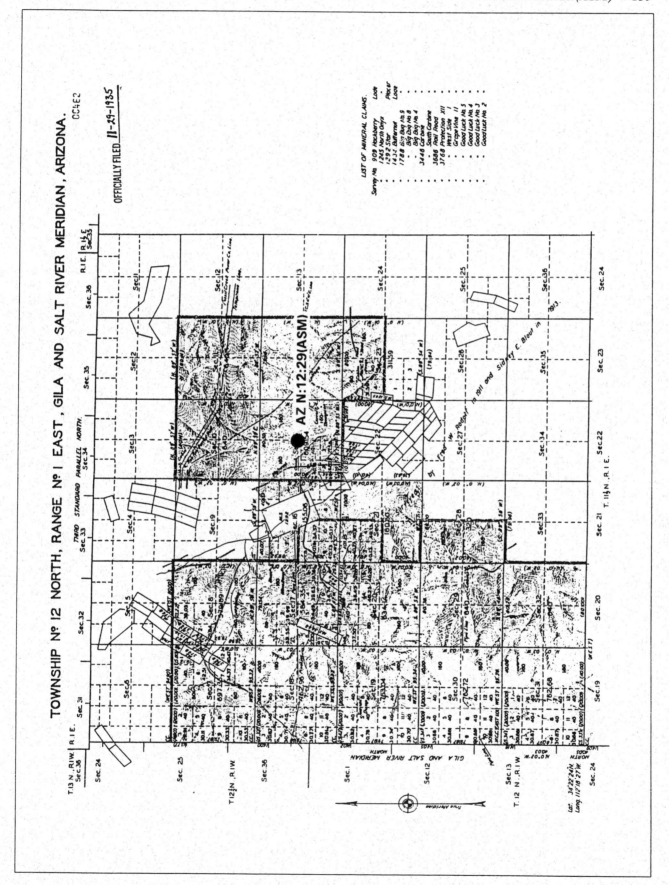

Figure 8.3. 1935 General Land Office map of Township 12 North, Range 1 East.

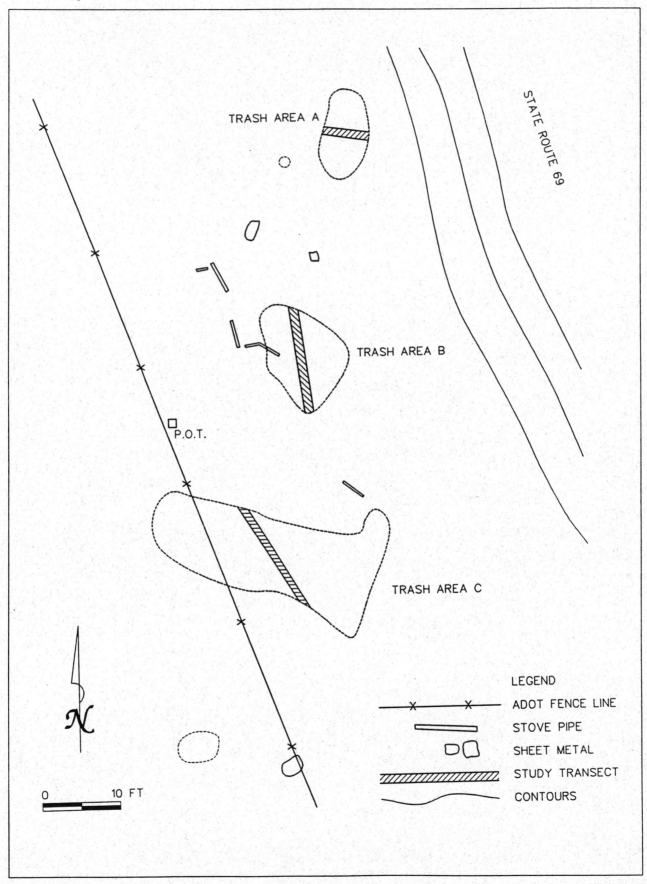

Figure 8.4. Site AZ N:12:29(ASM). Entire site is within proposed right-of-way.

Trash Area A, at the northern edge of the site, measured 11.5 feet north-south by 6.5 feet east-west. In terms of volume, all trash at this locus could have been transported to the site in one 10-gallon container. In terms of function, the items in the study transect represented seven categories: food (10 cans and bottles), food preparation and consumption (a fork and fragments of a plate), household furnishings (a metal tub), medicinal and health (a Mentholatum bottle), tools and hardware (chicken wire and a piece of strap metal), machinery (an oil can), and miscellaneous/unidentified (one pale yellow and one sun-colored amethyst [SCA] bottle). In terms of chronology, the most closely datable artifact from the entire trash area was a fragmentary pale green bottle bearing a circa 1905–1929 American Bottle Company basemark. Other temporally diagnostic artifacts were a white milk-glass Mentholatum bottle base dating 1906 ff.; an Eagle Brand milk can lid dating 1900 ff.; a piece of SCA glass (ca. 1880–1917); and pieces of a pale yellow glass bottle (ca. 1914–1930s). These data suggested that the trash had a domestic (household) origin and that the trash could have been deposited in one dumping episode, most likely during the late 1910s or early 1920s. A shovel test in the central and densest part of Trash Area A indicated that it contained no subsurface material.

Trash Area B measured 13 feet north-south by 11 feet east-west and was in the central part of the site 20 feet south of Trash Area A. A few pieces of sheet metal lay between the two areas, and several pieces of stovepipe lay immediately northwest of Area B. In terms of volume, all material from this locus could have been transported to the site in a 50-gallon drum. In terms of function, the items in the study transect represented six categories: food (9 cans), food preparation and consumption (fragments of two tumblers and one plate), architecture (a brick fragment and window glass), leisure and recreation (fragments of two beer bottles), tools and hardware (one ferrule and three bands of strap metal), and miscellaneous/unidentified (a lid from a can and pieces of a bottle). In terms of chronology, the most closely datable artifacts from the entire locus were a Homer Laughlin "Colonial" pattern plate (ca. 1905), a Homer Laughlin "Genessee" pattern plate (ca. 1915), and an Illinois Pacific Coast Company bottle basemark (ca. 1930–1932). Other temporally diagnostic artifacts were several fragments of an H. J. Heinz condiment bottle (1930 ff.). The analyst could not identify or date a pale green bottle base embossed "UNITED...BREW...." These artifacts suggested that the trash in Feature B had a domestic origin. If the Homer Laughlin plates (representing the relatively early dates of 1905 and 1915) were treasured possessions that had survived for a long period until finally breaking and being discarded, then all the trash in this locus could have been discarded in one episode, in the early 1930s. A shovel test in the central and densest part of Trash Area B revealed no subsurface material.

Trash Area C, at the southern edge of the site 15 feet south of Trash Area B, measured 31 feet east-west by 11 feet north-south. One piece of metal stovepipe was between the two loci. Trash Area C was the largest of the three loci in both area and number of artifacts. In terms of volume, all material from Trash Area C could have been transported to the site in two 50-gallon drums. In terms of function, the items in the study transect represented seven categories: food (14 cans and 2 bottles), food preparation and consumption (a tumbler), leisure and recreation (a pocket tobacco tin and a beer bottle fragment), medicinal and health (a fragment of a cold cream or Mentholatum jar), transportation (11 graphite cells from an automotive battery), tools and hardware (a piece of chicken wire and two pieces of strap iron), and miscellaneous/unidentified (fragments of aqua, pale yellow, and clear bottles).

Numerous closely datable artifacts were in this trash concentration. Bottle fragments bore a number of basemarks: Rockware Glass, Ltd. (1920–1930), John Duncan & Sons (1877–1920), Adolphus Busch Glass Manufacturing Co. (1886–1928), American Bottle Co. (1905–1929), Bishop & Co. (1890–1920), and the Illinois Glass Company (1916–1929). Other datable marks included H. J. Heinz & Co. (1888 ff.),

Armour & Co. (1867 ff.), and Mentholatum (1906 ff.). A tumbler base bore a patent date of 1906. Two closely datable objects were metal: a Log Cabin syrup can in the shape of a log cabin (ca. 1914–1928) and a galvanized plate from a Republic Motor Truck (1912–1929). The syrup can was particularly interesting because it had been converted into a toy by cutting out miniature windows and doors, suggesting that the article came from a household with a child.

These data suggested that Trash Area C, like Areas A and B, represented household refuse. The refuse could have been hauled to the site in one large load or several smaller ones, perhaps in a Republic Motor Truck. The trash was most likely deposited on the site in the 1920s. A shovel test in the central, densest part of Trash Area C indicated a maximum depth of one inch.

Archaeological data revealed no striking differences among the three loci in terms of function: all consisted predominantly of household refuse. In terms of chronology, the differences between them were subtle and not strong or convincing. Trash Area A may have been deposited in the late 1910s or early 1920s, B may have been deposited in the early 1930s, and C may have been deposited in the 1920s. By these dates, most mines in the immediate vicinity of the site were no longer active, and the only homestead in the immediate vicinity (the McMichael Homestead) was already patented. However, by these same dates, the Prescott-Phoenix highway near the site was becoming well established as an automotive route. The trash at AZ N:12:29(ASM) could have been deposited by any person or persons using this road system.

SUMMARY AND RECOMMENDATIONS

Testing indicated that Site AZ N:12:29(ASM) consisted mainly of household refuse that could have been deposited in as few as three episodes spanning the course of two decades. However, neither archival research nor on-site testing placed the site in any precise historic context. Situated along a well-traveled road, unknown users of that road likely deposited the trash at the site. The trash could have originated from a household in Phoenix or Prescott (or more distant points) as easily as it could have originated from a household in the immediate site area.

Testing at Site AZ N:12:29(ASM) revealed no qualities that would render it eligible for the National Register of Historic Places. The site consisted entirely of roadside trash unassociated with known persons, places, activities, or events. The site could not be placed in any meaningful historical context and therefore could not be expected to yield significant data relating to any context, nor was further study likely to yield important data. SWCA therefore did not recommend or conduct additional work at the site during the data recovery phase of the investigations.

CHAPTER 9

AZ N:12:30(ASM)
THE TREADWELL (GREAT WESTERN) SMELTER

Pat H. Stein
Elizabeth J. Skinner

MANAGEMENT HISTORY

Site AZ N:12:30(ASM) is in the E½NE¼NE¼NW¼ and the W½NW¼NW¼NE¼ of Section 26 in Township 12 North, Range 1 East on the USGS Mayer, Arizona, 7.5 minute quadrangle (Figure 9.1). The site is on the top and slopes of a northwest-facing hill overlooking the town of Mayer, at elevations ranging from 4380 feet to 4420 feet above sea level. Vegetation consists of dense transitional chaparral-desertscrub. The site is bounded on the east by Big Bug Creek, on the south by a modern garage, on the west by current State Route 69, and on the north by a modern trailer park. The archaeological site measures approximately 360 feet northeast-southwest by 200 feet northwest-southeast and encompasses a total of 1.65 acres on private land and an Arizona Department of Transportation (ADOT) easement.

Marked by a prominent smokestack, the site is a well-known local landmark, although it has occasionally been misidentified. In her article about the history of Mayer, Thorpe (1978:160) erroneously called this site the "Grey Eagle Reduction Company," referring to the smokestack as "Wagoner's Tower." As Chapter 10 of this report will show, the Gray Eagle Reduction Plant, associated with H. A. Wagner, was not at this location but 0.5 mile to the southeast.

GPI Environmental, Inc., first inventoried and correctly identified Site AZ N:12:30(ASM) as the Treadwell (Great Western) Smelter during preliminary investigations for SR 69 (GPI 1991). Archaeological Research Services, Inc., (ARS) subsequently reported the property in greater detail during the Class III cultural resource survey for the Mayer to Dewey segment of SR 69 (Hathaway 1992). The Class III survey noted 20 features, including the smokestack, concrete foundations, prospect holes, tailings piles, and cobble piles. ARS recommended that the site be considered potentially eligible for the National Register of Historic Places (NRHP), based on its apparent potential to yield scientific information pertaining to the early twentieth century mining industry of central Arizona.

ADOT staff estimated that the proposed construction would impact several features at the southwest end of the site, specifically, Features 19 and 20 and part of Features 2 and 16. During the testing program, SWCA conducted archival research, mapped the entire site, photographed each feature, documented the features to be impacted, tested the only right-of-way (ROW) feature that appeared to have depth, and conducted in-field analysis on all artifacts within the proposed ROW. While brushing the ROW, SWCA investigators discovered two additional features (21 and 22) and documented them in detail. SWCA did not recommend or conduct further work during the data recovery phase of the SR 69 project.

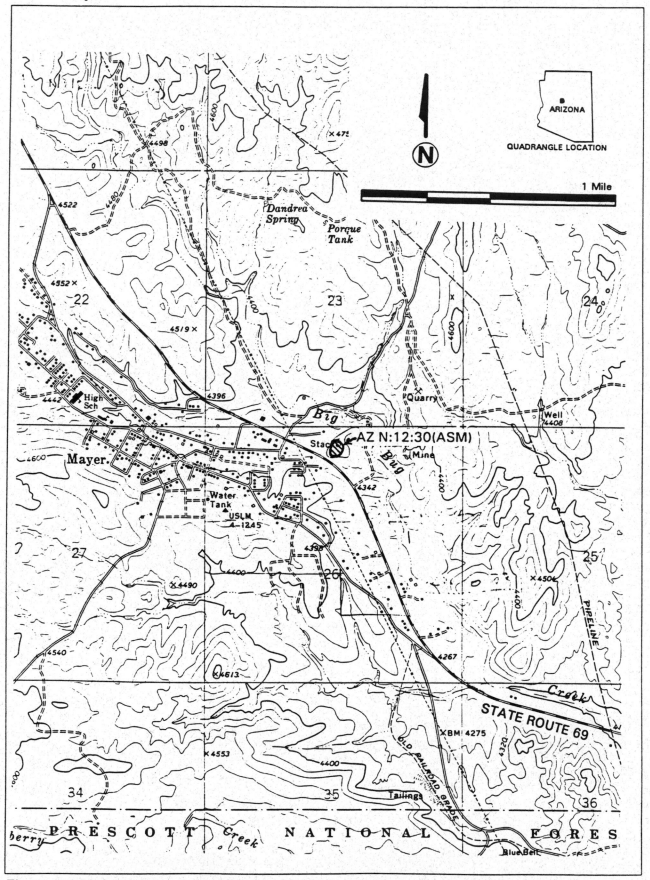

Figure 9.1. Location of Site AZ N:12:30(ASM), the Treadwell (Great Western) Smelter. Base map is Mayer, Arizona, USGS 7.5′ quadrangle, 1974.

HISTORICAL DATA

Mayer was a bustling town at the turn of the century. Under the guidance and care of Joe Mayer, the settlement had evolved from a stage station along the Prescott-Phoenix wagon road to a major shipping center for mines of the Bradshaw Mountains and Big Bug Mining District. The arrival of the Prescott & Eastern Railway in 1898 further enhanced the town's status as a major commercial center. When construction began in 1902 on the Bradshaw Mountain Railway—a branch of which would extend rail service from Mayer to the Crowned (also called Crown) King mines—Mayer's future could not have looked brighter (Sayre 1985:61–62).

Amid this atmosphere of economic hope, George A. Treadwell announced plans in 1902 to build a 250-ton smelter at Mayer. Treadwell had prior experience in smelting technology, having previously owned and operated, with William C. Green and Walter S. Logan, a smelter at Arizona City (Thorpe 1978:158; *The Weekly Reflex* 1899). Moreover, Treadwell, a San Franciscan, owned the George A. Treadwell Mining Company, a business with corporate offices in New York City and properties in the Big Bug and Verde mining districts of Arizona Territory (*The Prospect* 1902; Thorpe 1978:158; Treadwell n.d.). The company's Verde Mining District properties included the Cliff, Brookshire, Badger, Pastime, Crystal, Crystal Placer, Agua Fria, and Wallace mines. Its Big Bug Mining District holdings were the Boggs, Hackberry, and Iron Queen mines. Treadwell's Mayer smelter was designed specifically to process ores from the company's Big Bug properties. In 1902 the company built a narrow-gauge railroad from Mayer to the Hackberry mine and in 1904 began to extend the line to the Boggs and Iron Queen mines as well (*The Prospect* 1902, 1904). Treadwell built the Mayer smelter in 1902 and was conducting trial runs by early 1903 (*Mining and Scientific Press* [*MSP*] 1903; Thorpe 1978:158). A mining-trade article described the facility:

At Mayer, Yavapai County, Arizona, a furnace of unusual construction has been built to smelt copper ores by a process employing crude petroleum as fuel. The ore is crushed to nut size, no piece larger than will pass a 3/4-inch ring. This passes down what may be termed the inclined hearth of the furnace, constructed at an angle of about 45°, at the foot of which is a horizontal hearth or floor. Upon this the ore falls and extending upward on the inclined hearth is subjected to the powerful heat of the petroleum blast, the ore matting at and near the low hearth, melting and flowing over into a lower compartment, the slag being tapped at one opening, and the matte [next stage of ore reduction] at a lower one [*MSP* 1903].

The same article noted that the system was undergoing modifications and experiencing problems:

One important change suggested by M. P. Boss, the inventor of the process and furnace, is that of crushing the ore much finer, by which means it is expected more satisfactory results will be obtainable. The experimental runs have been made through the short period of two months under many disadvantages. When a constant supply of ore is available still more favorable results are anticipated in the application of this novel process [*MSP* 1903].

Two photographs published with the article showed how the facility looked in early 1903. One of the photographs (Figure 9.2) referred to the plant as a "hydro-carbon smelter." The other (Figure 9.3) indicated that the plant included a petroleum or water tank on a hilltop, a smelter terraced down the hillside, and several cabins of unspecified function on the flats below the smelter.

Figure 9.2. 1903 photo of Treadwell hydro-carbon smelter. (Photo courtesy Sharlot Hall Museum).

Figure 9.3. 1903 photo of Treadwell Smelter; view southeast (*Mining and Scientific Press* 1903).

The Treadwell Smelter operated infrequently from 1903 to 1906. It did not function as well as expected and had difficulty obtaining ore. To alleviate the latter problem, in October of 1904 the company made what a local newspaper termed "an important mining move" (*Arizona Journal Miner* [*AJM*] 8 October 1904): Treadwell hired a special agent, Frank Giroux, to visit all mines in the county and purchase the ores in their stockpiles. In this manner, the company would become owner of the ores on-site and would assume the cost of transporting them to the smelter. The company predicted that miners would welcome the arrangement, as they would no longer be required to bear the cost of shipment to smelters. The company also predicted that local miners would be particularly eager to do business with the Treadwell smelter and company, since the popular Humboldt smelter had burned in September of 1904 and had not been rebuilt. For reasons that are unclear, local miners did not embrace the proposed system, and the smelter continued to experience trouble obtaining adequate ore.

Despite problems with his plant, George Treadwell retained the facility and took steps to legally acquire the land on which it was situated. In 1904 he and his son, E. D. Treadwell, formally filed a mining claim with the Yavapai County Recorder. Their 16-acre "Smelter Placer Mining Claim" included the smelter site and acreage along both sides of Big Bug Creek (General Land Office Mineral Entry Survey 3991).

As his smelter continued to experience problems, Treadwell nonetheless took an active role in developing Mayer. With Joe Mayer and other associates, Treadwell and his son solved the town's water problem in 1902–1903 by constructing an 8-mile pipeline from Crystal Springs. The pipeline delivered 400,000 gallons of high-quality water each day, allowing the town to grow (Sayre 1985:63). In 1904 the Treadwells, George Scammel, and Joe Mayer incorporated the town of Mayer and marketed lots in the community. Lots in the 160-acre townsite sold for $100 to $500 apiece, and a frenzied period of real estate activity followed (Sayre 1985:63).

As the town enjoyed vigor following incorporation, it witnessed the evolution of not one but three ore-processing plants. An article published by the *Mining Reporter* (*MR*) in February of 1906 stated that the Rigby Mining and Reduction Company, the Crown Gold Mining Company, and the George A. Treadwell Mining Company were about to begin operating their respective plants at Mayer (*MR* 1906). The Rigby plant, a short distance north of town, employed a method known as the "Pohle-Crosdale volatilization process," developed for the reduction of highly siliceous gold, silver, copper, and other ores. The Crown Gold plant (the exact location of which is unspecified in historical records) had a 50-ton per day capacity and was designed to reduce ores using the "Wood process" of dry concentration, in which ores were crushed using a mechanical ore sizer. The same article stated that the Treadwell plant consisted of "a 250-ton Mitchell economic hot blast smelting furnace for the production of a high grade copper matte. The ores to be treated are mainly those from the Treadwell company's mines, which ores contain sufficient iron to render them self-fluxing" (*MR* 1906). The same article also contained a photograph (Figure 9.4) showing the new Mitchell hot blast furnace, near the base of the hill and adjacent to (southwest of) the hydro-carbon smelter. The furnace was in a long building with two smokestacks.

Several historical sources (Sayre 1985; Simpson 1975; *Yavapai* Magazine [*YM*] April 1917) indicate that the Treadwell smelter operated briefly and never achieved the desired results. From 1906 to 1915 it lay idle, during which time its buildings and machinery were wrecked and ransacked by petty thieves (Simpson 1975). Brief hope for the facility appeared in December of 1909, when a syndicate headed by David Miller of the Standard Exploration Company of New York leased the Treadwell facility and announced plans to build a 300-ton unit (*AJM* 23 December 1909). However, the plans were never carried out, and hopes for the smelter soon faded.

Figure 9.4. 1906 photo of Treadwell Smelter; view southeast (*Mining Reporter* 1906). Note addition of Mitchell furnace (in long building with two smokestacks).

The plant witnessed a rebirth in late 1916 or early 1917 when it was acquired by the Great Western Smelter Company. The smelter company was organized mainly to process ores from two unusually rich mines of the area, the Henrietta and the Butternut. The Henrietta Mine, 8 miles west of Mayer, was originally a gold property discovered in the 1860s by members of the Walker party (Dunning and Peplow 1959) and named for Henrietta Crossman, a pin-up girl of that era. Joe Mayer and associates successfully worked the mine in the 1890s, before the mine experienced hard times involving litigation and mismanagement. During a period of court-ordered closure, the mine caved in and filled with water. When the court order was lifted in 1899, miners re-entered its workings and discovered that flooding had exposed a rich new vein of gold with a high copper content. The Butternut Mine, about 3 miles northwest of Mayer, was not a gold but a copper property. Also developed by Joe Mayer and associates, the Butternut lay idle for many years following Mayer's death in 1909. During the period of idleness, its underground workings became waterlogged. When they were reopened in 1916, miners discovered that the mineral-saturated waters had coated all the iron fixtures of the mine—ore cars, rails, tools—with copper.

The richness of the Butternut and Henrietta mines became all the more attractive when World War I created high demand for industrial and precious metals. The Big Ledge Mining Company purchased the two properties in 1916, then arranged for their ores to be treated by the Great Western Smelter Company, which Big Ledge acquired in 1917. From its Treadwell days, the plant still contained

> a 2,000 ton ore bin system, coke bins of 1,000 tons capacity, a railroad trestle 250 feet long (all in a very bad state of repair), one blast furnace 42 × 120 feet (completely dismantled). In the power house there was one 150-h.p. engine direct connected to a No. 8 Connersville blower and two 80-h.p. boilers. All of this equipment was stripped of babbitt, brasses and valves, in fact everything that could be taken away [Simpson 1975:4].

The old plant was quickly rehabilitated for war-time use. A "blowing in" (first firing) ceremony was set for January 17, 1917 (*YM* January 1917). By April of 1917, the plant's managers reported that the smelting unit was treating 150 tons of ore per day, with an output of 15 tons of copper matte averaging 40% copper and $60 per ton in gold and silver. Based upon this level of productivity, the managers optimistically predicted that the unit would process 4,320,000 pounds of copper and $324,000 in gold and silver per annum (*YM* April 1917). To further expand the capacity of the plant, the Great Western Smelter Company hauled in and began to install two 48 × 240–foot blast furnaces, one 500-horsepower Cross Compound Corliss engine, two No. 8 Connersville blowers, a 150-kilowatt generator, and three 250-horsepower Marine-type boilers (Simpson 1975:5).

Historical photographs of the Great Western Smelter (Figures 9.5 and 9.6) reveal that the hilltop tank and the Mitchell blast furnace had been retained from earlier times. However, the original Treadwell hydro-carbon smelter was completely gone. In its place and spreading along terraces on the hillside was the new smelter, which would have a 600-ton daily capacity.

The rehabilitated plant was to include a new smokestack. Great Western contracted with the Weber Chimney Company of Kansas City to build the stack, and work began in 1917. The stack was designed to be 129.5 feet tall, with its foundation 65 feet above the top of the new furnace. The design was capable of creating an immense updraft that would generate intense furnace heat. Men worked for 36 cents an hour on the stack, pouring reinforced concrete in 5-foot sections (*Prescott Courier* [*PC*] 1971). The walls were made to taper in thickness, with the inside diameter 16 feet at the base and 10 feet at the top. The completed stack could withstand temperatures of 1300°F and 100-mile-per-hour winds.

Figure 9.5.   Circa 1917 photo of Great Western Smelter; view south.   (Photo courtesy Sharlot Hall Museum.)

Figure 9.6.   Circa 1917 photo of Great Western Smelter; view south-southeast.   (Photo courtesy Arizona Historical Society/Tucson. AHS#49,376.)

As the Great Western Smelter took form, winds of change blew through the corporate offices of its parent company. The Big Ledge Mining Company had been heavily promoted and highly capitalized. On a capital of 2 million shares, its stock reached a price of $6.00 per share in Boston in 1916—enough to have bought several big-ticket mining properties (Dunning and Peplow 1959). The inflated valuation of the stock caused uneasiness among minority stockholders, who in February of 1917 brought suit against company officials, charging fraud in the sale of stock. Minority owners specifically claimed that the stock was being converted to the use of an affiliate, the Big Ledge Development Company, and that this action effectively froze out the interests of the minority stockholders (Dunning and Peplow 1959).

On June 29, 1917, the Superior Court of Yavapai County ordered the Big Ledge Development Company and the Big Ledge Mining Company to turn over to Dr. Nester A. Young and other minority stockholders 105,000 shares of stock. By July of that year, as a result of the lawsuit, the Henrietta and Butternut mines closed. The loss of its ore supply, in turn, forced the closing of the Great Western Smelter (*YM* July 1917).

The Big Ledge Mining Company reorganized as a result of the lawsuit. To secure new capital, it increased its capital stock from 1.5 million to 3 million shares, with a par value of $5 per share. Big Ledge stated that some of the capital would be used to complete the acquisition of the Great Western Smelter, a transaction finalized by December of 1917. The company then announced plans to expand the plant by adding two new converters and a reverberatory furnace. It also announced that the smelter would henceforth operate as a custom mill, providing services to large as well as small producers (*YM* September 1917 14:2 and December 1917 7:4).

Although the April 1918 issue of *Yavapai Magazine* noted that Big Ledge had resumed mining operations at the Henrietta and Butternut mines, it did not mention the Mayer plant (Simpson 1975). In fact, no further announcements were made of any activity at the facility, which appears to have closed in late 1917. The two mines were reorganized in 1923 as the Huron Copper Mining Company. Walter Lytzen, a mining engineer of ability and integrity, made an earnest effort to make the two mines productive, but he found that their former owners had skimmed the cream (Dunning and Peplow 1959).

A final chapter was added to the history of the smelter in 1925–1926 when the land it occupied—the Smelter Placer Mining Claim—was at last patented. The Mineral Entry Survey plat (Merritt 1926) depicted only a few buildings remaining from the former smelter. The plat indicated the locations of three shallow prospect holes dug by claimants named J. E. and W. J. O'Brien, as part of the process of patenting their claim (Figure 9.7).

Abandoned for decades, the old smelter continues to draw visitors. People have often camped among its concrete foundations. A popular landmark is the smokestack, used by scout troops and high schoolers for campfires. On a dare, Mayer resident Martha Hickey once scaled the smokestack to its top; little did her challengers realize that Ms. Hickey had been raised in Switzerland and had conquered many Alpine slopes (*PC* 1971).

ARCHAEOLOGICAL DATA

The focus of on-site work during the testing phase was on remapping the site (Figures 9.8 and 9.9), photographing all its features, recording in detail features within the ROW, test excavating a feature that

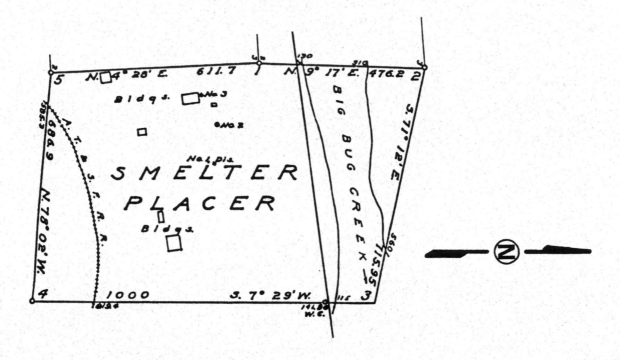

Figure 9.7. 1926 plat of the Smelter Placer Mining Claim (Merritt 1926).

appeared to have depth, and analyzing all artifacts within the ROW. Hathaway (1992) had recorded 20 features during the Class III survey. The SWCA testing crew relocated them easily, corrected a misplotted location for one feature (Feature 16), and found two additional features (Features 21 and 22). Using historical photographs and descriptions, SWCA personnel were able to identify the function and dating of several features.

Of the 22 features at the site, Features 2, 16, and 22 will be partially impacted by construction and Features 19 through 21 will be completely destroyed. Descriptions of each element follow.

Feature 1 was the smokestack at the top of the hill, measuring 129.5 feet in height. At its base, the stack had an external diameter of 18 feet and an internal diameter of 16 feet, with walls 1 foot thick. The stack tapered inward so that its top had an external diameter of 12 feet and an internal diameter of 10 feet. Built in 1917 by the Weber Chimney Company of Kansas City under contract to the Great Western Smelter Company, the stack is constructed of reinforced concrete laid in 5-foot sections. The present investigations did not support rumors that it was never used. The interior of the stack exhibits carbon deposits resulting from a heat so intense as to have vitrified some of the carbon. The vitrification undoubtedly resulted from industrial use rather than from recreational (campfire) use in modern times.

Feature 2 was a series of three linear concrete foundations excavated into the hillside at the southwestern edge of the site within an area measuring 47.3 feet northeast-southwest by 18 feet northwest-southeast (Figure 9.10). This feature was also of concrete, reinforced with 1-inch rebar set 7 feet apart. The central concrete slab had two "windows" measuring 12 × 11 inches and set 15 feet apart. The lowest (downhill) foundation differed from the upper two in being tapered in cross-section and exhibiting

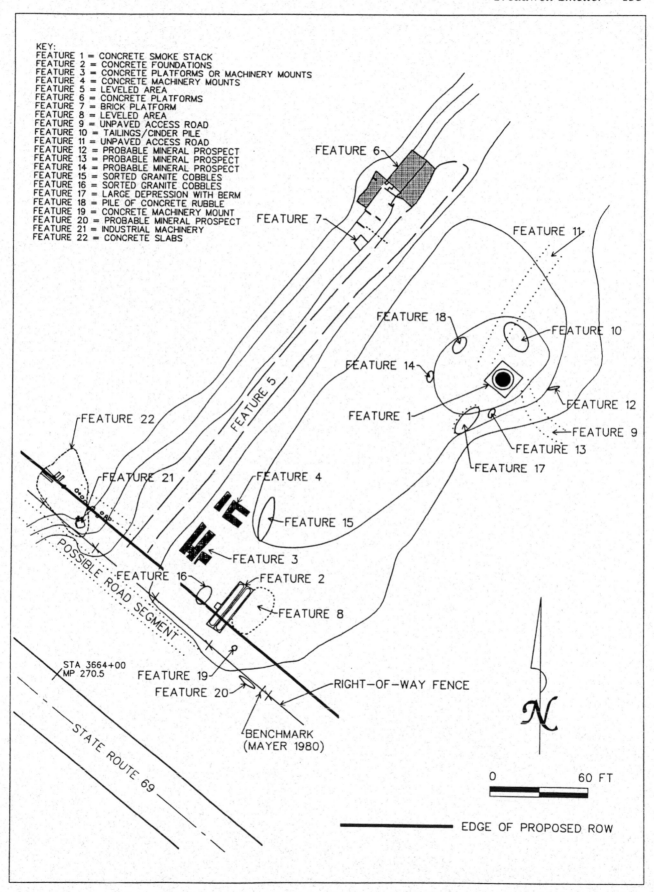

KEY:
FEATURE 1 = CONCRETE SMOKE STACK
FEATURE 2 = CONCRETE FOUNDATIONS
FEATURE 3 = CONCRETE PLATFORMS OR MACHINERY MOUNTS
FEATURE 4 = CONCRETE MACHINERY MOUNTS
FEATURE 5 = LEVELED AREA
FEATURE 6 = CONCRETE PLATFORMS
FEATURE 7 = BRICK PLATFORM
FEATURE 8 = LEVELED AREA
FEATURE 9 = UNPAVED ACCESS ROAD
FEATURE 10 = TAILINGS/CINDER PILE
FEATURE 11 = UNPAVED ACCESS ROAD
FEATURE 12 = PROBABLE MINERAL PROSPECT
FEATURE 13 = PROBABLE MINERAL PROSPECT
FEATURE 14 = PROBABLE MINERAL PROSPECT
FEATURE 15 = SORTED GRANITE COBBLES
FEATURE 16 = SORTED GRANITE COBBLES
FEATURE 17 = LARGE DEPRESSION WITH BERM
FEATURE 18 = PILE OF CONCRETE RUBBLE
FEATURE 19 = CONCRETE MACHINERY MOUNT
FEATURE 20 = PROBABLE MINERAL PROSPECT
FEATURE 21 = INDUSTRIAL MACHINERY
FEATURE 22 = CONCRETE SLABS

Figure 9.8. Site AZ N:12:30(ASM), the Treadwell (Great Western) Smelter.

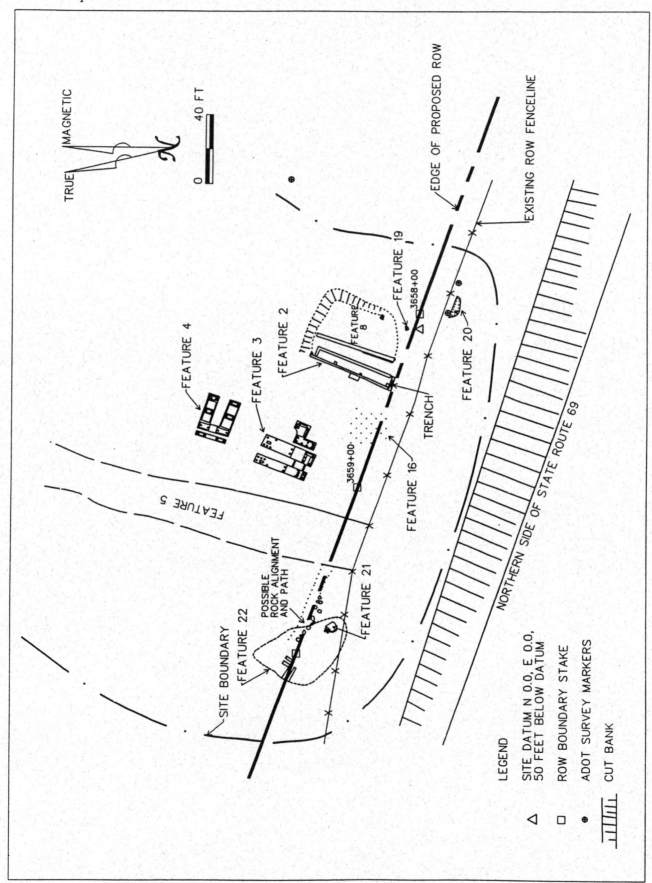

Figure 9.9. Site AZ N:12:30(ASM), detail of features in and near right-of-way.

Figure 9.10. Site AZ N:12:30(ASM), Feature 2, concrete foundations; view northwest.

buttressing. Its top was 1.6 feet wide, its base was 2.1 feet wide, and its four buttresses were on its downhill side and set 14.1 feet apart. The center of this foundation had a rectangular opening measuring 3.9 × 3.1 feet. The feature was tested by digging a trench between the central and lowest foundations. Testing revealed that the feature had no floor; the foundations terminated in concrete footers approximately 1 foot below the present ground surface. Testing revealed no artifacts. From historical photographs, this feature appeared to have been the support system for one of two large, vertically mounted wheels that were in this part of the site during the Great Western Smelter era (1917). The function of the wheels was unclear, but in form they resembled "sand" or "tailings" wheels, ingenious devices used at some mining sites to lift ores and tailings (Richards 1903:629). The wheels carried buckets on the inside of wide rims. The buckets were loaded with ore or tailings at the lowest point in the wheel's rotation, then discharged their contents into other parts of the milling system at the highest point in the rotation. The position of Feature 2 near the terminus of a railroad spur pictured in historical photos suggested that it was indeed part of such a conveyance system.

Feature 3 was a series of irregularly shaped reinforced concrete platforms within a 37 × 37–foot area. The platforms were built into the side of the hill a short distance northwest of Feature 2 and had walls 8.5 feet high. The numerous rebar and metal bands projecting from the platforms appeared to be machinery mounts. This feature likely dated to the Great Western Smelter period of the site; the earlier Treadwell phase did not generally extend into the site's southwestern area.

Feature 4 was two reinforced concrete machinery mounts (one U-shaped and one linear) in an area measuring 30 feet northwest-southeast by 20 feet northeast-southwest. The mounts were approximately 7 feet tall and were constructed into the hillside northeast of Feature 3. Like Features 2 and 3, they likely dated from the Great Western rather than the Treadwell phase of the site; the latter generally did not extend into this portion of the site.

Feature 5 was a leveled earthen area measuring 25–40 feet wide by 400+ feet long excavated into the northwestern side of the hill. This feature appeared to be a road. A comparison of its location with historical photos suggested that the road ran along the back (southeastern) side of the 600-ton smelting unit constructed in 1917. The road terminated at Feature 6, a feature likely constructed in 1902.

Feature 6 was a series of concrete platforms with associated concrete and cobble retaining walls constructed on the northwest hillslope at the northern end of Feature 5. The location of this feature and the fact that it was stepped down the hillside suggested that it was part of Treadwell's original 1902 hydro-carbon smelter. Historical photos indicated that this unit was removed during the Great Western phase of the site.

Feature 7 was a brick platform measuring 10 feet square and constructed into the hillslope south of Feature 6. Its proximity to Feature 6 suggested that it was part of the Treadwell hydro-carbon smelter. Its exact function is unknown.

Feature 8 was a leveled area measuring 45 feet northeast-southwest by 22 feet northwest-southeast excavated into soil adjacent to and immediately east of Feature 2. Its proximity to Feature 2 suggested that it was part of a large conveyance wheel dating to the Great Western Smelter phase of the site and was perhaps used to load and unload materials transported by rail.

Feature 9 was a 10-foot-wide unpaved access road. From the stack, the road extended approximately 800 feet east and eventually joined an unpaved road leading to SR 69.

Feature 10 was a 20 × 12-foot tailings/cinder pile immediately north of Feature 1. Its location adjacent to the smokestack suggested that it was associated with smelting activity of the Great Western Smelter period of the site.

Feature 11 was a 12-foot-wide unpaved access road extending from the north side of the stack (Feature 1) toward the direction of Big Bug Creek to the north-northeast.

Feature 12 was a prospect hole east of Feature 1. This was likely one of the three prospect pits excavated by J. E. and W. J. O'Brien in the mid 1920s while patenting the Smelter Placer Mining Claim.

Feature 13 was a prospect hole south of Feature 1. Like Feature 12, this was likely one of the three prospect pits excavated by the O'Briens to patent the Smelter Placer claim.

Feature 14 was a prospect hole west of Feature 1. Like Features 12 and 13, this was likely one of the three prospect pits dug by the O'Briens to show that they were actively developing the Smelter Placer claim.

Feature 15 was an area measuring 25 feet northeast-southwest by 10 feet northwest-southeast containing a pile of granite river cobbles. Cobbles within the pile had been sorted by size, suggesting that they might have been stockpiled for eventual use in construction. The source of the cobbles was likely Big Bug Creek, at the northern edge of the site.

Feature 16 was a 20-foot-diameter pile of unsorted river cobbles. The cobbles likely were gathered along Big Bug Creek and stockpiled at this location for an unknown purpose.

Feature 17 was a depression measuring 25 feet northeast-southwest by 8 feet northwest-southeast and 1.5 feet deep, with a slight berm of backdirt along its western edge. The function and date of this feature could not be determined, but it might have been associated with the same mine-patenting activity as Features 12, 13, and 14.

Feature 18 was a pile of concrete rubble in an area measuring 12 × 10 feet. The exact source of the rubble could not be determined. Both Treadwell and Great Western used concrete as a construction material at the site. The pile of rubble could have dated from either of those periods, or from later mine-patenting activity.

Feature 19 was a 4 × 3 × 3-foot chunk of concrete with two protruding lengths of rebar. The concrete fragment was near Feature 2 and appeared to have broken off that feature.

Feature 20 was a depression measuring 10 feet northwest-southeast by 5 feet northeast-southwest and 1 foot deep. This feature was originally reported as a probable mineral prospect. Clearing it of brush disclosed that the site was not a mineral prospect but a water pipe. The 1-inch pipe bore the inscription "WATEROUS / OPEN (arrow) / DF 906754." Water was seeping from the pipe and could be heard gurgling within it.

Feature 21 was an iron artifact so large and heavy that it was given its own feature designation (Figure 9.11). SWCA field personnel found this artifact while brushing the ROW during testing; it did not appear to be in situ. Made of 1/4-inch sheet iron, the object was custom made and was fastened with riveted and welded joints. It had two main parts: a "body" and a "neck." The tubular body was 44 inches long with a diameter of 44 inches. One end of the tube was closed and the other was open. The neck was joined to the body at a right angle by 1/2-inch rivets set 1-1/4 inches apart. Resembling a small smokestack, the neck was 17 inches long and 29 inches in diameter and terminated in a flaring rim with a diameter of 37 inches. The object was identified by the Arizona Department of Mines and Mineral Resources as an elbow of a duct from an old boiler.

Feature 22 was an L-shaped concrete trough at the upper end of an area of steep relief on the northwestern side of the hill. The feature was 6 inches tall, with its long arm measuring 8.7 × 3.25 feet and its short arm measuring 3.5 × 2.7 feet. The function of this small feature could not be determined.

Analysis of artifacts within the ROW sought clues to the function and dating of the southwestern part of the site. The artifacts were scattered sparsely throughout the area and did not cluster around any particular feature or features. Thirty fragments represented a minimum of 23 objects of metal, ceramics, glass, fabric, rubber, and polyethylene (PET) plastic. Glass objects included one whole, clear glass bottle with an Owens-Illinois basemark (1954 to the present), a fragment of sun-colored amethyst (SCA) glass (made from 1880 to 1917), and the bases of two modern "NO DEPOSIT-NO RETURN" beer bottles. Metal items were most numerous and included a bolt shank with nut, a steel cable, three cummerbund-shaped belts, two pocket tobacco tins, a hole-in-cap can fragment (pre-1922), a small lid stampe "PAT 1966887 / IMPORTANT / LIFT HERE," a 40d wire nail, a piece of baling wire, a modern sanitary can with its price sticker still visible, and a modern, barely rusted fish can. Ceramic items consisted of a corner of a red cinder brick and a piece of a porcelain electrical fixture bearing the trademark of the

Figure 9.11. Site AZ N:12:30(ASM), Feature 21, iron artifact.

General Electric Company (post-1891). The remainder of the objects consisted of four tiny fragments of rubber, a fragment of a pine board, a modern cotton sweatshirt, and a modern PET plastic "SUNNY DELIGHT" juice bottle. Excluding obviously modern items (such as the sweatshirt, PET juice bottle, and so forth), the assemblage represented functional categories indicative of the industrial nature of the site and, to some extent, the diversions of its employees. Functional categories represented by the historic trash included machinery and hardware (five items), architecture (two items), recreation and leisure (three items), food (one item), and miscellaneous/unidentified (four items).

SUMMARY AND RECOMMENDATIONS

A popular story in central Arizona is that the Treadwell/Great Western Smelter was part of a fraudulent scheme designed to bilk eastern investors of money. SWCA's investigations revealed a far more complex history and suggested that the smelter was part of an ambitious and well-intentioned plan that went awry.

The smelter witnessed not one but four periods of construction. Each was designed to remedy flaws, modernize equipment, and ultimately deliver better service to customers. The first period occurred in 1902 when George Treadwell built his hydro-carbon smelter. Despite technical problems with the smelter and difficulties in obtaining ore, Treadwell and his son E. D. Treadwell continued to improve and expand the system, adding a 250-ton Mitchell blast smelting furnace by 1906 in the second period of construction. The Treadwells seemed to have a genuine interest in nurturing their struggling business and, with it, the town of Mayer. They improved the town's water system and helped incorporate the townsite.

The third period of construction was in late 1916 and early 1917 when the Great Western Smelter Company acquired the property and rebuilt the Mitchell blast furnace. The *general* impetus for reopening the plant was the frenzied market for metals prompted by World War I. The *specific* impetus was the desire to process ores from the Henrietta and Butternut mines at a locus near those two rich sources of minerals and thus keep transportation costs low. The reopening of the plant was followed in 1917 by the fourth period of construction, which added two additional blast units, including the smokestack. The smelter fell on troubled times when minority stockholders sued the Big Ledge Mining Company, forcing closure of the Butternut and Henrietta mines. The smelter was not an instrument of fraud, but a victim of war-time speculators whose risks (in overinflating the value of company stock) did not yield the benefits anticipated.

On the basis of testing results, SWCA recommended that the site be considered eligible for the National Register of Historic Places. The site has yielded, and appears capable of continuing to yield, significant information about historical mining technology in central Arizona and possesses values that make it eligible under Criterion D of the NRHP. The proposed construction will impact several features at the southern edge of the site; the majority of the site will remain undisturbed following construction. Testing documented the features and artifacts that will be impacted and determined that additional significant data would not likely come from the ROW portion of the site. SWCA did not recommend or conduct additional work during the data recovery phase of the SR 69 investigations.

CHAPTER 10

AZ N:12:39(ASM)
THE GRAY EAGLE REDUCTION (MAYER CUSTOM) PLANT

Pat H. Stein
Elizabeth J. Skinner

MANAGEMENT HISTORY

Site AZ N:12:39(ASM) is in the N½SW¼NE¼SE¼ and the S½NW¼NE¼SE¼ of Section 26, Township 12 North, Range 1 East on the USGS Mayer, Arizona, 7.5 minute quadrangle (Figure 10.1). It is on the west side of Big Bug Creek and the east side of current State Route 69 approximately 0.65 mile southeast of Mayer. The site extends from the floodplain of the creek up the side of a northeast-facing slope overlooking the creek. The slope and floodplain have been modified by historic and modern construction and are covered with moderately dense riparian and chaparral vegetation. The archaeological property measures 300 feet east-west by 200 feet north-south, encompassing a total of 1.4 acres on private land and an Arizona Department of Transportation (ADOT) easement.

Archaeological Research Services, Inc., (ARS) first inventoried the site during the cultural resource survey for the SR 69 Mayer to Dewey segment (Hathaway 1992). The 13 features recorded consisted of 9 concrete foundations (including two with machinery mounts), 1 wood-frame structure, 1 wood and corrugated metal structure, and 2 corrugated metal structures. Using information provided in Sayre (1985:72–73), the ARS survey identified the site as the Gray Eagle Reduction Plant, an ore-processing facility constructed in 1915 and closed in 1917. Taking into account information provided by ADOT and local informants, the ARS surveyors hypothesized that (1) Feature 1 represented the remains of the C & C Cafe (constructed after 1957, demolished after 1989); (2) Feature 2 represented the remains of a storage shed and loading platform along the Gray Eagle railroad spur; (3) Features 3 through 7, 12, and 13 represented the remains of the reduction works; and (4) Features 8 through 11 represented the remains of structures built after the dismantling of the reduction plant.

On the basis of the survey report, ADOT, the Arizona State Historic Preservation Office, and other agencies concurred that the site should be considered eligible for the National Register of Historic Places (NRHP). Design analysis by ADOT engineers determined that the proposed SR 69 project would impact the western portion of the resource. The ADOT request for proposals for this project stipulated that testing should consist of archival documentation, mapping, the collection of surface artifacts within the right-of-way (ROW), and limited subsurface testing within the ROW.

The scope of archaeological testing changed when ADOT staff learned that the site contained hazardous materials. Following a preproposal meeting in August of 1993, ADOT contracted to have soils at the site tested for potentially contaminated materials; since the site had been used for ore reduction, the possibility existed that its soil might contain concentrations of heavy metals or other toxic substances. Results of these tests indicated detectable levels of arsenic, cadmium, chromium, lead, mercury, and silver. The level of lead in the soil was particularly high, exceeding by ten times the Arizona Department of Environmental Quality acceptable level. Subsequent analysis by an industrial hygienist (Butler 1994) determined that the lead posed a potential health hazard for archaeologists. ADOT therefore instructed SWCA to conduct no work on-site and to limit testing investigations to intensive historical research. The following sections present the results of the historical research and interpret the features of the site in terms of those findings.

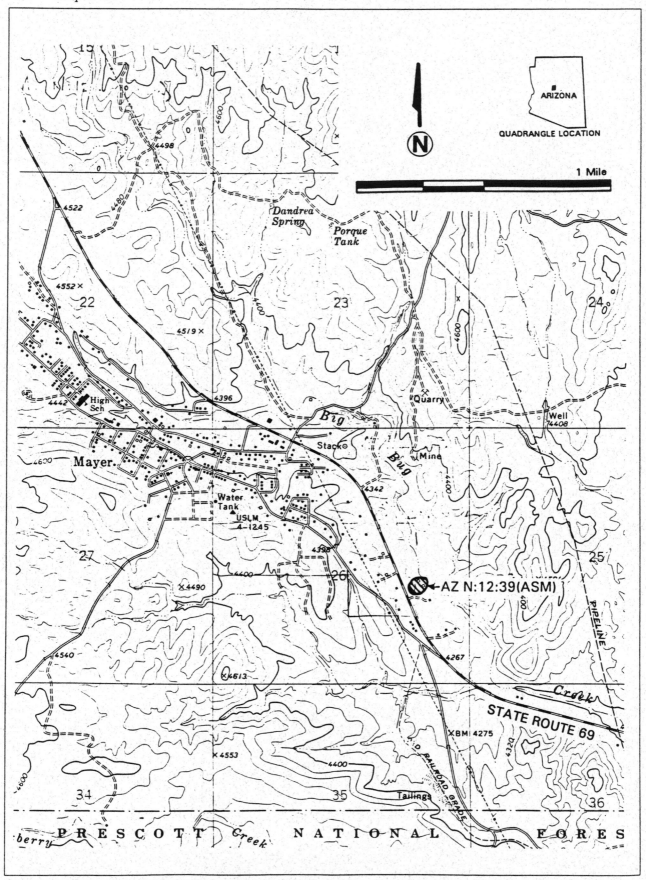

Figure 10.1. Location of AZ N:12:39(ASM), the Gray Eagle Reduction (Mayer Custom) Plant. Base map is Mayer, Arizona, USGS 7.5′ quadrangle, 1974.

HISTORICAL DATA

Master Plat Title Indices at the State Office of the Bureau of Land Management (BLM) indicated that the land occupied by Site AZ N:12:39(ASM) first passed from government to private ownership as the result of homesteading. Long before the site became the Gray Eagle Reduction Plant, it was part of a homestead settled by William P. Murphy.

Murphy was born in County Cork, Ireland, in 1849. During the Great Potato Famine, his family immigrated to the United States, where William became a naturalized citizen in 1890. During the spring of 1890, William Murphy settled on acreage straddling Big Bug Creek a stone's throw southeast of Joe Mayer's town. In February of 1890 the creek had flooded, devastating much of Mayer but leaving in its wake rich alluvial soils. The alluvium attracted farmers such as Murphy, who proceeded to establish farmsteads along the floodplain. He continued to live at the Big Bug Creek property for the next 16 years, but as a squatter rather than as owner of the land; he was unable to acquire legal title because the U.S. government owned the land and had never designated it for private entry. (William Murphy was no relation to Frank M. Murphy, builder of the Prescott & Eastern and Bradshaw Mountain railways.)

Murphy's status changed following passage of the Forest Homestead Act of 1906, designed to put tillable, non-mineral inholdings within Forest Reserves into the hands of farmers. Squatter Murphy was given a preferential right of entry to the Big Bug Creek tract, a right he exercised by filing a homestead entry (Serial No. 01352) in late 1907 or early 1908 (General Land Office [GLO] Homestead Entry Survey [HES] 41). For a brief but frustrating period, Murphy's application became caught in a bureaucratic limbo between the Washington and Phoenix offices of the General Land Office (GLO). Eventually his application was allowed, and Murphy assumed the legal status of homesteader. In October of 1908 he filed his final proof, and in November of 1910, at the age of 61, Murphy acquired his Certificate of Title to the land (GLO HES 41).

Records obtained from the National Archives and from the State Office of the BLM provided a great deal of information about the Murphy Homestead. The property was an approximately 53-acre tract that encompassed Site AZ N:12:39(ASM). Two detailed maps of the homestead exist: a 1907 preliminary plat (Figure 10.2) and a 1909 plat that became the final official survey of the property (Figure 10.3). The earlier plat showed the location of a reservoir, barn, cultivated land, and a house; just off the west side of the claim, it also showed the location of the Bradshaw Mountain Railway. The later plat excluded the reservoir from the claim, indicated the same barn and house as on the 1907 plat, and indicated that a well and corral had been added to the property. The insert in the latter figure, taken from a 1935 GLO map, indicates the exact location of the Murphy homestead in relation to quarter and quarter-quarter sections of Section 26. The corral, barn, and house lay within the boundaries of Site AZ N:12:39(ASM).

The case file for the Murphy Homestead (National Archives [NA] Homestead Case File [HCF] 01352) revealed that the 1907 and 1909 plats indicated only the *major* improvements made by Murphy. When Murphy proved up on the land, he listed *all* improvements, including minor ones: "a 4-room lumber house 20 × 30. Barn 20 × 30. Wagon shed. Corn crib. Cellar. Well. Chicken house. Blacksmith shop. About 30 acres fenced. Reservoir pipeline [illegible]. Value about $1800.00" (NA HCF 01352). Murphy further testified that he grew alfalfa, grain, hay, corn, beans, and some vegetables on 20 cultivated acres on the east side of Big Bug Creek. His living quarters and facilities for livestock were on the west side. Murphy's description of improvements was verified by four witnesses, the most notable of whom was George Ruffner, a Prescott pioneer who later became Yavapai County Sheriff.

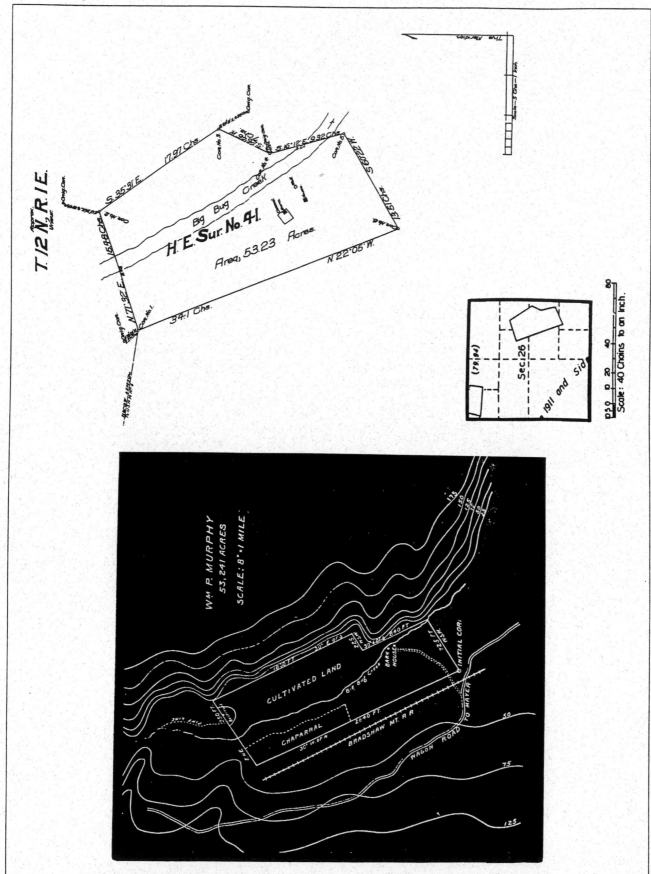

Figure 10.2. Preliminary 1907 plat of the William Murphy homestead (General Land Office Homestead Entry Survey 41).

Figure 10.3. Final 1909 plat of the William Murphy homestead (Merritt 1909).

William Murphy died shortly after receiving title to the land. The bachelor's 53-acre estate passed to his sister, Nellie, on October 4, 1912 (Yavapai County Recorder [YCR] Bood of Deeds [BD] 95:537). Described as a spinster living in Chicago, Nellie Murphy sold a warranty indenture on the property for $1.00 to the Gray Eagle Reduction Company on March 4, 1915 (YCR BD 100:569). This transaction marked the dawn of a new era of development at the property.

The Gray Eagle Reduction Company was a firm based in Springfield, Illinois, but doing business principally in Arizona. The owners formed the company in response to the outbreak of World War I in Europe and the increased demand for metals occasioned by the war. In the first known reference to the company's activities in Arizona, *Yavapai Magazine* reported in the summer of 1914 that the Gray Eagle Company had been formed and had secured options on a 20-stamp mill and other buildings owned by the Tiger Gold Company in the vicinity of Crown King (*Yavapai Magazine* [YM] June 1914 16:2). By early 1915 Gray Eagle had gained control of all mines within a 10-mile radius of Crown King (*YM* 15 February 1915 13:3). By January of 1915 the reduction company was making plans to build a plant at Crown King that would process 50 tons of ore per day. Using the"Wagner electric process," the plant planned to treat complex ores at a fraction of the normal price of smelting (*YM* January 1915 13:1). In February of 1915 the State Mine Inspector paid a visit to the construction site, and *Yavapai Magazine* reported his findings:

> He [the State Mine Inspector, a Mr. Bolin] says that an interesting feature of development work in Yavapai county at the present time is the new plant in the process of installation at Crown King for the treatment of ores by the electrolytic process. The company which has the project under way claims that all ore values can be extracted by such a course of treatment, and Mr. Bolin thinks if its contention proves to be well founded it will mean a big thing for the whole district, and a course which will probably be imitated generally over the state concerning the grade of ore which is now not handled. Many grades of ore are being taken from the mines which cannot be worked at all with profit, and this new process is depended on to place this stuff in the profit column. The Crown King experiment is attracting a great deal of attention by local mining men, and it is stated by many in Prescott that if it proves successful there will at once be many such plants installed in this part of the state [*YM* March 1915 8:4].

A postscript added that shortly after Bolin's inspection, the Gray Eagle Reduction Company moved to Mayer, where its reduction plant would be built on the old William Murphy homestead. The postscript stated that management decided to move the plant mostly for reasons of transportation; using the local rail system, it would be easier to ship ore and products into and out of Mayer than Crown King.

By May of 1915, a railroad spur to the Mayer plant site had been built and the Gray Eagle Reduction Plant was rapidly taking form (Sayre 1985:72; *YM* 4 May 1915 12:1). Interest in the emerging facility grew when the company announced ore-processing rates that were considered low and extremely reasonable for their time:

> The scale of charges of the Gray Eagle Reduction Company, whose plant at Mayer will be in operation about October 1, promises to make profitable the working of many mines which have not been mined in the past because the values did not warrant the costs of reduction. In a circular the new company gives the following scale of prices:
>
> > There will be no penalties of any kind charged. A specialty is made of ores high in zinc or insolubles. A reasonable treatment charge will be made on ores, based upon the

character of the ore, its chemical composition and its assay value. Payment will be made on the following basis:

Gold: 100% of assay value at $19.00 per ounce on all ores containing over .05 ounces per ton.
Silver: If 22 ounces or more per ton contained, 95% at New York quotation.
Copper: Deduct 20 pounds of copper per ton of ore and pay for remainder at quotation for electrolytic wire bars less 2-1/2c per pound.
Lead: 95% of assay value at 3 cents per pound on all ores containing over 1%.
Iron: Under certain conditions an allowance may be made for iron.
Zinc: Will not be paid for on account of no penalty being added for ores high in zinc [*YM* June 1915 11:3].

Hopes for the plant floundered in the fall of 1915. For reasons that are not clear, the company decided to install its own power plant rather than obtain power from the Childs hydroelectric system (see Chapter 3). It is possible that the Gray Eagle company could not become a customer; by 1915 the Childs system had many potential customers on its waiting list and was in the process of expanding. At any rate, the decision by Gray Eagle to install its own power plant delayed the opening of its facility (*YM* September 1915 13:2). The company ordered a 150-horsepower diesel engine and received it in late fall of 1915. By the close of the year, the company was busily installing the engine but had not fixed a date for the blowing in of the plant (*YM* December 1915 13:1).

The Gray Eagle Reduction Plant was completed in early 1916, developed problems of an unspecified nature, and promptly closed (*YM* November 1917 15:2). It lay dormant through the rest of 1916 and most of 1917 as its controlling company experienced financial turbulence. Finally, by November of 1917, Dr. H. A. Wagner, the metallurgist/engineer who had designed the plant and supervised its construction, gained control from the Gray Eagle company. As General Manager, he renamed the facility the Mayer Custom Plant (also called the Mayer Ore Purchasing Company) and announced plans to immediately commence operations (*YM* November 1917 15:2).

Wagner spent approximately $75,000 altering and equipping the plant. His goal was to offer a thoroughly modern works where miners could find solutions to various problems encountered in exploiting complex or low-grade ores. Wagner envisioned a plant with four distinct departments. By June of 1918 the Sampling, Concentrating, and Custom Assay departments were functioning, and a fourth section, the Leaching Department, was under construction. News articles of the period reported how the plant and its sections operated (*YM* March 1918 12:3–4, May 1918 13:2, June 1918 7:1–4), while historical photographs (Figures 10.4–10.7) depicted the plant's appearance. The following summary is drawn from these sources.

The Mayer Custom Plant (Mayer Ore Purchasing Plant) was set up on a hillside to take advantage of gravity whenever possible for transporting materials from one milling step to another. From the railroad spur, incoming ore normally went first to the Sampling Department. The ore was weighed on a Fairbanks railroad scale and then dumped into a bin from which it was carried by an 18-inch-wide conveyor belt to a "grizzly," a device that separated the larger rock and dropped it into a crusher, which reduced the ore to stones of 1-1/2 inches or less in diameter; this process served to reduce the volume of the ore in order to diminish the expense of shipping and further treatment. After crushing, the ore was transported by conveyor belt to the railroad spur track. The Sampling Department offered an additional service: it bought ores of practically all kinds in quantities ranging from small consignments to rail-car lots, thus providing

Figure 10.4. 1918 photo of Mayer Custom Plant, view west (*Yavapai Magazine* June 1918).

Figure 10.5. 1918 photo of Mayer Custom Plant's receiving platform, showing conveyor belt (*Yavapai Magazine* June 1919).

Figure 10.6. 1918 photo of Mayer Custom Plant, showing tram for carrying concentrates to spur track (*Yavapai Magazine* June 1918).

Figure 10.7. 1918 photo of bunkhouse and garage of Mayer Custom Plant (*Yavapai Magazine* June 1918).

a market for small producers. The Sampling Department stockpiled the ores purchased and assembled them into rail-car lots for more economical reduction on-site or for shipping to smelters in various parts of the country. The department had a capacity of 120 tons of ore per day.

The next reduction area, the Concentrating (milling) Department, was equipped with an Allis-Chalmers ball mill, Dorr classifier, Allen cone, Oliver filter, Butchart tables, and K & K flotation machine. It had a capacity of 80 tons per day and concentrated ores using processes known as table concentration and flotation. The machinery of this department was housed in galvanized iron buildings and was electrically driven by a 250-horsepower diesel engine. A 600-gallon-per-minute centrifugal pump provided water for the milling activity.

The flotation unit of the Concentrating Department was of special interest to miners who worked with complex ores. Flotation is the separation of minerals from each other and from waste matter by inducing (through the use of reagents) relative differences in their abilities to float in a liquid medium. The first successful flotation plants in the United States were developed at Butte, Montana, in 1911 and in Miami, Arizona, in 1915 (Noble and Spude 1992:30). The flotation unit of the Mayer Custom Plant was innovative in having the capability to adapt its machinery to the varying needs of different clients with different ores. All types of precious and base metals were handled by the unit and given either of two tests, termed "short cut tests" and "mill tests" by the plant's management. By means of short cut tests, it was possible to determine, in a general way, the milling process that would likely be most applicable to the ore in question. No elaborate details were derived from short cut tests: they simply served to outline the basic treatment that would be best for the ore at hand. Mill tests, on the other hand, gave extremely detailed results. The desired mineral end product would be decided in advance and then arranged by finely adjusting the machinery of the flotation device. In this way, ore would pass through the flotation unit as if the unit had been especially designed for the ore at hand. During the run, periodic samples would be weighed and assayed and further adjustments made in the flotation equipment. The results of mill tests yielded not only the desired mineral product but also a process flow chart (a metallurgical "recipe") documenting exactly how the desired result was achieved. Wagner's flotation device took the treatment of complex ores out of the realm of guesswork and into the realm of science.

The next department of the plant, the Custom Assay Department, tested the content, type, and quality of metal in ores using various methods, including fire assay and acid tests. The department was run by an experienced assayer, and all results were guaranteed to be accurate. The Mayer Custom Plant offered discounts for large numbers of assay samples submitted at one time and also provided a "rush" service for samples needing rapid analyses.

The last department of the plant, the Leaching Department, was designed to be used for the treatment of oxidized copper ores and was expected to handle 40 tons of ore a day. By June of 1918, construction of the unit was underway, with large concrete tanks already in place. In late 1918 *Yavapai Magazine* referred to the leaching unit being in operation, but did not provide details about how it worked.

Beginning in the summer of 1918, the company experienced a recession. During the month of August, Dr. Wagner reported that his plant

suffered from a shortage of ore. Quite a number of our principal shippers were closed down during the entire month. Previous to this our different departments have been kept quite busy. The principal shippers were Silver Belt Consolidated Mining Company; the Swansea Lease, Inc.;

manganese, shipped by M. B. Schurman, etc. Now that the cool weather has set in, we are in hopes that we will receive sufficient ore to operate to capacity [*YM* September 1918 16:3–4].

Cooler weather returned but not the hoped-for new orders of ores. In his November report, Wagner reported:

Our custom concentrator suffers from an acute shortage of ore. Our sampler is also not operating to capacity, although we are handling a little material. Our ore testing [assaying] department has been fairly busy. We have conducted a number of cyanide, flotation, and leaching tests for clients all the way from Mexico to Montana. At this time we have several commissions on our books for tests, ranging from a few pounds to carload lots, principally for concentrator and flotation [*YM* December 1918 9:4].

This was the last reference to any activity at the plant. It closed in 1919 as World War I ended. As the plant was dismantled, its equipment was salvaged and sold. Table 10.1 lists all of the salvaged material.

The property has experienced little activity in late historic and modern times. A small residence (occupant unknown) was built at the northern edge of the property and occupied until recent times. Circa 1960, the C & C Cafe was built on the western edge of the property, adjacent to SR 69. The residence still stands but is abandoned; the cafe is in ruins.

ARCHAEOLOGICAL DATA

This section interprets the archaeological remains at Site AZ N:12:39(ASM) in terms of information derived through archival research. The interpretation is facilitated by a series of historical photographs, homestead records, articles describing how the Gray Eagle/Mayer Custom Plant functioned, and miscellaneous other records.

Thirteen features have been recorded at the site (Figure 10.8). Hathaway (1992) described them as:

(1) A 25-foot-square poured concrete foundation/pad, with an 8-foot-square foundation/pad attached to the northeast corner of the larger foundation.

(2) A 2-foot-tall, linear concrete foundation and attached structural feature within an area measuring 50 × 12 feet, with one section slotted for the installation of 8 × 8–inch timbers/railroad ties.

(3) A 15 × 10-foot, 8.5-foot-tall poured concrete foundation/basement, constructed into the hillslope.

(4) A series of 5–10-foot-tall poured concrete foundations/tanks and associated machinery mounts constructed into the hillslope, within an area covering 30 × 30 feet.

(5) A 30 × 10–foot poured concrete foundation/tank adjacent to Feature 4, approximately 8 inches thick and 2.5 feet tall.

(6) A second 30 × 10–foot concrete foundation adjacent to Feature 5, with a wooden platform covering the northwestern portion.

Table 10.1. Material Salvaged at Closure of the Mayer Custom (Gray Eagle) Plant

---

1 50–100 ton hardinge ball mill, 6 feet × 22 inches, mill No-1212, weight mill and liners, 14 tons, geared by link belt reduction drive, to 50-HP, GE-AC-440-60c-3P, Amps-61Sec Amps103-RPM-no load-900-full load-865-motor serial No-1376787. Mill-6 feet in the clear inside diameter, between liners-19 feet in circumference-12 feet-six inches over all long, Challenge feeder with K&K oiler and Simplex all steel classifier.

1 Telsmith 9 × 18 jaw crusher (Primary crusher) with starter box and Telsmith No-2F-gyratory crusher, size 4 feet × 56 inches, flat belted to 50-HP-GE-AC Electric motor, material belts, shafting, screens, gates, elevators, starter boxes, etc. (50 HP motor runs both crushers and elevators).

1 Minerals separation system of North America, flotation system, straight air lift type, 6 cell unit (4 roughers, two fine) connected to 8 inch outlet, Root Blower, size 2, No-35076, geared direct to 25 HP-GE-AC-motor, serial No-14034010-440-60C-3P-Type KT-526-6-26-1200-Form-B-RPM-full load 1135, complete with all risers, values and fittings.

1 Dorr Thickener-9½ feet × 10 feet, redwood stave tank-with machinery, electric overload alarm and electric motor.

1 American type disk filter, vacuum tank and gauge, vacuum compressor, class-ER-1-5 × 4 Ingersoll-Rand, material belts, motor, etc.

1 50,000 gallon redwood mill supply water tank, round steel bands.

1 Four unit, 28 gage galvanized steel mill building, Oregon fir nailed framing, building in excellent condition. This mill unit, rated from 50 to 120 tons, depending on the mesh ground is 100% new, only being used a few hours to test out equipment.

1 75 gallon boiler

20 tons 20-pound mine rail

1 5 ton ore scale

1 lot of ore cars

1 Ingersoll-Rand-Leyner No-5 drill sharpener, with complete set of chucks, dies and blocks and odd lot of hollowdrill steel

1 15 HP, Vulcan single drum, variable speed electric hoist, complete with direct geared GE-electric motor, controller box, steel frame, grid, n excellent condition

1 30 HP, electric hoist, same as the above, except 30 HP, complete

1 two stage Sullivan center fly wheel-505 cu ft compressor, flat belt drive to 50 HP GE-AC induction motor-serial No-455916-440-60c-3p-type 1-8 form k-RPM-900-62-volts, speed full load 865. Cylinder size 14 × 9 × 10

1 Ingersoll-Rand compressor 12 × 10 single stage, 270 C.F., serial No-27219, flat belted to 50 HP GE-AC-440-60c-3p-electric motor. Serial No-1046910-type KT-343-6-50-1200-Form B-Amps 60 RPM-full load 1160

1 Telsmith jaw crusher, size 9 × 18, with starter box

1 24 × 24 × 48–inch ball bearing skip car

1 4 × 10–foot heavy steel air receiver, with brass pop-off and brass whistle, and 4 inch pipe connections

2 small air receivers

Table 10.1. Material Salvaged at Closure of the Mayer Custom (Gray Eagle) Plant, continued

1   Ingersoll-Rand compressor, single stage, 270-foot-sized-12 × 10 cylinders, serial No-27219, flat belted, short belt, to 50 HP GE-AC-440-60c-3p, electric motor, serial No-1046910-Type-Kt-343-6-50-Form-B-RPM- no load-1200-full load-1160-Amps-6011

1   Sullivan two-stage compressor, cylinder size 14 × 9 × 10–class WJ-serial No-1131-505-foot cap-center flywheel, flat belt drive with idler pulley to 50 HP-GE-AC-440-60c-3p-electric motor-serial No-455916, type-ITS-50a-RPM-900-Form-K-AMOS-62-RPM-full load 865.

Above compressors connected to horizontal type heavy steel, receiver size 4 × 12 feet, complete with all pipe connections, brass pop-off and large brass mine whistle

General lot of odds and ends, mine supplies

2   small underground mine air receivers

1   15 HP-single drum variable speed, reversible, Vulcan electric hoist direct connected to 15 HP GE-AC-440-60c-3p-motor. Steel I beam hoist base, with controller box and grid, in small metal house.

1   Cameron sinker No-5

1   Fairbanks-Morse-5 × 4 × 6 outside pack

3   V type, side dump, ball bearings, 20-foot capacity

9   plain bearing, swing around, 16-foot capacity

1   5 ton cap, ore scale with rails, weights, etc.

20 tons   20-pound weight, with switches, fish plates (NEW) odd lot of new spikes, switch points. Odd lot of different weight nails.

1   Ball bearing skip car with end valve, size 24 × 24 × 48 inches

1   Ingersoll-Rand-Leyner, with a complete set of dollies-blocks-dies and extra parts.

1½ tons   hollow drill steel

1   blacksmith small air hammer

odd lot of drill carriages, hammers and small blacksmith tools

1   Rumsey triplex air pump, 2¼ × 4 inches

1   small snow boiler feed pump

1   75 gallon steel boiler with water valve

15,000 ft heavy and odd sized copper core insulated cable, with small transformer

(Source: Special Collections, Arizona State University)

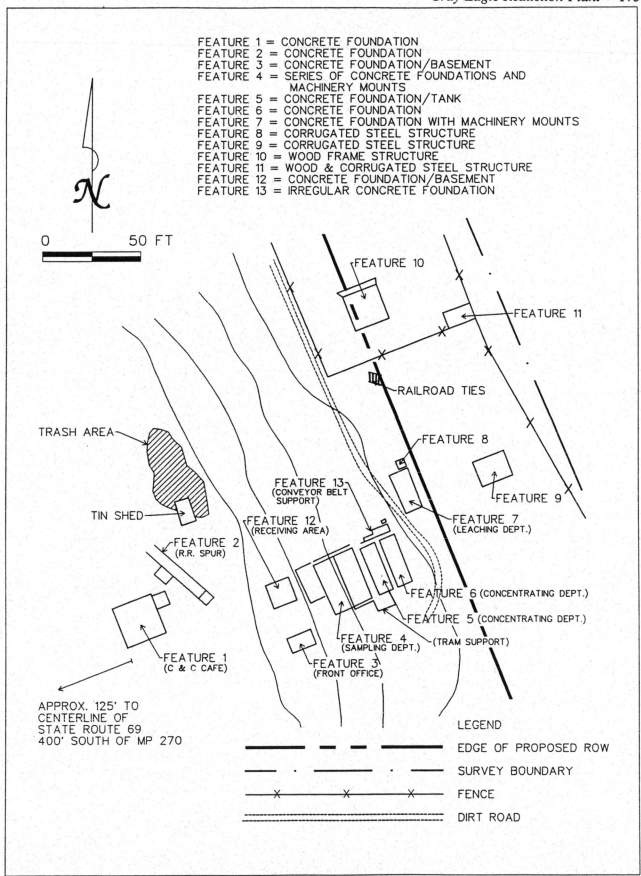

FEATURE 1 = CONCRETE FOUNDATION
FEATURE 2 = CONCRETE FOUNDATION
FEATURE 3 = CONCRETE FOUNDATION/BASEMENT
FEATURE 4 = SERIES OF CONCRETE FOUNDATIONS AND
            MACHINERY MOUNTS
FEATURE 5 = CONCRETE FOUNDATION/TANK
FEATURE 6 = CONCRETE FOUNDATION
FEATURE 7 = CONCRETE FOUNDATION WITH MACHINERY MOUNTS
FEATURE 8 = CORRUGATED STEEL STRUCTURE
FEATURE 9 = CORRUGATED STEEL STRUCTURE
FEATURE 10 = WOOD FRAME STRUCTURE
FEATURE 11 = WOOD & CORRUGATED STEEL STRUCTURE
FEATURE 12 = CONCRETE FOUNDATION/BASEMENT
FEATURE 13 = IRREGULAR CONCRETE FOUNDATION

0   50 FT

FEATURE 10

FEATURE 11

RAILROAD TIES

TRASH AREA

FEATURE 8

FEATURE 9

FEATURE 13
(CONVEYOR BELT
SUPPORT)

TIN SHED

FEATURE 12
(RECEIVING AREA)

FEATURE 7
(LEACHING DEPT.)

FEATURE 2
(R.R. SPUR)

FEATURE 6 (CONCENTRATING DEPT.)

FEATURE 5 (CONCENTRATING DEPT.)

FEATURE 4
(SAMPLING DEPT.)

(TRAM SUPPORT)

FEATURE 1
(C & C CAFE)

FEATURE 3
(FRONT OFFICE)

APPROX. 125' TO
CENTERLINE OF
STATE ROUTE 69
400' SOUTH OF MP 270

LEGEND

—————————— EDGE OF PROPOSED ROW

———— · ———— SURVEY BOUNDARY

———×———×———×——— FENCE

============= DIRT ROAD

Figure 10.8. Site AZ N:12:39(ASM), the Gray Eagle Reduction (Mayer Custom) Plant (from Hathaway 1992). Notations in parentheses indicate probable functions of features.

(7)   A 25 × 15-foot poured concrete foundation with attached machinery mounts.

(8)   A 5-foot-square shed-roofed standing structure of corrugated steel adjacent to Feature 7.

(9)   A 20 × 15-foot corrugated steel standing structure.

(10) A 20-foot-square wood-frame standing structure, within a fenced enclosure with Feature 11.

(11) A 15 × 10-foot shed-roofed, wood and corrugated steel structure, within a fenced enclosure with Feature 10.

(12) A 15-foot-square poured concrete semisubterranean foundation/basement, above Feature 4 and northwest of Feature 3.

(13) An irregularly shaped concrete foundation within a 15 × 5-foot area, northwest of Features 5 and 6.

The following paragraphs interpret the functions of these features in chronological order (that is, according to period of association).

The Murphy Homestead Era

The fence enclosing Features 10 and 11 matched the location, size, and orientation of a corral shown on the 1909 plat of the Murphy Homestead (Figure 10.3). There is virtually no doubt that this enclosure was first built when Murphy homesteaded the land. However, no other elements of AZ N:12:39(ASM) appeared to relate to this early period of occupation. Features 10 and 11, within the fenced area, matched neither the platted locations nor the descriptions of any improvements that Murphy made to his homestead. For example, it is known that Murphy's barn was situated adjacent to and within the east side of the fenced area; it is also known that the barn measured 20 × 30 feet. None of the site's archaeological features matched these locational and descriptive data.

The Gray Eagle/Mayer Custom Plant Era

Many features of AZ N:12:39(ASM) matched elements of the site's industrial period (1915 to 1919). Historical photos (Figures 10.4 through 10.7) and newspaper articles helped interpret the function of features associated with this era.

* SWCA concurred with Hathaway's (1992:55) assessment that Feature 2 was related to the Gray Eagle Spur, a railroad grade that connected the industrial plant with the Prescott & Eastern/Bradshaw Mountain railways. The spur was at the western end of the plant's receiving platform and conveyor belt, elements pictured in Figure 10.5.

* Feature 3 is clearly pictured in Figures 10.5 and 10.6. This was the "front office" for the works and served several functions. It was the main office that customers encountered when entering the plant. Assay samples were received and likely analyzed here. It was also the point at which

concentrated products could be inspected before loading onto railroad cars; a tram along the south side of the plant (see Figure 10.6) carried concentrates up to the back of this building.

- Feature 13 and a southern projection of concrete between Features 4 and 5 appeared to have been the support system for the conveyor belt and tram, respectively. The conveyor belt carried ores through the Sampling Department, while the tram carried material through the Concentrating Department.

- Feature 4 represented the Sampling Department. Figures 10.5 and 10.6 indicate that part of this building had two stories. The conveyor belt on the north side of the plant carried ore from the spur to this unit, where it was mechanically crushed, then loaded back onto the spur line for shipment elsewhere or for further treatment at this plant. If the crushed material was to be shipped, it would be passed uphill via the conveyor belt to the spur line. If it was to be further treated within the plant, it would be sent downhill to the next unit, the Concentrating Department.

- Features 5 and 6, located downhill from the Sampling Department (Feature 4), were probably the remains of the Concentrating Department where table concentration and flotation techniques separated the ores. Once material was concentrated in this unit, it was passed along a tramway (located along the south side of the plant) uphill to the main office and spur line. Concentrated material could be inspected by the customer in the front office.

- Feature 7 is clearly depicted in Figures 10.4 and 10.6. It was a free-standing building having a door and three windows on its south side. Its function is unspecified in historical records. It may have been the Leaching Department, a facility added to the plant a bit later than the Assaying, Sampling, and Concentrating departments. The slightly later date of the Leaching Department might account for the physical separation of Feature 7 from the main group of features at the site; also, it was not as integral and central to the design of the plant as the other departments and therefore may have been physically separate from those units. The function of Feature 8, immediately north of Feature 7, is similarly unclear.

- The location of Feature 9 coincided with the location of an element of the Mayer Custom Plant shown in Figure 10.4. The building in the photo was dark colored, had a main roof gable oriented east-west, and had a shed-roofed addition to the south. The building was on the edge of a riparian thicket along Big Bug Creek. Its function is unknown.

- Feature 12 was likely the receiving area of the Sampling Unit, an area depicted in Figure 10.5. The receiving area included a railroad-type scale for weighing ores submitted to the plant. This semisubterranean feature may have housed the scale mounts.

- Three substantial buildings associated with the plant (and shown in Figure 10.4) apparently left no archaeological remains. The historical photograph showed two buildings northeast of the main plant and one building southeast of it. Although the functions of the two northeastern buildings were not identified in historical documents, the southeastern building was clearly identified as the bunkhouse and garage (Figure 10.7). None of these three buildings matched the locations and descriptions of any features at AZ N:12:39(ASM).

The Late Historic/Modern Era

From informant data, Hathaway (1992:55) suggested that Features 10 and 11 were associated with the post-industrial occupation of the site; he further hypothesized that Feature 1 was the remains of the C & C Cafe, a circa-1970 facility. The SWCA investigators reached similar conclusions; these three features are not shown on earlier maps and photographs of the property and do, indeed, appear to be of late historic/modern vintage. However, SWCA researchers disagreed with the assessment that Features 8 and 9 were also associated with the post-industrial era. A historical photograph (Figure 10.4) suggested that Feature 9 was present when the plant functioned. The proximity of Feature 8 to Feature 7 suggested that the former was an element of the plant as surely as the latter.

SUMMARY AND RECOMMENDATIONS

Testing revealed that Site AZ N:12:39(ASM) had three periods of occupation. The first, the Murphy Homestead Era, dating from 1890 to Murphy's death circa 1912, was weakly represented by physical remains at the site. The second period, associated with the Gray Eagle/Mayer Custom Plant and dating from 1915 to early 1919, was strongly represented by physical remains; indeed, most features at the site dated to this era. The third period of occupation, representing the late historic and modern eras, was represented by Feature 1 (a concrete foundation), Feature 10 (a wood-frame structure), and Feature 11 (a wood and steel structure).

SWCA made the following recommendations regarding eligibility of this site for the National Register of Historic Places on the basis of the testing results. The Murphy Homestead component of the property, marked only by a fence of no particular distinction, represents an important phase of the property's development but, unfortunately, lacks sufficient integrity to be considered of National Register quality. The industrial component (Gray Eagle/Mayer Custom Plant) is significant for its data content and possesses strong integrity and therefore is eligible for the NRHP under Criterion D. The third component, which began in late historic times and continued into modern times, lacks sufficient age and is not of sufficient significance to be considered eligible for the National Register.

The proposed SR 69 project will impact a major portion of the (Register-eligible) industrial component of this site. SWCA's study documented the history of this component, described its units and how they interrelated, located historical photographs and narrative descriptions of the plant, and even found an exhaustive list of all items salvaged from the facility upon its closure. While it is possible that data recovery could glean additional tidbits of information about the site, such information would likely be minor in relation to what has already been learned. Moreover, the potential health risks would outweigh the scientific benefits of retrieving data from the contaminated soils of the site. In light of these considerations, SWCA did not recommend or conduct additional work at Site AZ N:12:39(ASM) during the data recovery phase of the SR 69 investigations.

CHAPTER 11

AZ N:12:40(ASM)

Pat H. Stein

MANAGEMENT HISTORY

Site AZ N:12:40(ASM) is in the SW¼NE¼SW¼NE¼ of Section 26 in Township 12 North, Range 1 East on the USGS Mayer, Arizona, 7.5 minute quadrangle (Figure 11.1). It is on the southeast edge of Mayer, on the top of a low, flat, gravel terrace on the west side of Big Bug Creek. An unnamed tributary of the creek cuts along the northern base of the terrace. The site lies in dense desertscrub and chaparral vegetation; dense desert riparian vegetation lines the creek to the east and the tributary drainage to the north of the site. Current State Route 69 runs along the west side of the property. The site is on private land and on an Arizona Department of Transportation (ADOT) easement.

Hathaway (1992) discovered Site AZ N:12:40(ASM) during the Class III cultural resource survey for SR 69 from Mayer to Dewey by Archaeological Research Services, Inc. Hathaway reported the site as a low-density trash scatter approximately 200 feet in diameter. He saw no concentrations of material or other features but noted that the dense vegetation could be obscuring any features that might exist. The cultural material—consisting of sun-colored amethyst (SCA) and amber bottle glass, tableware sherds, fragments of hole-in-cap cans, buckets, enamelware, personal and clothing-related items, hardware, and construction items—appeared to date from the late nineteenth and early twentieth centuries. A preliminary records check during the survey suggested that the site lay on the old William Murphy property (see Chapter 10). Hathaway concluded that the site was potentially eligible for the National Register of Historic Places and recommended that it be avoided or subjected to an archaeological testing program to formally determine its Register eligibility.

ADOT staff found that avoiding the site was not feasible. At first ADOT engineers thought that construction would impact only the western part of the site. However, when they had staked the proposed right-of-way (ROW) and SWCA initiated testing, it became apparent that construction would impact virtually all of the resource. SWCA's testing program consisted of archival research plus on-site archaeological work that included brushing, mapping, photodocumentation, controlled surface collection, and testing of two features discovered during brushing. As a follow-up to fieldwork, the SWCA archaeologists invited Yavapai-Prescott tribal representatives to visit the site and interviewed those who attended the session. The following discussion presents the results of the testing program. SWCA did not recommend or conduct additional work during the data recovery phase of the SR 69 investigations.

HISTORICAL DATA

Master Plat Title Indices at the State Office of the Bureau of Land Management (BLM) indicate that the land occupied by Site AZ N:12:40(ASM) passed from government stewardship to private ownership as a result of homesteading. The land occupied by the site was not part of the Murphy Homestead, as previously thought (Hathaway 1992:56). The Murphy property actually lay southeast of this property (see Chapter 10), and the land occupied by this site was part of the John A. Martin Homestead. Martin was, according to BLM records, the only party to attempt to acquire this parcel from the government in historic times.

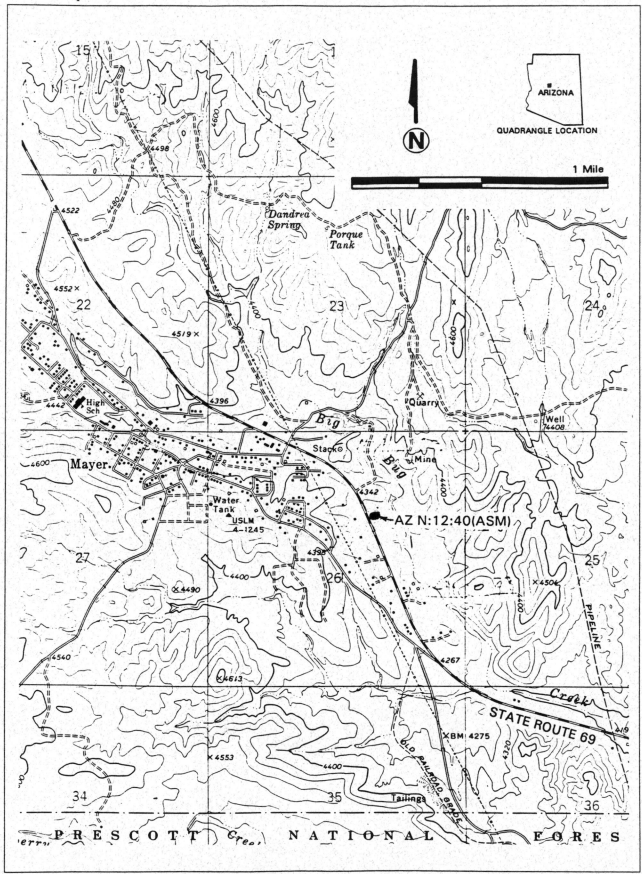

Figure 11.1. Location of Site AZ N:12:40(ASM). Base map is Mayer, Arizona, USGS 7.5′ quadrangle, 1974.

John A. Martin was born in 1854 in Greene County, Tennessee. By 1897 he had moved to Arizona Territory and was residing in Mayer, although his exact place of residence in that community is unknown. He lived in Mayer for 57 years and, at the time of his death in 1954, owned considerable property, including the town water works (Sharlot Hall Museum [SHM] Obituary Book [OB]:n.p.).

The date Martin first settled on his homestead is unclear from historical records. He may have squatted there as early as 1897 or as late as 1915. In October of the latter year he formally filed an application for a homestead. He submitted his final proof on the claim in 1919 and was issued a title patent for it in June of 1920 (USDI Bureau of Land Management Phoenix Serial Record 028509).

Martin's homestead consisted of 150 acres. Its legal description was Lots 3 and 6, plus the SW¼NW¼ and the SE¼NW¼ of Section 26 in Township 12 North, Range 1 East. His claim would have been the more usual 160-acre size were it not for the fact that his neighbor to the southeast, William Murphy, had made a prior homestead claim that cut 10 acres out of Lots 3 and 6 (Figure 11.2).

The General Land Office (GLO) never produced a plat map of Martin's homestead. There was no need to; by the time Martin filed his claim in 1915, the GLO had already (1914) conducted a survey of the township, dividing it into sections, quarter sections, and quarter-quarter sections. The Martin homestead could be accurately described and recorded on the basis of that existing GLO survey. Unfortunately, the lack of a plat for the Martin homestead means that the historical researcher cannot tell where, within the 150-acre homestead, Martin sited his house and other improvements necessary for "proving up" on the claim. A comparison of the location of AZ N:12:40(ASM) with the location of the Martin Homestead indicates that the site would have been within Lot 3 of the Martin property. Was the site, then, directly associated with Martin? As shown in the next section, archaeological data obtained through testing suggested a different conclusion.

Grantee/Grantor indices at the Yavapai County Recorder's Office indicated that John A. Martin retained the 150-acre tract through the duration of the historic period. Upon his death in 1954, his estate passed to his nephew, G. I. Martin, who had helped him conduct his Mayer business (SHM OB n.p.).

ARCHAEOLOGICAL DATA

SWCA's field crew began archaeological testing by removing brush. The site had a dense vegetative cover, and its removal helped to define the site's extent, condition, and nature and revealed data that altered previous impressions of the site. It was not a low-density trash scatter unassociated with any features (as previously reported), but an area of historic trash of low to moderate density associated with two features. The features were assigned the designations A and B; Figure 11.3 shows their locations within the site. Testing revealed that one of the features was cultural and the other was natural.

Feature A was a crude stone circle measuring 12 feet in diameter (Figure 11.4). Six of the rocks were closely spaced to form an arc. The remaining four were located at various distances to complete the circle. The rocks were very slightly (less than 2 inches) embedded into the earth. A 3 × 5-foot test trench excavated and screened along the arc revealed that there were no courses of rock beneath those on the surface and that the feature did not have either a floor or subsurface artifacts.

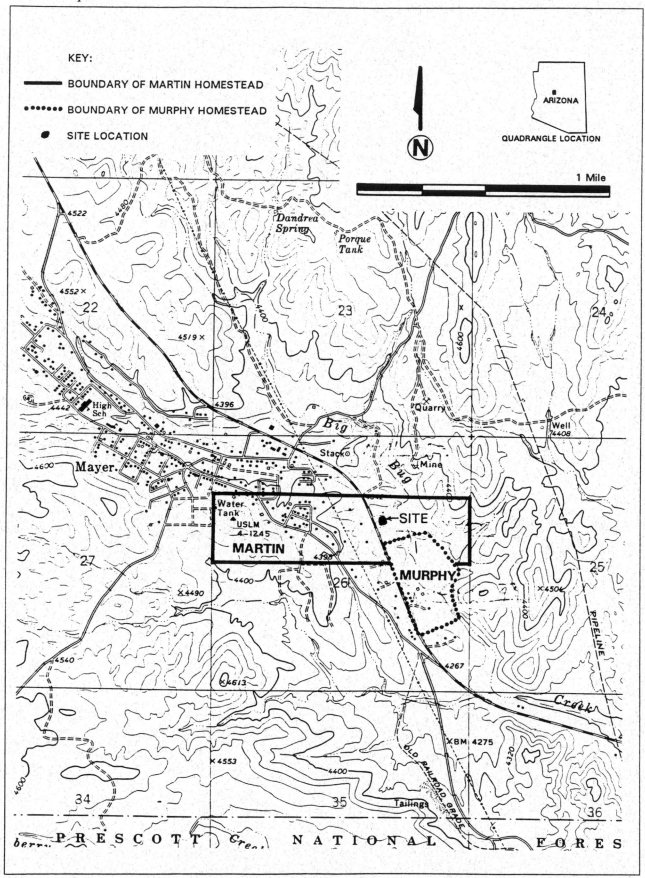

Figure 11.2. Locations of Martin and Murphy homesteads in relation to Site AZ N:12:40(ASM). Base map is Mayer, Arizona, USGS 7.5′ quadrangle, 1974.

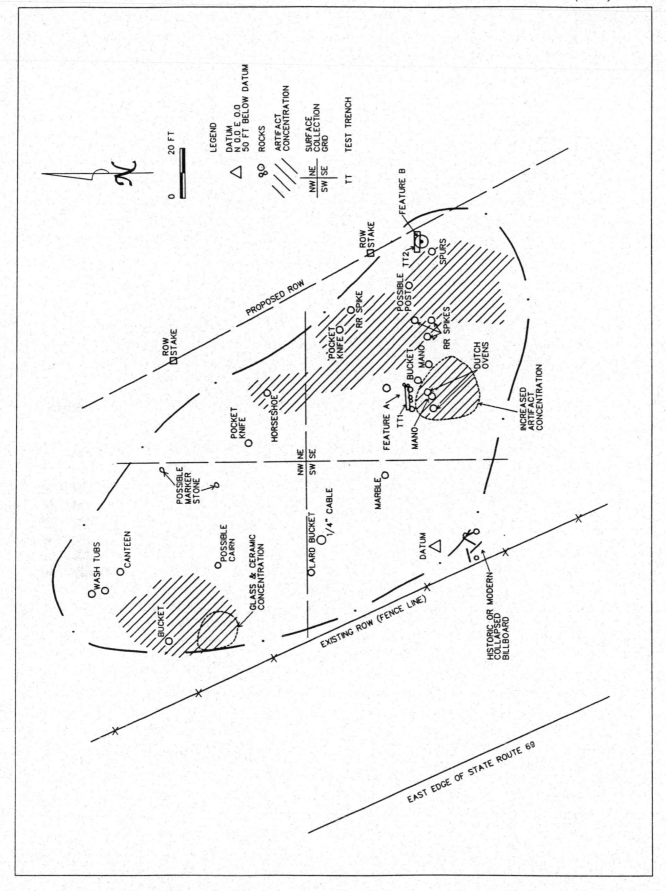

Figure 11.3. Site AZ N:12:40(ASM).

Figure 11.4. AZ N:12:40(ASM), Feature A, stone circle; view east.

South of this feature, artifacts were denser than elsewhere on the site. The assemblage had a decidedly domestic (household) character. The artifacts included pieces of a Dutch oven (base embossed "7H"), two white enamelware cups, a lard bucket, a cold cream jar fragment, fragments of a hard-paste earthenware plate and two bowls (no maker's marks), and a harmonica reed. Also present were a Union Metallic Cartridge Co. No. 12 "Climax" shotgun shell (ca. 1900) and a 20d wire nail. Two whole manos completed the assemblage. The first mano was of vesicular basalt and measured 7.2 × 3.3 × 2 inches (18.3 × 8.5 × 5.0 cm). It had been carefully shaped by pecking, was subrectangular in form, and was plano-convex in cross section. It was slightly burned and had one use surface, with no evidence of multiple function (for example, it had not been used as a hammerstone). The second mano, of granodiorite, measured 4.5 × 3.5 × 1.6 inches (11.5 × 9.0 × 4.2 cm), was unshaped, had one use surface, exhibited no evidence of multiple function, and was of a natural oval shape with a bi-planar cross section.

The artifact assemblage suggested that Feature A was a habitation unit. However, the unit did not appear to be a standard Euroamerican type of habitation, as on the entire site only one nail and no other architectural material (lumber, window glass, hardware, etc.) was present. The circular arrangement of stones, the size of the circle, and the presence of the two manos suggested that the habitation was historic American Indian in origin.

Feature B was a slight depression measuring 4 feet in diameter by 6 inches deep on the southeastern edge of the site. The field crew shovel-scraped the surface to delineate the feature's plan and then tested it by means of a 3 × 5-foot trench. The fill, which consisted of a soft loam, was screened through 1/4-inch mesh. Artifacts recovered from the fill consisted of the partial base of an amber bottle, a spoon without a handle, an alarm clock resonator, a piece of coiled wire, tiny fragments of tin cans, and a metal strip with tack holes. The feature ended at a depth of 3 inches below the present ground surface and therefore was not a privy. It appeared to be the remains of an old packrat midden or animal den.

The archaeologists divided the site, which measured 240 feet northwest-southeast by 110 feet northeast-southwest, into quadrants for more detailed field study. They pinflagged all artifacts to gain a sense of their distribution; with the exception of the area immediately south of Feature A, artifacts were sparse in all areas of the site. Although artifact concentrations were slightly denser in the northwestern and southwestern quadrants of the site, the distribution of materials in these areas could still be characterized as sparse.

Some items merited special note. The southeastern quadrant (which contained Features A and B) contained four railroad spikes (doghead type) that appeared to have been anchors for a tent or tarp. Three of the spikes were in situ, still embedded in the ground and forming three corners of a rectangle, while the fourth was uprooted and a short distance from the other three. The southwestern quadrant contained remnants of a late historic or modern wooden billboard; the iron base for the billboard was still in place along current SR 69. The northwestern quadrant contained three small rock piles that resembled cairns. The testing crew carefully picked them apart and examined them, but they bore no inscriptions or other identifying marks and appeared to be natural, not cultural.

Artifacts identified at the site were of ceramic, glass, metal, and other materials. Summary descriptions follow. Definitions of terms used to describe historical artifacts appear in the Glossary.

Ceramic fragments represented at least 12 different objects. Ten items were of hard-paste earthenware and two were porcelain. The hard-paste earthenware items were fragments of a white storage container, plate, cup, saucer, and bowl; a cup with teal green floral design on a white background; a flow-blue plate; a rice bowl with blue design on an eggshell background; a cup with gold paint on a white background; and a blue-glaze Chinese shipping jar. The porcelain items were fragments of a white vessel lid and a vessel of unknown form with a raised, molded design.

Only the saucer and blue-glaze shipping jar exhibited a mark, design, or form that could be more closely identified. The saucer bore a maker's mark indicating that it was a piece of Royal Ironstone China manufactured by the East End Pottery Company of East Liverpool, Ohio (established 1891). The shipping jar fragment—a globular body sherd— suggested that the jar once held sauce or perhaps a distilled liquor called *Ng Ky Py* (Goodman 1993:174–175). Shipping jars of this type were made in South China for centuries but were exported to Chinese emigrants in North America starting in the era of the California Gold Rush (ca. the mid 1800s). The jar fragment found at AZ N:12:40(ASM) likely made its way to Mayer and this site via Chinese laborers. For example, Joe Mayer employed a steady stream of Chinese cooks to help him run his stage station and restaurant at Mayer (Thorpe 1978:143). Most got homesick for their native country and did not stay long in the area. (Trouble once erupted when Joe Mayer inadvertently hired members of rival *tongs* to work in his kitchens [Thorpe 1978:151–152].)

Glass fragments represented at least 13 glass items. Glass container fragments came from four brown beer bottles, a sun-colored amethyst (SCA) panel bottle, and a pale green panel bottle. At least two of the beer bottles, marked "Dispose of Properly" and "Please Help Fight Litter," had been left on the site recently. The SCA panel bottle bore a basemark used by the Illinois Glass Company circa 1916–1929; the SCA color suggested a date of manufacture near the beginning of this temporal range (SCA glass was manufactured ca. 1880–1917). Other glass items included fragments of a thermometer, a possible "slag" marble, an SCA press-molded footed candy dish, an SCA ink bottle, an amber bottle stopper, and a milk-glass cold cream or Mentholatum jar. Only the ink bottle bore an identifying mark, "Carter's," a company that has been in operation since 1858.

Metal artifacts were by far the most numerous items at Site AZ N:12:40(ASM). Cans, the most common artifacts, included the following types: hole-in-cap (2 specimens), hinge-top pocket tobacco (1), meat with rolled top (1), crimped round meat (3), evaporated milk (1), rectangular syrup (1), rectangular fuel (1), baking powder with reclosable lid (1), meat with scored-strip opening (2), and sanitary (7). These items provided clues to the dating of the site. Three cans with interlocking side seams indicated a manufacture date circa 1885–1903. The evaporated milk can was of a size and style made circa 1917–1919. The syrup can was made by Karo beginning in 1906. The pocket tobacco tins dated post-1913. The sanitary cans were made in the twentieth century. A "Schilling's Best" spice can suggested a manufacture data circa 1890–1947.

Metal items of particular interest included two gray enamelware wash basins that had been purposely destroyed by slashing their bases with an axe or knife (Figure 11.5). They were found on the northern edge of the site. The practice of ritually "killing" metal objects in this manner has been documented among the Yavapai and Apache of central Arizona (Gifford 1936; Heider 1955; Schroeder 1974), typically in association with the death of the owner.

Figure 11.5. Two "killed" washtubs recovered from northern edge of Site AZ N:12:40(ASM).

Several items associated with horses and tack were present. They consisted of a horseshoe, two harness buckles, two spurs, a hobble chain, a halter bolt from a wagon or coach, and small strips of metal from leather tack.

Several items associated with horses and tack were present. They consisted of a horseshoe, two harness buckles, two spurs, a hobble chain, a halter bolt from a wagon or coach, and small strips of metal from leather tack.

A variety of other metal objects included lard buckets (5), a round-nose shovel with ferrule, a suitcase frame and hinge, a white enamelware bowl, an "equal end" jackknife, a 2-blade jackknife, a piece of a candle holder or lamp, an alarm clock resonator, a Union Metallic Cartridge Co. No. 12 "Climax" shell (ca. 1900), the tin cap from a gun powder can, a funnel, wire mesh, a canteen, a cobalt-blue "marbleized" wash basin, and a few miscellaneous nuts, washers, and pieces of strap metal. One item was associated with clothing: a 24-ligne brass rivet, probably from jeans, marked "B-L @."

One metal artifact in the assemblage exhibited reuse: a solder-top can with a nail inserted through its top and bottom. The function of the modified can was not apparent.

Two artifacts at AZ N:12:40(ASM) were of substances other than glass, pottery, or metal. They were a 22-ligne shell button and scraps of a leather shoe.

SUMMARY AND RECOMMENDATIONS

Archival research indicated that the only individual of record to lay claim to the land containing Site AZ N:12:40(ASM) in the historic era was John A. Martin. The Tennessee native filed his homestead claim in 1915, submitted his final proof in 1919, and obtained his title patent in 1920. Artifacts at AZ N:12:40(ASM) suggested that this was a habitation site. The dating of the artifacts further suggested occupancy sometime between 1900 and 1920. The chronology of the site (based on datable artifacts) was consistent with the era of Martin's homesteading effort. Was the site, therefore, Martin's residence?

Archaeological data led to a different conclusion. The general absence of architectural remains (nails, window glass, building hardware) and the presence of two "killed" wash basins and two manos suggested that the site was associated with American Indians during the early twentieth century. Moreover, Feature A resembled the base of a type of mud and brush structure used by the Yavapai in historic times. Archaeologists often refer to these ephemeral rock features as "wickiup rings." However, the Yavapai-Prescott prefer that such features be called were "*awah 'puunvah* rings," from the Yavapai word for "shelter" (personal communication, Robert C. Euler and tribal elder Ted Vaughn 22 April 1997). A visit by the Yavapai-Prescott Tribal Archaeologist (then Mr. Kevin Harper) and a tribal member (Mr. Lonnie Morgan) confirmed that Feature A indeed resembled the base of a Yavapai *awah 'puunvah*.

The conclusion that Site AZ N:12:40(ASM) was Yavapai, not Euroamerican, did not conflict with historical and ethnohistorical data regarding central Arizona. Mayer and Big Bug Creek formed part of the vast traditional territory of the Northeastern Yavapai (Gifford 1936:248; Schroeder 1974). Hunter-gatherers who practiced limited agriculture, the Yavapai were organized in bands that exploited distinct territories in pursuit of game and ripening plants. According to Gifford (1936:249–250), the group of Yavapai based in the Mayer-Big Bug area in ethnohistoric and historic times was called the *Mathaupapaya*; their place name for Mayer was *Wikido'yo'*. The U.S. government forcibly placed the Yavapai on reservations from the 1860s to the 1890s, but allowed them to return to their traditional homelands around the turn of the century. By the late 1890s, there was a large Yavapai camp along Big Bug Creek at Mayer (Thorpe 1978:156). According to a daughter of Joe Mayer (Thorpe 1978:156), the American Indians in the encampment eked out a livelihood by making baskets and water jugs, which they sold to travelers using the Prescott & Eastern Railway (completed in 1898). The same source states that their diet included traditional recipes such as woodrat stew, cooked in large cans over a fire. When E. W. Gifford conducted his ethnographic fieldwork in 1932, Yavapai were still living in Mayer. In fact, one of his Yavapai informants, Jim Miller, was a Mayer resident.

Assuming that Site AZ N:12:40(ASM) was a Yavapai encampment dating to the early twentieth century, what can be said about the lifestyle of the people who lived there? Artifacts suggest that their material culture included a wide variety of manufactured items and processed (canned) foods. Wild plants and animals may have formed part of the diet; certainly, procurement and processing of such foods would have been facilitated by the occupants' 12-gauge shotgun, jackknives, and milling stones. For transportation, they used one or more horses and perhaps also owned a coach or wagon. Aside from the horse(s), tack, and wagon/coach, their most expensive and cherished item may have been their Dutch oven. They eschewed Yavapai ceramics (perhaps traditional wares were no longer being made when this site was occupied), favoring instead enamelware and manufactured pottery as serving utensils. The Chinese shipping jar was an unusual but not entirely inexplicable artifact within this historic context. Like the Yavapai, the Chinese occupied Mayer in the early twentieth century, and the presence of this artifact simply suggested contact between the two cultural groups. Judging from its form, the jar could have contained sauce or a distilled liquor. The artifact inventory from Site AZ N:12:40(ASM) indicated that the occupants indulged in recreational activities that included occasional tobacco consumption and playing the harmonica.

How many people resided at the site? This was difficult to determine, but the occurrence of only one *awah 'puunvah* ring suggested that the number did not exceed one nuclear family. The Yavapai, even in historic times, were organized in bands that lived in clusters of wickiups. For example, Keller and Stein (1985) studied a cluster of early twentieth-century *awah 'puunvah* rings at an archaeological site in Prescott. Although no such cluster was observed at this site, other *awah 'puunvah* may have been along adjacent terraces of Big Bug Creek, outside the SR 69 ROW. It was difficult to determine the age and gender of the occupants of AZ N:12:40(ASM). A marble at the site could have been a child's toy or simply an intriguing bauble/talisman acquired by an adult resident of the site during his or her travels. Age/gender-diagnostic artifacts for early twentieth century Yavapai sites have never been defined.

The testing program at Site AZ N:12:40(ASM) allowed the SWCA archaeologists to develop a historic context for the resource and obtain data that contributed significant information to that context. The site is eligible for the National Register of Historic Places because it has yielded important information regarding ethnicity and acculturation among American Indians in early twentieth century Mayer. The site lacked depth; the investigators fully studied its surface remains during testing, and it was unlikely to yield additional significant data. SWCA therefore did not recommend or conduct additional work at the site during the data recovery phase of the SR 69 investigations.

CHAPTER 12

LINEAR RESOURCES: RAILROAD AND ROAD SEGMENTS

John D. Goodman
Pat H. Stein

Seven segments of a historic railroad, nine sections of a historic road, and a series of discontinuous unpaved roadbeds lie within or immediately adjacent to the project area (Figures 12.1–12.4). Macnider and Sawyer-Lang (1990) first recorded some of the railroad segments and road sections; Hathaway (1992) first recorded others during the Class III inventory of State Route 69 from Mayer to Dewey. The Arizona Department of Transportation (ADOT) requested that SWCA conduct additional documentation of these elements during the archaeological testing phase of the current project. This chapter presents the results of that documentation. SWCA did not recommend or conduct additional work on the railroad segments or road segments during the data recovery phase of the SR 69 investigations.

HISTORIC RAILROAD SEGMENTS
(SITES AZ N:7:44[ASM], AZ N:8:29[ASM],
AZ N:11:28[ASM]/AR-O3-O9-03-365, AZ N:12:41[ASM])

Management History

Seven sections of the abandoned Prescott & Eastern Railway (P&E) grade lie within or immediately adjacent to the project area.   Because they are discontinuous, the seven railroad segments had previously been assigned four different site numbers in conformance with the Arizona State Museum's (ASM) linear-site recordation policies. ASM requires one site number for discontinuous segments of the same linear feature within a given quadrant and separate site numbers for segments within other quadrants (e.g., all segments within the AZ N:7 quadrant have one site number, segments within AZ N:8 another number, and so forth). Thus, the known segments of the P&E and associated railroad features (such as trestle remains and water-control devices) had been recorded as Sites AZ N:7:44(ASM), AZ N:8:29(ASM), AZ N:11:28(ASM)/AR-03-09-03-365, and AZ N:12:41(ASM). Hathaway (1992) first inventoried most of these segments, although Macnider and Sawyer-Lang (1990) initially recorded the segment in the AZ N:7 quadrant. Hathaway (1992) designated the segments by the numbers 1 through 7, assigning the lowest number to the southernmost segment. That designation system was retained during SWCA's work.

Although many portions of the P&E grade have been destroyed by modern development (Macnider and Sawyer-Lang 1990:3), several sections of the grade within the project area are relatively intact (Hathaway 1992:62). The seven sections along the project area, as well as many portions outside of that corridor, appeared to retain archaeological integrity. The Class III inventory report recommended that the intact railroad segments be either avoided and protected or subjected to an archaeological testing program if they were to be impacted by the SR 69 project.

SWCA's documentation of these seven linear resources involved walking closely spaced (20-foot-wide) transects along the length of each segment. The field crew characterized the construction methods of each segment, recorded all features and artifacts observed, took overview photographs of each segment, and took additional photographs of significant features such as water-control devices, retaining walls, and rail-

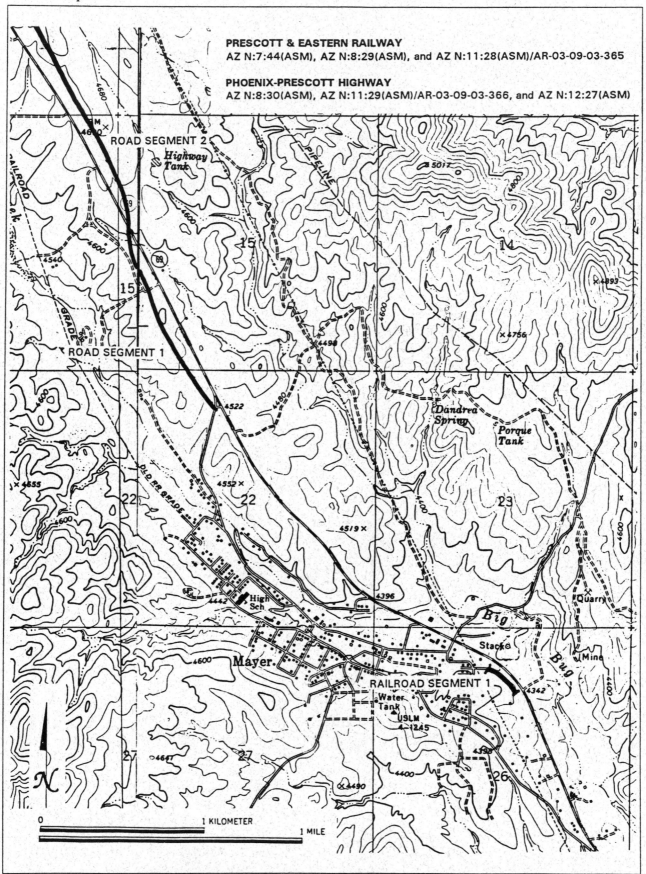

Figure 12.1. Locations of railroad and road segments. Base map is a combination of Mayer, Arizona, 1974, and Poland Junction, Arizona, 1975, USGS 7.5′ quadrangles.

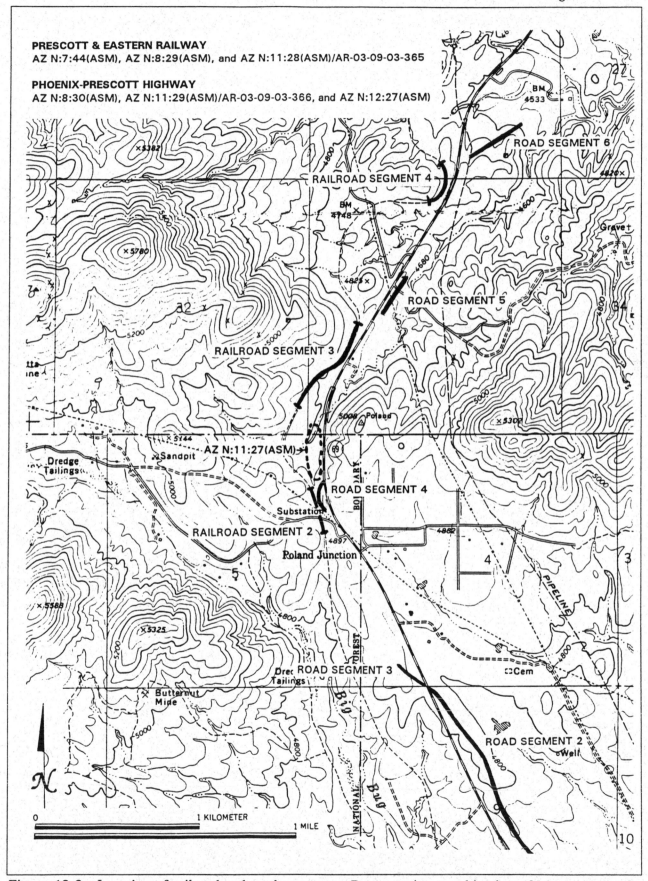

Figure 12.2. Location of railroad and road segments. Base map is a combination of Mayer, Arizona, 1974, and Poland Junction, Arizona, 1975, USGS 7.5′ quadrangles.

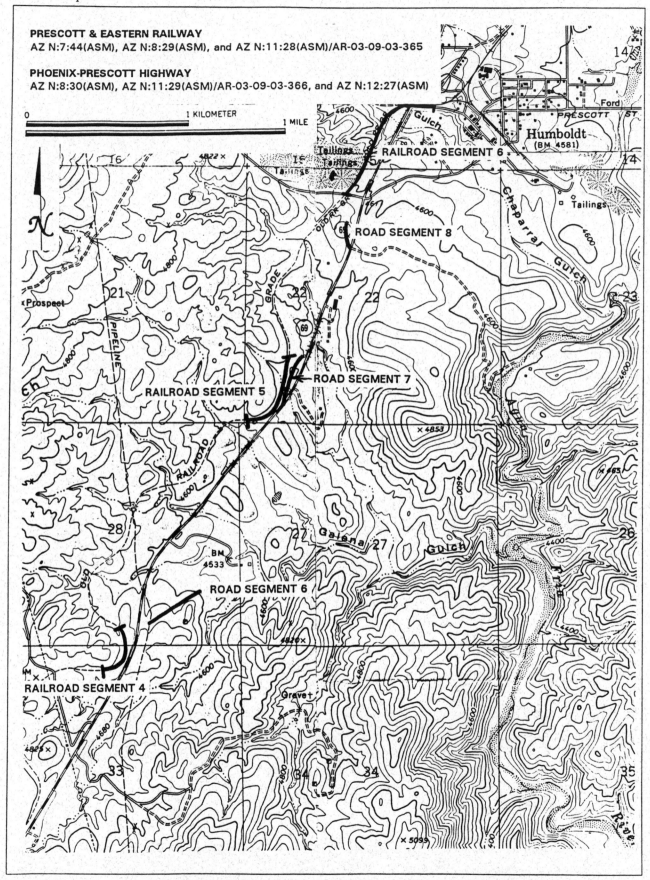

Figure 12.3. Locations of railroad and road segments. Base map is a combination of Humboldt, Arizona, 1973, Mayer, Arizona, 1974, and Poland Junction, Arizona, 1975, USGS 7.5′ quadrangles.

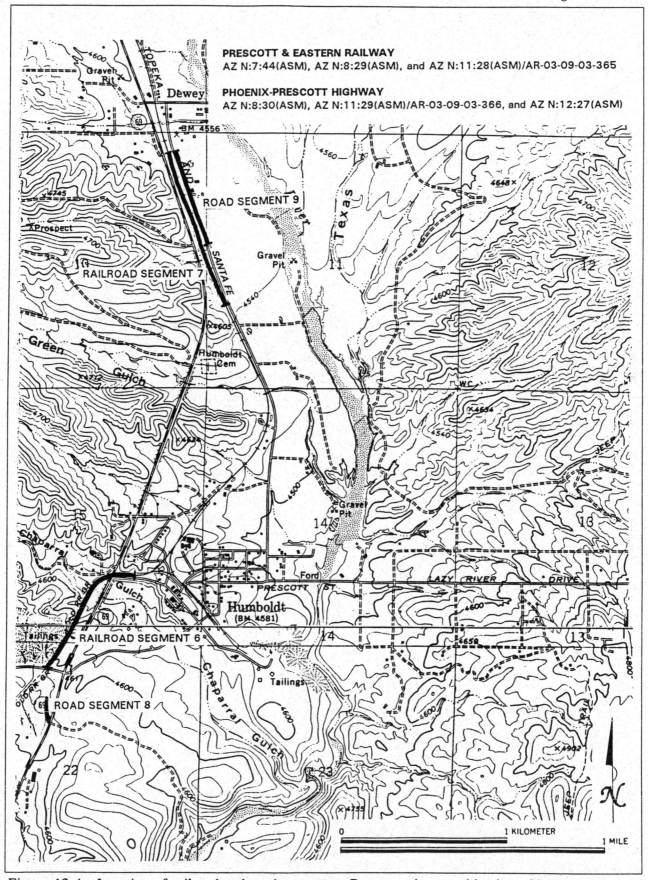

Figure 12.4. Location of railroad and road segments. Base map is a combination of Mayer, Arizona, 1974, and Humboldt, Arizona, 1973, USGS 7.5′ quadrangles.

road trestle remains. They took taped measurements of each segment and associated features, measured some artifacts (such as milk cans or isolated railway appliances), recorded maker's marks, and illustrated specimens of unknown function or type. No artifacts were collected. Analysts consulted appropriate references for historic materials (see Chapter 2) in identifying artifacts. The works of Barry (1876), Moore (1879), Myrick (1968), Glover (1984), Sayre (1985), Robertson (1986), and Swenson (1988) facilitated identification of railway appliances and an understanding of the history of railroads of the area. Archival research provided specific historical data pertaining to the individual segments and the areas around them. Sources included accounts of local and regional history and early survey maps showing roads, mining claims, and other features.

Historical Data

The arrival of railway transportation had an immense impact on the development of mines and towns near the project area. Prior to the arrival of the Prescott & Eastern Railway in 1898, transportation systems in the area were slow, cumbersome, and expensive. Ore was hauled by mule teams; over a 12-hour period, a team of mules might move several tons approximately 40 miles, if they encountered no obstacles. Stagecoaches transported other cargo and passengers. Horse teams that drew stagecoaches needed changing every 12 hours, which required the building of many stations along the longer routes. In and near the project area, stations such as Dewey (then called Agua Fria), Humboldt (formerly Val Verde), and Mayer (Big Bug) were established in the nineteenth century. As mining increased, these stations became increasingly active and grew into settlements.

Transportation in the area began to undergo a transformation with the arrival of the transcontinental railroads: the Southern Pacific Railroad across southern Arizona Territory in 1880 and the Atlantic & Pacific Railroad (A&P) across the northern part of the territory in 1882. These two carriers gave rise to a network of major and minor railways that eventually spread throughout Arizona (Figure 12.5). Sleepy outposts and stagecoach stops along railway corridors became bustling towns in a matter of years. Trains transported heavy ore-processing machinery quickly and efficiently for the construction of mills and smelters. Trains also carried thousands of board-feet of shoring timbers to mines that began excavating deep shafts and tunnels for the extraction of metals. Everything from pianos to pistachios was now carried along the rails to once-remote areas.

In *Ghost Railroads of Central Arizona*, Sayre (1985) provides thorough descriptions of the railroads, stations, and towns that developed along the Dewey-Mayer corridor. Robertson's (1968) *Encyclopedia of Western Railroad History* contains specific data on the various railroad companies, railway statistics, and locomotive engines associated with railroads of the study area. A summary of their information follows.

In 1886 construction of the Prescott & Arizona Central Railway from the A&P station at Seligman to Prescott established a rail link connecting a transcontinental carrier with the heart of Yavapai County. When this railroad experienced numerous difficulties because of poor management and other problems, Prescott entrepreneur Frank Murphy built a railroad from the A&P main line at Ash Fork to Prescott in 1893. Murphy was responsible for convincing the Arizona Territorial Legislature of the need for a second railroad to Prescott, and he organized the Santa Fe, Prescott & Phoenix Railway Company (SFP&P) in 1891. The Atchison, Topeka and Santa Fe Railway Company (AT&SF) invested in Murphy's project,

Figure 12.5. Map showing abandoned and operating railroads in Arizona in 1965 (from Myrick 1968). Arrow indicates project area.

supplying the line with second-hand rail in exchange for stock (Sayre 1985:7). The prosperous SFP&P from Ash Fork to Prescott was nicknamed the "Pea Vine" due to its steep route and many twisting curves.

With the success of the Pea Vine assured, Murphy and his wealthy Chicago associates realized the advantages to be afforded by a railway link from Prescott to mines in the Bradshaw Mountains and the Agua Fria valley. They proposed a 26-mile-long route, beginning from the Pea Vine north of Granite Dells and extending along the Agua Fria valley to Mayer. The railroad was to be a standard-gauge line, with rails spaced 56-1/2 inches apart. The Montana and Arizona Construction Company began building this line, christened the Prescott & Eastern Railway, in early March of 1898.

The construction company completed the P&E over a period of six months, the exact time specified in the contract. Two construction camps initially were set up along the line, one near Granite Dells and the second approximately two miles to the south (Sayre 1985:9). Seventy men began working southward from the northern end of the line, and 33 men and 27 wagon teams worked northward from the southern camp. Ultimately the project employed over 350 men, who performed the grading with pick and shovel, although rudimentary scrapers and leveling devices attached to wagons were also used (Sayre 1985:9). Most of the workers on this line were Greeks and Italians imported to do the grading and rail-laying. No Chinese crews worked on the line, although some Mexicans and American Indians apparently did (Sayre 1985:9). When labor shortages occurred, vagrants, hobos, and petty criminals who had been arrested in nearby towns were given the option of either sitting behind bars or working on the railway. At the end of two months, the grade had been completed to just north of Dewey, and two miles of rail had been laid. Crossing low areas required as much as 18 feet of fill, and trestles at the larger drainages. By late July of 1898, the rails crossed approximately 20 miles of the route. The line to Mayer was completed by the end of August, and the first scheduled train arrived in Mayer on October 15, 1898.

The P&E constructed small train stations at Cherry Creek near Agua Fria (Dewey), Val Verde (Humboldt), Huron, and Mayer. The stations included standard 24-foot-diameter wooden water tanks to fill the boilers of the steam locomotives. Long sidetracks ran in back of some stations for loading and storing railcars. At the stations, the railway company sometimes constructed houses for agents, dormitory-style housing for railroad laborers, warehouses, tool houses, sheep stockpens, and ore bins. Sayre (1985) provides detailed descriptions of these stations with accompanying maps, illustrations, and historic photographs.

With the Prescott & Eastern in place, mines began transporting immense ore shipments along the rails. With thousands of laborers hired to work in the busy mines, substantial communities developed around the mines and railway stations.

The transportation of ore by rail accelerated with construction of spurs and branch lines directly to many of the mines in the early 1900s. With the encouragement and backing of Frank Murphy, two branch lines extended into core mining areas. In 1901 Murphy incorporated the Bradshaw Mountain Railway and in the same year constructed a branch line that began at Poland Junction (on the P&E) and terminated at the rich Poland Mine. The Bradshaw Mountain Railway also built a branch line that began at Mayer, passed through the Tiger and Pine Grove mining districts, and extended to the Crown King Mine, completing this branch in the spring of 1904 (Figure 12.6). In 1907 the railway extended the Poland Branch, via tunnel, to the Hassayampa Mining District (Spude n.d.:7–8). The Prescott & Eastern and Bradshaw Mountain railways built spurs, sidings, and narrow-gauge railroads to various mines and ore-processing facilities along the route.

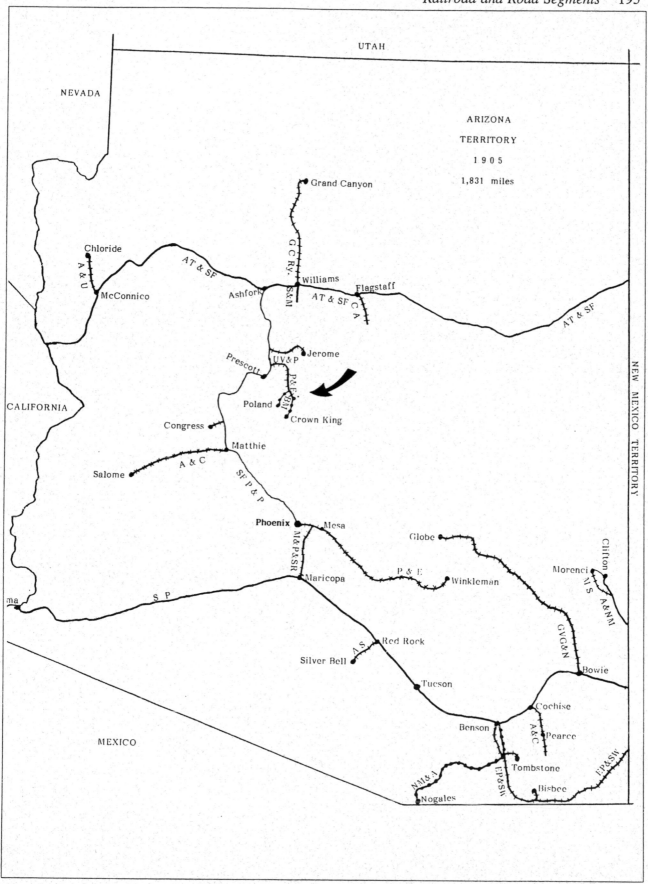

Figure 12.6. Map showing operating railroads in project area circa 1905 (from Robertson 1976). Arrow indicates location of the Prescott & Eastern Railway and the two branch lines of the Bradshaw Mountain Railway.

The Prescott & Eastern and Bradshaw Mountain railways were legally independent entities, although the Santa Fe, Prescott & Phoenix Railway Company held the stock of both. The two smaller lines did not own any rolling stock (locomotives and cars) of their own, using equipment of the parent company. At first, the SFP&P reserved sole use of engines 1 through 9, and engine numbers 10 through 12 were assigned to the two smaller railroads. However, as activities accelerated along the P&E, the SFP&P loaned the "Lucky Seven Spot" as well as engines 8 and 9 to that line. These engines were""4-6-0" coal-burning locomotives (a "4-6-0" engine had four small rolling wheels at the front and six large driving wheels). The Crown King Branch of the Bradshaw Mountain Railway posed an arduous climb to the upper Bradshaws and used stronger "2-8-0" oil-burning engines on that route. The six locomotives assigned to this line were numbered 51 through 56. Figure 12.7 shows four of the engines that worked along the P&E and Bradshaw Mountain railways.

The success of these railways depended on the prosperity of local mines. For a variety of reasons, many mines in the area that boomed around the turn of the century had become unprofitable by 1910 (see Chapter 1). As a direct consequence of mine closures, by the end of the first decade of the 1900s trains along the Agua Fria and into the Bradshaws were running a maximum of only three times per week rather than daily. During World War I the railroads experienced a resurgence as mines reopened in response to the increased demand for metals. However, at the end of the war, metal markets were saturated, and most of the mines again ceased operations. The smelter at Humboldt closed, and most miners and merchants there moved to other locations and opportunities. The last train to the Crown King Mine ran in the fall of 1926; the line to the Poland Mine was abandoned in 1939. Service along the Prescott & Eastern to the Blue Bell Siding near Mayer continued until 1958, then was withdrawn to the Iron King Spur near Humboldt. Along these abandoned lines, ties deteriorated and trestles rotted until the railroads finally removed them. All remaining P&E rails and ties were unceremoniously salvaged in 1974. The towns along the P&E became shells of their former selves, and once-bustling stations such as Huron became virtual ghost towns.

Archaeological Data

Railroad Segment 1

This railroad grade segment crosses private land at the southeastern edge of the town of Mayer (Figure 12.1). The segment is on the west side of SR 69 and southwest of Site AZ N:12:30(ASM), the Treadwell (Great Western) Smelter. It is between survey stations 3545+00 and 3660+00 in the NE¼SW¼NE¼, the SW¼NW¼NE¼, and the SE¼NE¼NW¼ of Section 26 in Township 12 North, Range 1 East on the USGS Mayer, Arizona, 7.5 minute quadrangle.

The northern end of Segment 1 where it enters southwest Mayer has been obliterated by the urban sprawl of the town. The central portion of the segment, directly southwest of a Circle K convenience store, includes a small, visible segment of railroad grade that appears to have been excavated into the hillside to a depth of approximately 30 feet below the original ground surface. Perhaps modified for the construction of a trailer pad, or possibly associated with the Treadwell Smelter spur line, this small terraced area runs northwest-southeast approximately 150 feet and is approximately 50 feet wide. This portion of the grade and the surrounding area were recently the scene of a brush fire. The southern portion of Segment 1, directly southwest of the abandoned Treadwell Smelter, remains largely intact. This portion consists of

Figure 12.7. Four engines used on Prescott & Eastern and Bradshaw Mountain railways (Sayre 1985). A and B are 4-6-0 locomotives; C and D are 2-8-0 locomotives.

a berm of local gravel and sand across an area of low relief that follows the general contour of the land and curves to the southeast following the base of a low hill. The berm has a general height of approximately 7 feet and a width of approximately 14 feet. The northern end of this portion of Segment 1 terminates at an automobile wrecking yard and dirt road (Figure 12.8).

One feature is present along Segment 1, a box culvert across a small drainage in the southern portion of the segment (Figure 12.9). The culvert consists of a series of stacked-and-staggered 2 × 4–inch boards on the sides, a plate of aligned 2 × 4–inch boards on the base, and a plate of aligned 3 × 10–inch boards on the top. The rectangular aperture measures 24-1/2 inches high by 24 inches wide. The boards are well preserved, suggesting construction during the final years of the railway's use.

A general scatter of modern trash along Segment 1 includes recent beverage bottles, cans, and plastic items. The only artifact of historic vintage observed along the segment was a single fragment of sun-colored amethyst (SCA) glass from a container. SCA glass was manufactured between 1880 and 1917.

Railroad Segment 2

This abandoned railroad segment is within the boundary of the Prescott National Forest, on the west side of SR 69 and extending north and south of the Poland Junction Substation. It is on the lower hillside of a chaparral-covered slope that faces to the northeast (Figure 12.2). Upper Big Bug Creek is approximately 0.3 mile to the west. Historic Road Segment 4 lies to the east of the railroad grade and west of SR 69 along the northern portion of the grade. Directly to the northeast, downslope from the northern portion of the segment, is Site AZ N:11:27(ASM), a series of discontinuous roadbeds not directly associated with the old Prescott-Phoenix highway (discussed below). Railroad Segment 2 is in the NW¼SE¼NE¼, the SW¼NW¼NE¼, and the SE¼NW¼NE¼ of Section 5, in Township 12 North, Range 1 East on the USGS Poland Junction, Arizona, 7.5 minute quadrangle. It lies between survey stations 3906+00 and 3918+00.

The average width of most of the grade is approximately 9 feet. To the north of the substation, the grade cuts into the hillside to a depth of 4-8 feet. South of the substation, the grade cuts through schist bedrock to a depth of approximately 25 feet. Cinder ballast was deposited on the grade throughout this section. The grade is not visible at the substation and appears to have been obliterated during the rebuilding of that facility in 1969.

The number "318" in black paint appears on an exposure in the rock cut south of the substation. The investigators could not determine the significance of this number. It did not appear to relate to any locomotive engine number that traveled these rails. Two railroad ties found in situ along the southern portion of the grade appeared to have been milled out of fir posts cut into 8-foot lengths. One of the ties measured 7 × 6 inches in cross section and the other measured 8 × 6 inches. The only other artifact in direct association with Segment 2 was a fragment of a 5-gallon barrel or drum of sheet metal found on the southern grade portion.

Figure 12.8. Railroad Segment 1; view northwest.

Figure 12.9. Railroad Segment 1, wooden box culvert.

Railroad Segment 3

Segment 3 is approximately 0.3 mile north of Segment 2 on the west side of SR 69 (Figure 12.2) on private and Bureau of Land Management (BLM) land. It is between survey stations 3930+00 and 3951+00 in the E½SE¼SE¼ of Section 32 and the E½SW¼ of Section 33 in Township 13 North, Range 1 East on the USGS Poland Junction, Arizona, 7.5 minute quadrangle. The northern portion of this segment is within Site AZ N:11:23(ASM) (Huron Station; see Chapter 6).

The elevated grade, built of local sand and gravel, is 6 feet above the ground surface on the eastern side of the grade and 3–4 feet above the ground surface on the western side of the grade. The top of the grade is approximately 8-1/2 feet wide.

Segment 3 has four associated features: the remnants of a wooden trestle, a box culvert, and two retaining walls. All that remains of the trestle are the truncated posts of its framework (Figure 12.10). The framework consisted of six rows of posts, each 16 feet long and spaced 12 feet apart. Five of the extant rows contain six posts, while the sixth row has five posts. The average diameter of the posts is 12–14 inches, and the spacing between the posts within each row averages approximately 3 feet. It is evident that the posts were treated with creosote or another preservative. Most of the posts protrude approximately 2 feet above the ground surface, the height at which they were truncated when the railway removed the trestle for safety reasons. The posts on the east side of the drainage average 5–8 feet in height. Hathaway (1992:60) suggested that this trestle was originally 80 feet long, 29 feet wide, and 18 feet high. The present investigations supported this assessment.

The box culvert (Figure 12.11) is also in the southern portion of the segment. The 3 × 10-inch and 3 × 12-inch boards of which the culvert is constructed are joined by large (over 20d) wire nails. The aperture of the culvert is 24-1/2 inches wide by 12-1/2 inches high. Like the box culvert on Segment 1, this feature is in a good state of preservation. Several nails stamped with the number "25" observed in a few of the boards may refer to 1925, perhaps the year when this culvert was constructed.

The two retaining walls are free-standing structures of schist slabs. One of the walls is in the southern portion of the segment on the west side of the grade. This wall measures 20 feet long by 8 inches high; for most of its length it is two courses high. The second retaining wall is on the east side of the grade at the northern end of the segment, near Huron Station. This wall is 16 feet long, has an average height of 3-1/2 feet, and is generally three to four courses high.

Associated artifacts included a standard railroad spike and a decomposing iron tie plate with a flat dorsal surface and a ridged ventral surface. Rectangular holes in the plate suggested that spikes secured this device to railroad ties; the ventral ridges probably helped to hold it in place. Other artifacts observed along Segment 3 were a heavy-gauge rectangular wire frame (probably from a suitcase), a machine-made strand of barbed wire (post-1873), two pieces of aquamarine glass (from the lower, "petticoat" portion of an insulator, with "drip points" around the base), one thick fragment of aqua glass (probably from an early "export" beer bottle, ca. 1880–1920), and one SCA glass fragment (1880–1917).

Figure 12.10. Railroad Segment 3, remains of dismantled trestle; view southwest.

Figure 12.11. Railroad Segment 3, wooden box culvert.

Railroad Segment 4

This short railroad segment is on the west side of SR 69 approximately 1.3 miles north of Poland Junction and approximately 1 mile southeast of Galena Gulch. It curves around a southeast-facing hill base that merges into the impact zone and at this point enters the SR 69 ROW (Figure 12.2). This segment crosses BLM land between survey stations 3977+00 and 3987+00 within the NE¼NE¼NW¼NW¼ and NW¼NW¼NE¼ of Section 33 and the SW¼SW¼SE¼ of Section 28 in Township 13 North, Range 1 East on the USGS Poland Junction, Arizona, 7.5 minute quadrangle.

The surface of this segment is a ballast of local gravel and sand. The top of the grade is 10 feet wide and is 4 feet above the ground surface to the west and 10 feet above the ground surface to the east.

No associated features occur along this short segment. The most interesting artifact was an iron railway appliance that was likely a type of rail chair, a device for securing rails to ties. It was a mask-like cast-iron object with a central nose-like dome and two lateral rectangular "eyeholes" for securing the piece to ties with spikes. The object measured 6 × 7 inches and had the number "55" stamped in its base. Other metal artifacts included five standard railroad spikes, one piece of thin-gauge strap iron, and a 3-inch metal brad with tapered edge (probably designed for preventing end-splitting on ties).

Glass artifacts sparsely distributed along the segment included a brown bottle base manufactured by the Owens-Illinois Glass Company (ca. 1929–1955), one pale green bottle fragment, four thick brown beverage bottle fragments (probably from export or "short quart" beer bottles), and two thick aqua fragments (also probably from early beer or beverage bottles). The beer bottles from which these aqua shards derived were of a common type manufactured after 1873, when bottled beer became possible after pasteurization processes were refined. Such bottles held about 24–26 fluid ounces and typically had a length of 11-1/2 inches. This type of heavy beer bottle generally was not manufactured after the development of fully automatic bottle machines (patented in 1903 and common by the 1920s).

Railroad Segment 5

Railroad Segment 5 is above and to the west of SR 69, approximately 1.1 miles southwest of Humboldt (Figure 12.3), and follows the lower eastern slope of the undulating hills east of Galena Gulch. Historic Road Segment 7 lies directly below and to the east of this railroad segment and generally follows the same hillside contours as the railroad grade. The railroad segment crosses private land between survey stations 4037+00 and 4053+00 and is within the SW¼SW¼ of Section 22 in Township 13 North, Range 1 East on the USGS Poland Junction, Arizona, 7.5 minute quadrangle.

The northern portion of this elevated grade consists of a berm, composed of local gravel and sand, that averages 8 feet in width. The ground surface on the west (uphill) side of the grade lies approximately 10 feet below the top of the grade, and the ground surface on the east side of the grade is approximately 15 feet below the top of the grade. Continuing southward, the grade crosses a small drainage and then cuts through a schist outcrop. The prism formed by this cut is approximately 14 feet deep.

Within the northern end of Segment 5 are the remains of a box culvert constructed of 2 × 12–inch boards, presently visible only on the east side of the grade. South of this culvert is a structure of poured concrete that combines a culvert and a retaining wall (Figure 12.12). The date "1927" inscribed into the headwall of this feature probably indicates the year of its construction. Made by pouring concrete into 6-inch wooden forms, the structure required 12 pouring courses to complete. The upper (western) headwall is 6 feet long, 6 feet wide, and 2 feet thick. Support buttresses to either side of the retaining wall are approximately 7 feet long, 3-1/2 feet high where they join the headwall, and 1 foot thick. The aperture of the culvert is 3-1/2 feet in diameter and is lined with a piece of riveted and galvanized corrugated sheet metal.

A dry-laid schist retaining wall runs along the eastern side of Segment 5 near its southern end where it cuts through the schist outcrop (Figure 12.13). The wall is approximately 300 feet long, from four to seven courses high, and an average of 3 feet in height. Numerous initials and "love signs" have been carved into the rocks on either side of the cut: "PB + MMM," "BB +," "PT, RT, ET" (inscribed twice), "RUDY GOTA," "ZL + CT," "WM + MW 1958," "AB + G," and several hearts with piercing arrows. Hathaway (1992:59) noted the date "Sept. 23, 1909" engraved along the rock cut, but SWCA's field personnel did not relocate this inscription.

Artifacts observed along Segment 5 included a railroad tie measuring 8 feet in length and 6 × 4 inches in cross section with "80" or "08" stamped into one end. Four railroad spikes, a section of a 1/2-inch-diameter bolt with a square nut, a portion of a rail plate with a ridged ventral surface, a piece of galvanized corrugated sheet metal, and a piece of canvas-like woven material (perhaps a wick from a lantern) were also noted. Glass objects included a petticoat fragment from an aquamarine wire insulator (embossed "NG"), four brown glass fragments (probably from beer bottles), a crown-cap bottle finish (made by a technique developed after 1903), and one emerald glass fragment from a beverage bottle. Other artifacts were a tobacco snuff can lid embossed "COPENHAGEN SATISFIES" (manufactured circa 1937 to 1977) and several church-key-opened beer cans (ca. 1935 to the 1960s).

Railroad Segment 6

The southern end of this segment begins on the north side of the Iron King Mine road 0.4 mile southwest of Humboldt (Figure 12.4). Current SR 69 crosses and has obliterated the northern portion of this segment. Most of the segment is west of SR 69; east of the highway, a spur line formerly branched southeastward to the Humboldt Smelter. Segment 6 lies between survey stations 4090+00 and 4113+00 on private land within the NE¼NE¼NW¼ of Section 22 and the SE¼SE¼SW¼, the E½SW¼SE¼, and the SE¼NE¼SE¼ of Section 15 in Township 13 North, Range 1 East on the USGS Mayer and Humboldt, Arizona, 7.5 minute quadrangles.

Most of this segment consists of an immense berm, constructed of thousands of tons of local gravel and sand, that stretches across Chaparral Gulch (Figure 12.14). The berm is approximately 30 feet high; its top, capped by a sand and gravel ballast, is 9-1/2 feet wide.

A trestle, the remains of its framework still visible, once formed the central 70 feet of Segment 6. A wooden platform tied the trestle into the berm at each end (Figure 12.15). The platforms consisted of a row of at least 12 beams, measuring 4 × 12 inches in cross section, set perpendicularly into the berm in a row 18-1/2 feet wide. Spanning the bottom of the drainage were five rows of round (11-inch diameter) and rectangular (12 × 16–inch) posts. Many of the posts in the drainage had washed away, making it difficult to discern the number of timbers originally present in each of the five rows. One of the posts had

Figure 12.12. Railroad Segment 5, concrete retaining wall and culvert. Headwall is inscribed "1927."

Figure 12.13. Railroad Segment 5, cut through schist. Note dry-laid retaining wall in center.

Figure 12.14. Railroad Segment 6, berm of railroad grade; view south-southeast.

Figure 12.15. Railroad Segment 6, remains of trestle platform.

a crosspiece attached by a tie rod with a 3-inch octagonal nut. A date nail stamped "25" in one of the posts may indicate construction in 1925.

The best-preserved of four decomposing railroad ties found near the trestle was 8 feet long and 4 × 6-1/2 inches in cross section, with "P. 90" stamped on one end. West of the trestle were two more ties, each measuring 8 feet long and 6-1/2 × 8 inches in cross section. One of these ties had the inscription "B38" stamped on one end. Other artifacts noted included two railroad spikes, 14 SCA fragments from a pumpkin-seed whiskey flask (manufactured ca. 1880–1917), an aqua crown-cap finish (manufactured by a fully automatic bottle machine after 1903), two brown glass bottle fragments, and one milk-glass fragment (probably from a Mentholatum jar, dating ca. 1900–1952).

Railroad Segment 7

The northern end of this segment begins 0.2 mile south of Highway 168 in the town of Dewey (Figure 12.4). The segment parallels SR 69 on the east side of the highway, running in a northwest-southeast direction. Historic Road Segment 9 is directly east of the railroad grade and currently is used as an access road for residences and farms on the east side of SR 69. Segment 7 is on private land between survey stations 4170+00 and 4215+00 within the NW¼NW¼SW¼ and the SW¼SW¼NW¼ of Section 11 in Township 13 North, Range 1 East on the USGS Humboldt, Arizona, 7.5 minute quadrangle.

Distinguishing and recording Segment 7 was difficult. A power line had impacted much of the grade, and fruit trees had been planted along and across the northern portion, which had also been disced or mowed. In this portion of the segment, the grade averaged only 1-1/2–2 feet high on its eastern edge, and the western side was nearly level with the surrounding ground surface. The southern end of the segment was more prominent. In that portion, the grade stands approximately 3 feet above the surrounding ground surface, has an average width of approximately 17 feet, and has a ballast of local sand and gravel.

Segment 7 has no associated features but has a light scatter of modern trash on and around the grade and a few artifacts of historic age along the berm. Glass objects included 4 brown beer bottle fragments, 5 aqua bottle fragments (including a hand-applied finish made ca. 1892–1903), 1 brown press-molded piece with cross-hatching in relief, 3 clear glass fragments, and a few pieces of window glass. Several fragments of a stoneware rice bowl with a blue, hand-painted underglaze floral design may have been of Japanese origin. Fragments of several double-crimped sanitary cans also were present, and one railroad spike was embedded in nearby Road Segment 9.

Summary and Recommendations

The Prescott & Eastern Railway, represented in the project area by Segments 1 through 7, appears eligible for the National Register of Historic Places mainly for the information it has yielded regarding railroad technology and construction methods in the late nineteenth and early twentieth centuries, making it eligible under Criterion D. Although associated with a significant event or process in history, the railroad does not appear to be eligible under Criterion A; modern development has segmented the line, diminished its visual quality, and weakened its ability to convey a sense of the railroad's historic association.

During testing SWCA archaeologists documented the seven segments of railroad grade, their features, and their artifacts. Since additional archaeological work at these segments was unlikely to yield additional important information, SWCA did not recommend or conduct additional archaeological work at these segments during the data recovery phase of the SR 69 investigations.

THE PHOENIX (ROCK SPRINGS)–PRESCOTT HIGHWAY (SITES AZ N:8:30[ASM], AZ N:11:29[ASM]/AR-03-09-03-366, AZ N:12:27]ASM])

Management History

Nine historic road segments are within or immediately adjacent to the project area (Figures 12.1–12.4). Aerial photographs and highway construction plans indicate that these segments were once connected as part of the Phoenix (Rock Springs)–Prescott Highway (Hathaway 1992:62). The roadbed segments had previously been assigned three different ASM site numbers because of their locations in different quadrants, in conformance with ASM linear-site recordation policies. Macnider and Sawyer-Lang (1990) recorded road segments in the AZ N:12 quadrant. During the Class III inventory of SR 69 from Mayer to Dewey, Hathaway (1992) revisited the AZ N:12 segments and recorded additional segments in the AZ N:8 and N:11 quadrants, assigning numbers 1 through 9 (from south to north) to these roadbed segments. SWCA retained Hathaway's designations for the current study.

Some of the nine segments are still well-defined, in-use tracks; others are relatively subtle and are becoming obscured by erosion and vegetation. Hathaway (1992:66) noted that the nine segments along the project ROW, as well as several segments outside the ROW, appeared to retain archaeological integrity. He recommended that the ROW segments be avoided by construction, or subjected to an archaeological testing program if they were to be impacted.

During the testing phase, SWCA personnel documented the road segments by walking closely spaced (20-foot-wide) transects along the lengths of the segments and recording all features and artifacts. No artifacts were collected. The widths of the segments and associated features were measured in standard English units. Overview photographs were taken of each segment, and additional photographs were taken of accessory features such as retaining walls and culverts.

Historical Data

The Phoenix (Rock Springs)–Prescott Highway evolved from earlier wagon and stagecoach routes that linked Yavapai County with the Salt and Gila river valleys. State Route 69 evolved, in turn, from the Phoenix–Prescott Highway. A chronological overview of the development of transportation through this corridor follows.

The earliest known precursor of the Phoenix–Prescott Highway was an 1860s wagon road that connected Fort Whipple with Fort McDowell. The two military forts had been established by the United States government to protect miners and other settlers in the region from American Indian resistance to Euroamerican expansionism (Brandes 1960:75). Contemporaries sometimes referred to the wagon road as the "Woolsey Trail" after King Woolsey, the "Indian-fighter" who lived along the trail near present-day Dewey (Federal Writers' Project [FWP] 1940). The road was perilous. It was the scene of several hostile encounters between travelers and American Indians or, more often, between travelers and bandits, and it was difficult to negotiate where it emerged from the central plateau and descended to the lowland desert. At dangerous one-way grades where drivers awaited each other at turnouts, they sounded long tin horns to warn others of their presence: a long blast on the horn meant an approach, and two blasts signaled acknowledgment.

During the 1870s the Black Canyon Stage Line route along the Agua Fria valley followed most of the course of the older wagon road. As mining developed in the 1870s and 1880s, mule teams increasingly used the stage route to haul ore and goods to and from the mines. Numerous stage stops such as Agua Fria (present-day Dewey) and Big Bug (present-day Mayer) that were established along the stage route became the nuclei for small communities. A trip along the stage route was long and arduous. A Concord stagecoach leaving Prescott at six in the morning did not arrive in Phoenix until noon the following day.

The route of the Black Canyon Stage Line came to be called the Black Canyon Highway. In the first decades of the twentieth century, the highway was an unpaved, slow, tortuous road with little traffic; nonetheless, it was one of the main routes between the Yavapai County seat in Prescott and the territorial (later, state) capital in Phoenix.

As the Black Canyon Highway entered the automotive age, transportation along the road continued to move at a slow and leisurely pace by today's standards. When the Arizona State Highway Commission proposed a state highway system in 1927, the Black Canyon Highway was not among the routes thus designated (Cross, Shaw, and Scheifele 1960:223). Helen Swenson (1988:51), a long-time resident of Humboldt, described the road as a twisting, narrow, dirt road where travelers saw more deer and antelope than cars. She described a milk wagon that traveled daily between Humboldt and Dewey, noting that "people would bring their pitchers, bottles or pots and the milk was dipped up with a quart measuring pitcher and poured into the containers" (Swenson 1988:54). A Model T Ford with a bakery box bolted to the back and a pie rack on the running boards traveled the road twice a week. Customers would place their orders in their mailboxes in the morning; the baker would leave the desired items in the boxes and collect payment on his return trip. By 1940 a state travel guide (FWP 1940:303) described the route as a "maintained graveled road with many curves and steep grades; some sections very narrow. Limited accommodations; garages in Canon [Black Canyon] and Mayer."

The Black Canyon Highway entered the modern age in the mid 1950s when the State Highway Department (now ADOT) significantly improved the route. At that time, the road officially became the Rock Springs–Prescott Highway and was incorporated into the state highway system (Figure 12.16). A series of 1954 "As-Built" maps (ADOT 1954) document the improvements made by the state agency in cooperation with the federal government. Highway crews graded the route, straightened curves, erected road signs, and partially paved the surface (with mixed-in-place gravel as well as asphalt). The improvement project also regraded the route to eliminate many of the dips that posed an ever-present danger to motorists and erected culverts to prevent flooding in low areas. In earlier days of highway construction, roads simply followed the contour of the land. As a result, washes crossed the highway at intervals of half a mile or less; normally dry, these washes could carry considerable water after rains. The culverts were among the most costly items in the 1954 budget (Cross, Shaw, and Scheifele 1960:226)

Construction of modern SR 69 has obliterated much of the earlier road system that once passed through the project area. However, as the following sections indicate, nine segments of that system are still visible.

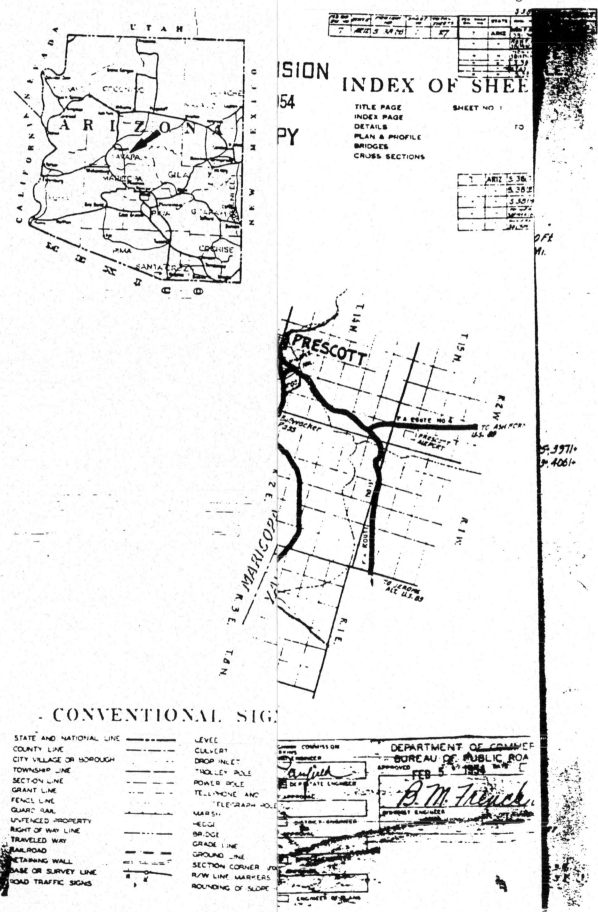

Figure 12.16. Route of Phoenix (Rock Springs

Archaeological Data

Road Segment 1

The southern end of this segment begins north of Mayer and proceeds northwestward along the west side of current SR 69 for approximately 0.8 mile (Figure 12.1). This segment is on a wide, southeast-trending ridge 0.3 mile east of Big Bug Creek. It traverses private and BLM land between survey stations 3738+00 and 3779+00 in the W½NE¼SW¼ of Section 22 and the SW¼SE¼SW¼ and W½SW¼ of Section 15 in Township 12 North, Range 1 East on the USGS Mayer and Poland Junction, Arizona, 7.5 minute quadrangles.

Most of this abandoned road segment is approximately 16 feet wide and less than 6 inches above the surrounding ground surface (Figure 12.17). Decomposing asphalt is present in many areas of the roadbed, especially in drainage areas where the asphalt was laid more heavily. Along most of this segment the asphalt appears to have been several inches thick, resting on a thin prepared bed of sand and gravel. Plant roots are rapidly breaking the asphalt, and sheetwash is eroding it away.

The single feature in Road Segment 1 is a poured concrete culvert (Figure 12.18), visible mainly on the east side of the segment. The headwall of this structure is 6-1/2 feet long, 3 feet high, and 1 foot wide. The circular aperture is 17 inches in diameter and has a riveted corrugated sheet-metal lining.

Artifacts observed along the segment include a Permaguard Antifreeze can (approximately 15 feet north of the road), a crushed coffee can, a sanitary can with the embossed partial word "ESTAB" on the lid, a one-pint oil can bearing the embossed words "GASITE OIL," a tin spout embossed "SIMPLEX" (perhaps from a large, rectangular oil can), a few wire nails, and several washers. In the south-central portion of the segment, a refuse concentration in a 10 × 10–foot area contains one press-molded SCA tableware fragment (perhaps from a vase), one aqua bottle fragment, 16 pieces of a brown beer bottle, a clear jar fragment (manufactured by the Owens-Illinois Bottling Company in 1954), and five sanitary church-key-opened beer cans (ca. 1935–1960s).

Road Segment 2

The southern end of Segment 2 begins on the eastern shoulder of SR 69 2.0 miles northwest of Mayer and immediately across SR 69 from the northern end of Road Segment 1 (Figures 12.1 and 12.2). Obviously a continuation of Road Segment 1 to the west of the highway, Road Segment 2 parallels the east side of SR 69 in a northwesterly direction for a distance of 1.75 miles, crossing private land and land administered by the BLM and the Arizona State Land Department. The segment follows a long southwest-facing ridge approximately 0.5 mile east of Big Bug Creek. The chaparral-covered rangeland has relatively low topographic relief. The segment is between survey stations 3778+00 and 3867+00 in the W½SW¼ and NW¼ of Section 15, the E½NE¼ and NE¼ of Section 16, and the NE¼E½NW¼ of Section 9 in Township 12 North, Range 1 East on the USGS Poland Junction, Arizona 7.5 minute quadrangle.

Several residences are to the east of this segment. While scouting the northern portion of the segment, a young man with a high-powered rifle accosted the SWCA crew. Apparently the northern end of this segment had become an access road to one of the private residences on the east side of SR 69 (the young

Figure 12.17. Road Segment 1; view south.

Figure 12.18. Road Segment 1, concrete culvert.

man emerged from this residence). Because of his extremely aggressive behavior, the crew aborted further work on this segment. There is no reason to assume that the intact portions of this segment differ substantially from Road Segment 1, of which it is a continuation. Hathaway (1992:64) reported that portions of Segment 2 were paved with asphalt, and he did not locate any features.

Road Segment 3

The southern end of this segment begins on the west side of SR 69 opposite the northern end of Segment 2, where the historic roadbed veers to the northwest and has been cut by the SR 69 ROW (Figure 12.2). This short segment is on the same southwestern-facing ridge system as Segments 1 and 2 and is a continuation of those segments. Its northern end terminates at the point where it passes out of the project area. Historically the road probably continued to Poland Junction, 0.5 mile to the north, and connected with what is now the southern end of Road Segment 4. Segment 3 crosses private land between survey stations 3867+00 and 3872+00 and is in the SE¼SW¼SW¼ of Section 4 in Township 12 North, Range 1 East on the USGS Poland Junction, Arizona, 7.5 minute quadrangle.

Segment 3 is subtle and distinguishable primarily by its lack of vegetation. The road surface is generally level with the surrounding ground surface and is approximately 16 feet wide. No structural features such as ditches or culverts occur along the segment, nor are there visible traces of asphalt. The only cultural material observed was a single piece of modern sheet aluminum.

Road Segment 4

The southern end of Road Segment 4 begins directly north of Poland Junction on the west side of SR 69, arcs to the northwest for approximately 300 feet, curves back to the northeast for an additional 300 feet, and terminates at the western shoulder of SR 69 (Figure 12.2). It is on the western slope of a low hill and follows the hill's general contours. This segment crosses land administered by the Prescott National Forest between survey stations 3895+00 and 3916+00 in the NE¼NW¼SE¼NE¼ and SE¼SW¼NE¼NE¼ of Section 5 in Township 12 North, Range 1 East on the USGS Poland Junction, Arizona, 7.5 minute quadrangle.

Segment 4 is approximately 11 feet wide, but the edges have experienced erosion (Figure 12.19). The eastern side of the road cuts into the hill; the fill was used to level the western side. No evidence of asphalt or other road-surfacing material was visible along this segment.

One culvert and three retaining walls are associated with Segment 4. The poured-concrete culvert is in a drainage in the southern portion of the segment. Loosely stacked schist rocks at either end of the structure probably provided reinforcement (Figure 12.20). The culvert is 7-1/2 feet high by 22-1/2 feet long and its headwall is 1 foot thick. The aperture measures 17-1/2 inches in diameter and is lined with a riveted circular piece of corrugated sheet metal. Northwest of the culvert is a poured-concrete retaining wall measuring 7-1/2 feet long, 1 foot wide, and 2 feet high. On the east side of the road segment across from the concrete retaining wall is a dry-laid retaining wall of schist slabs stacked three courses (1 foot) high. This wall is 13 feet long. Nearly 300 feet north of these features and on the west side of the segment is another retaining wall made of dry-laid schist slabs; this one is approximately 50 feet long and from five to seven courses (4-1/2 feet) high.

Figure 12.19. Road Segment 4; view north.

Figure 12.20. Road Segment 4, concrete culvert with rock reinforcement.

Artifacts noted along this segment include two bundles of baling wire, two pieces of thin-gauge strap metal, a plastic plate fragment, a church-key-opened can, and a nearly complete SCA glass pumpkin-seed whiskey flask with an applied double-ring finish. The plastic and the can suggest a twentieth-century association; the flask was likely made in the late nineteenth or early twentieth century.

Road Segment 5

Road Segment 5 is on the east side of SR 69. It begins approximately 0.8 mile northeast of Poland Junction and continues in a northeasterly direction parallel to SR 69 for a distance of 0.2 mile. This segment is on private land between survey stations 3950+00 and 3964+00 in the NW¼NE¼SW¼ and SW¼NW¼ of Section 33 in Township 13 North, Range 1 East on the USGS Poland Junction, Arizona, 7.5 minute quadrangle.

The average width of the roadbed is 10 feet. The surface of the road is slightly below the surrounding ground level, with shallow ditches excavated along both sides of the northern end. There is no evidence of asphalt or other surfacing material.

One poorly preserved feature of indeterminate function along Segment 5 consists of two sections of masonry wall. The sections are 22-1/2 feet apart, on opposite sides of a small drainage. The larger wall section is 7 feet long, 40 inches wide, and 10 inches thick; the smaller wall is too fragmentary for accurate measurement. Wire nails associated with these wall sections suggest that the walls were support pillars for a small wooden bridge that once spanned the drainage.

Artifacts noted along this roadbed included several lengths of galvanized hog wire, a tire tread, a possible chain guard for an early motorcycle or bicycle, and miscellaneous pieces of sheet metal. Other isolated artifacts included several sanitary fruit or vegetable cans, a score-strip meat-can top embossed with "ESTAB," a small fuel can with a continuous-thread cap, a hard-paste earthenware plate fragment, and a 7-Up soda bottle (manufactured in Clifton, Arizona, in 1947). A trash concentration on the east side of the roadbed in the southern portion of the segment included the base of a brown Duraglas Clorox jug (post-1940), a clear bottle finish with a continuous-thread closure, 12 sanitary fruit or vegetable cans, several coffee cans, and a rectangular 1-gallon fuel can.

Road Segment 6

Road Segment 6 begins 1.4 miles northeast of Poland Junction on the east side of SR 69, veers to the east, then rejoins SR 69 1.1 miles to the northeast (Figure 12.2). This segment traverses private land and is between survey stations 3985+00 and 4035+00 in the SE¼ of Section 28 and the W½NW¼SW¼ and W½NW¼ of Section 27 in Township 13 North, Range 1 East on the USGS Poland Junction, Arizona, 7.5 minute quadrangle.

Segment 6 is approximately 10-1/2 feet wide and slightly below the surrounding ground surface. Decomposing asphalt fragments indicate that portions of this segment were paved. The tracks of off-road vehicles help define the roadbed. The southern end of this segment has been disturbed by the construction of a pipeline, a transmission line, and a fiber optic line. Dumping of modern trash is evident as well. A dirt track leading to the Montezuma mining claim branches southeast from the central portion of the segment; close to this track was a 2 × 2-inch orange stake with an attached metal tag stamped "MONTEZUMA / DM."

This segment has no associated features. Metal artifacts within the roadbed or adjacent to it include many wire nails, a metal plate with "LOC MC 82" embossed on its base, a spice-can top, a hole-in-cap can lid with four holes punched in it, a hinged tobacco tin lid, and a 5-lb coffee can. At least 50 sanitary cans were close to the segment, and many more were in the general vicinity. Glass items included six SCA fragments, one of them a piece from the base of a pumpkin-seed whiskey flask (1880–1917), several jars manufactured by Duraglas (post-1940), and one brown jar base manufactured by the Owens-Illinois Glass Company in 1945.

Road Segment 7

The southern end of Road Segment 7 is 1.5 miles south of Humboldt on the west shoulder of SR 69 (Figure 12.3). Continuing northward, the segment veers slightly away from SR 69 to the west, then curves toward the highway again around the base of a small hill. Directly west of Road Segment 7 is abandoned Railroad Segment 5. Road Segment 7 is on private land between survey stations 4045+00 and 4070+00 and is within the E½SW¼SW¼ and SE¼NW¼SW¼ of Section 22 in Township 13 North, Range 1 East on the USGS Poland Junction, Arizona, 7.5 minute quadrangle.

Road Segment 7 is approximately 19 feet wide and 1/4 mile long. The central 190 feet of the segment cut through a schist outcrop. The prism of this cut is 3 feet deep on its uphill (eastern) side. The schist excavated from the cut is the material used to construct a dry-laid retaining wall, four to five courses (3 feet) high, on the downhill (western) side of the road. Artifacts observed along this segment consisted of two brown glass bottle fragments (one embossed "X / NET CONTENTS 11 OZ"), a crushed sanitary milk can, and a red brick measuring 7 × 3-1/4 × 2-1/4 inches.

Road Segment 8

Road Segment 8 is on the west side of SR 69 approximately 0.5 mile southwest of Humboldt (Figure 12.3). The former railroad spur and the automobile road to the Iron King Mine are approximately 0.2 mile north of the northern end of this 500-foot segment. The segment traverses private land and is between survey stations 4080+00 and 4087+00 in the N½NE¼SE¼NW¼ of Section 22 in Township 13 North, Range 1 East on the USGS Mayer, Arizona, 7.5 minute quadrangle.

The segment has an average width of 27 feet. The grade was made by cutting its uphill (western) side from an adjacent slope and filling its downhill (eastern) side with the excavated material. The downhill side consequently stands approximately 3 feet above the surrounding ground surface. The absence of asphalt and other surfacing material suggests that this segment was never paved. Dense vegetation currently grows across part of this segment (Figure 12.21).

Segment 8 has no associated features but has a relatively large number of scattered artifacts. The most interesting item was a globe-shaped oil-burning signal light with the embossed words "SIG-NA-LITE / THE TOLEDO PRESSED STEEL CO. / TOLEDO. O. USA" and a circular ring soldered onto it. The light appeared to have originally been painted black and may have been a roadside warning device.

Figure 12.21. Road Segment 8; view south-southeast.

Other artifacts included a piece of sheet metal, a coupling device made of hog wire, a single barrel hoop, an oil filter, a crushed evaporated milk can embossed "PUNCH HERE" (made ca. 1935–1945), a cone-top beverage can (ca. 1935–1950s), 11 crushed double-crimped sanitary cans, several sanitary beverage cans opened with church keys, a crushed 1-lb sanitary coffee can, an oval fish can embossed "NORWAY," 25 brown beverage bottle fragments, and a sherd of white hard-paste earthenware.

Road Segment 9

The northern terminus of Road Segment 9 is approximately 0.2 mile south of State Highway 169 in Dewey (Figure 12.4). The segment is on the east side of SR 69, parallel with the highway, and is 0.5 mile long. Railroad Segment 7 lies between SR 69 and the road segment. The field crew could not determine the width or other attributes of the historic road because it lies beneath a well-used and well-maintained 17-foot-wide access road (Figure 12.22). Road Segment 9 is on private land between survey stations 4170+00 and 4215+00 in the NW¼NW¼SW¼ and the SW¼SW¼NW¼ of Section 11 in Township 13 North, Range 1 East on the USGS Humboldt, Arizona, 7.5 minute quadrangle.

A great deal of modern dumping has occurred in this area. The only artifact of historic age observed along this segment was a standard railroad spike embedded in the road.

Figure 12.22. Road Segment 9; view north-northwest.

Summary and Recommendations

The Phoenix (Rock Springs)–Prescott/Black Canyon Highway, represented in the project area by Road Segments 1–9, appears eligible for the National Register of Historic Places under Criterion D mainly for the information it has yielded regarding road construction methods from the early to the mid-twentieth century. Although associated with a significant event or process in history (automotive transportation from the early to the mid-twentieth century), the road does not appear to be eligible under Criterion A; modern development has segmented the old road, diminished its visual quality, and weakened its ability to convey a sense of the property's historic association.

During testing SWCA archaeologists documented nine segments of the road, their features, and their artifacts. Since additional significant information from these segments was unlikely, SWCA did not recommend or conduct additional archaeological work during the data recovery phase.

OTHER ROAD SEGMENTS
(SITE AZ N:11:27[ASM]/AR-03-09-03-364)

Management History

Several discontinuous short road segments are in a small area approximately 0.2 mile north of Poland Junction (Figure 12.2). The segments begin north of Road Segment 4 and Railroad Segment 2, yet do not appear to relate to either of these historic properties. They are in a low area that is bisected by a northeast-trending drainage and are in an extremely poor state of preservation, having been severely eroded by the drainage. The segments lie on BLM and Prescott National Forest land between survey Stations 3915+00 and 39+00 in the W½NE½NE¼ of Section 5 in Township 12 North, Range 1 East, and the W½SW¼SW¼ of Section 33 in Township 13 North, Range 1 East on the USGS Poland Junction, Arizona, 7.5 minute quadrangle.

Hathaway (1992) first recorded these road segments during the Archaeological Research Services, Inc., (ARS) Class III inventory of the SR 69 Mayer to Dewey segment. The ARS surveyors recorded four short, more-or-less parallel road segments (designated A through D) and hypothesized that they were segments of an early roadway between Mayer and Dewey; however, archival records shed no light on the identity of these segments. The Class III survey report (Hathaway 1992:67–68) recommended that these resources be considered potentially eligible for the National Register based on their potential to yield information pertaining to transportation in the late nineteenth and early twentieth centuries in central Arizona. The report also recommended that the segments be avoided, or subjected to an archaeological testing program to further assess their Register eligibility.

ADOT engineers determined that construction would impact most of these road segments, and agency staff stipulated that the testing phase for the SR 69 project was to include the documentation of this resource. SWCA's documentation methods consisted of conducting archival research, walking closely spaced (20-foot-wide) transects through the site, and taking photographs, notes, and measurements.

Historical Data

In spite of careful archival research, SWCA personnel were not able to determine the historic context of these road segments. Examination of historical records, including historical maps, produced negative results. The segments did not correspond with any abandoned road segments noted on the "As-Built" highway construction plans (ADOT 1954), nor did they match the locations of roads shown on General Land Office or other historic maps. While it is possible (as Hathaway [1992:67] suggested) that the segments represent an early route between Mayer and Dewey (such as the Fort McDowell–Fort Whipple wagon road or the Black Canyon stagecoach route), research produced no direct evidence for this hypothesis. Another possibility, also neither proven nor refuted by the historical data, is that these segments were sections of roads that led from Poland Junction to the Poland Mine or to other nearby mines. A third possibility is that these roads were associated with the construction or maintenance of the Poland Substation or its power lines.

Archaeological Data

These road segments were so ephemeral and in such a poor state of preservation (because of erosion) that they were difficult to discern. In general, however, SWCA field personnel concurred with Hathaway's (1992) assessment that Site AZ N:11:27(ASM)/AR-03-09-03-364 consisted of four discontinuous unpaved road beds. Segment A was 600 feet long by 10 feet wide. Four dry-laid retaining walls along its western (downhill) side measured 10, 30, 30, and 12 feet long and crossed drainages, suggesting a check-dam/erosion-control function. Segment B was 750 feet long by 12–15 feet wide; in some places cobble alignments lined the road, as if to retain soil. Segment C consisted of three adjacent road segments ranging from 255 feet to 375 feet long and from 9 feet to 15 feet wide. The three segments paralleled one another and followed the contours of a slope; between two of the sections defining this segment was a 26-foot schist retaining wall. Segment D was 12–15 feet wide and approximately 1200 feet long.

Artifacts were extremely sparse and provided little insight into the date of the site or its various segments. Sheetwash had impacted virtually the entire area; the few artifacts observed were likely the result of redeposition. The artifacts consisted of an SCA glass bottle bearing a basemark of either the Adolphus Busch Glass Manufacturing Company (ca. 1904 to 1907) or the American Bottle Company (1905–1929), a tire-patch tool, and numerous fragments of modern brown beer bottles.

At the conclusion of fieldwork, the SWCA researchers' overall impression of the site was that its maze of roads represents a single transportation system that has washed out and been rebuilt numerous times. Extensive erosion has impacted the site area in modern times and appears to have done so in the past as well. The parallel nature of the segments, the obvious efforts to build check-dams along them, and their present eroded state all suggested that the builders of these segments ultimately waged a losing battle against nature.

Summary and Recommendations

Intensive archival research failed to identify Site AZ N:11:27(ASM)/AR-03-09-03-364 or to establish its historic context. The site has experienced extensive erosion and is in a poor state of preservation. The extremely sparse artifacts present appear to be the result of redeposition. The site appears to lack any qualities that would render it eligible for the National Register of Historic Places. Since the survey and testing programs documented the site, and it was unlikely that important information would come from the site in the future, SWCA did not recommend or conduct additional archaeological work at the site during data recovery.

CHAPTER 13

CONCLUSIONS

Pat H. Stein

SWCA, Inc., Environmental Consultants, conducted archaeological investigations for historic sites along State Route 69 between Mayer and Dewey, Yavapai County, Arizona, in accordance with clear management objectives and research goals (outlined in Chapter 2). SWCA researchers examined a total of 12 historic sites, consisting of three linear and nine nonlinear properties, in the testing phase of the investigations and excavated two of the nonlinear sites during data recovery. The final chapter of this report integrates data from both phases to summarize what was learned about the project area.

SWCA's research design for the SR 69 archaeological investigations proposed to investigate the sites in the context of three thematic categories from the Prescott National Forest's overview: Demography, Technology and Industry, and Transportation and Communication. Data from this study addressed all three of these issues.

FINDINGS RELATED TO DEMOGRAPHY

Archival and archaeological data from the SR 69 sites provided glimpses of the melting pot that characterized the Mayer-Dewey area in the late nineteenth and early twentieth centuries. Site AZ N:12:40(ASM), on the outskirts of Mayer, contained the remains of a type of Yavapai shelter called an *awah 'puunvah*. A fragment from a ceramic jar that probably once contained a sauce (such as soy sauce) or a liquor known as *Ng Ky Py* indicated contact with Chinese people. A group of three Hispanic and three Euroamerican miners had originally claimed a portion of one of the mining sites (the Montezuma portion of Site AZ N:11:23[ASM]), suggesting some measure of cooperation between the two ethnic groups. The remainder of the sites in the project area were of Euroamerican origin.

An interesting finding of the study was that ethnicity was sometimes expressed in the archaeological data set from a site but not in archival data. The converse was also sometimes true. For example, the archaeological profile of Site AZ N:12:40(ASM)—with its "killed" vessels, milling stones, and *awah 'puunvah* remains—was distinctly Yavapai, yet no archival records directly indicated this important aspect of the site. Conversely, the Hispanic affiliation of the Montezuma portion of Site AZ N:11:23(ASM) was reflected in the archival data but not in the archaeological data set. Similarly, although archival records indicated that Greek and Italian workers built the Prescott & Eastern Railway (Sites AZ N:7:44, N:8:29, N:11:28, and N:12:41[ASM]), nothing in the archaeological record reflected this aspect of the railroad's history. These findings underscored the importance of looking at both types of data when studying historical-archaeological properties.

The investigations revealed demographic diversity even among the Euroamerican sites. Archival data indicated that the persons associated with these sites came from far-flung areas. William Murphy, a homesteader associated with Site AZ N:12:39(ASM), was an Irishman who had escaped his native country's potato famine. Charles P. Wingfield, an entrepreneur associated with Sites AZ N:11:20(ASM) and AZ N:11:23(ASM), was born in Arkansas and lived in the Verde Valley of Arizona before moving to the Mayer-Dewey area when he found a job with the Prescott & Eastern Railway. George Hull, a mining magnate associated with Site AZ N:11:23(ASM), was born in Massachusetts but found his fortune in the West. Frank Nester, a saloon keeper and miner associated with Site AZ N:11:23(ASM), was a native of Michigan. The three persons associated with Site AZ N:11:19(ASM)—Mary Van Patten, Ezekiel Van Patten, and John Nelson—originally hailed from Ohio, New York, and Sweden, respectively. George Treadwell, the industrialist who developed the Treadwell Smelter, Site AZ N:12:30(ASM), was from San Francisco. H. A. Wagner, who developed and operated the Gray Eagle Reduction/Mayer Custom Plant, Site AZ N:12:39 (ASM), was from Chicago. And John Martin, a homesteader associated with the land on which Site AZ N:12:40(ASM) was located, was a native of Tennessee who moved to the Mayer area before the turn of the century. These findings revealed the attractiveness of the Mayer-Dewey area to people from different places of origin and walks of life. The findings also suggested the factors—opportunities in mining, agriculture (homesteading), and transportation (railroading)—that attracted people to the area in historic times.

Although westerners as well as easterners were drawn to the Mayer-Dewey area, their love affairs with the project area were not, as a rule, long-lasting. Most sites in the project area were occupied or used for short periods of time, although not *unusually* short periods by Arizona standards. Mining *claim* sites (such as AZ N:11:19, AZ N:11:20, and part of AZ N:11:23[ASM]) for both placer and lode claims were relatively short lived; from test data, it would appear that these sites never matched their owners' expectations of productivity and were abandoned or sold shortly after being located. Two sites in the project area (AZ N:12:39 and AZ N:12:40[ASM]) had been the scene of homesteading activity; in the first case, the homestead was sold to industrialists shortly after patenting and the death of its owner, but in the latter case, the homesteader retained his property (patented in 1920) through the rest of the historic period. The two mining *plant* sites in the project area were relatively short lived as well, although they did experience multiple episodes of utilization and reuse. The Treadwell Smelter (Site AZ N:12:30[ASM]), constructed at Mayer in 1902, was reincarnated as the Great Western Smelter in 1916–1917, but then permanently closed in late 1917. The Gray Eagle Reduction Plant (Site AZ N:12:39[ASM]), built at Mayer in 1915–1916, enjoyed new life as the Mayer Custom Plant in 1917 before closing in 1919. Linear resources such as the Prescott & Eastern Railway and the Phoenix (Rock Springs)–Prescott Highway enjoyed longer lives spanning several decades, although the real heyday of the railroad occurred during a relatively brief period, circa 1898–1910.

Investigations at Site AZ N:11:23(ASM) provided insights into the factors that caused local populations to grow and decline. Huron Station, founded as a stop along the Prescott & Eastern Railway in 1898, took on a life of its own, existing mainly to provide a variety of goods and services to outlying mines and mining camps, especially the McCabe Mine. Some of the services provided were telegraph and telephone lines, freighting, a Wells Fargo office, and blacksmithing. From the Wingfields' store and Nester's saloon, Huron also offered a variety of goods and libations. But as the outlying mines' fortunes declined after 1907, Huron's prospects faded. Despite a brief resurgence during World War I, the community witnessed a period of depopulation in the 1910s from which it never recovered. After World War I, Huron Station was essentially a ghost town.

The longest-used site in the project area was the Poland Junction Substation (Site AR-03-09-03-238), constructed in 1909 or 1910 and still active today. The key to its longevity lies in the fact that it provided a commodity—electricity—that is just as essential today as it was in the early twentieth century. Its long period of use is also due to the fact that the facility has been able to adapt to change as the technology for delivering power to customers has evolved. However, as the investigations indicated, site longevity (the continuing contribution of a property to history) is no guarantee of eligibility for the National Register of

Historic Places. The Poland Junction Substation has been modernized and modified so extensively that it has lost its historic integrity and therefore any potential for National Register eligibility.

The investigations provided some insight into the gender and age characteristics of persons associated with various sites. Women did not have a strong presence in either the archival or the archaeological data sets for the project area sites. Archival records suggested strong associations with women for only two sites (AZ N:11:19[ASM] and the Montezuma portion of AZ N:11:23[ASM]). In both cases, the women located or helped to locate mining claims but did not hold their claims for long. In terms of the archaeology of all the sites, women were almost invisible; that is, few artifacts associated strongly and specifically with women were found. The absence of female-diagnostic artifacts does not mean, however, that women were absent from the sites. Five sites yielded a few objects associated with children: AZ N:11:19, AZ N:11:23, AZ N:11:25, AZ N:12:29, and AZ N:12:40(ASM).

Within the theme of demography, SWCA researchers hoped to study the issue of the acculturation of American Indians into Euroamerican society and were able to address this issue using data from the Yavapai *awah 'puunvah* site, AZ N:12:40(ASM). Information from the site indicated an interesting blend of native and non-native material culture dating to the early twentieth century. At the "traditional" end of the cultural spectrum, the inhabitant(s) of the site lived in a traditional brush structure, used grinding stones, and followed tribal customs that included the deliberate "killing" of two vessels. At the "modern" end of the spectrum, these occupants used Euroamerican enamelware wash basins that were the objects for the "killing," cooked in a Dutch oven, ate on Euroamerican cups and plates, played a harmonica, and traveled by horse and wagon. To some degree, the occupants ate canned foods; the extent to which they relied on wild plants and animals could not be determined. The 12-gauge shotgun, jackknives, and grinding stones they possessed certainly could have been used to procure and process traditional foods. The level of acculturation reflected by material remains at AZ N:12:40(ASM) strongly resembled that noted by Teague (1980) at contemporaneous American Indian sites in southern Arizona and by Keller and Stein (1985) at Yavapai sites in Prescott.

FINDINGS RELATED TO TECHNOLOGY AND INDUSTRY

The SR 69 investigations provided a great deal of information pertaining to the industry of mining. The information obtained through testing revealed how mines and mining plants were organized, how the tasks of mineral exploration and processing were phased, what equipment was used, and how technologies differed through time and among sites.

Mineral extraction and prospecting took place at the Bay View Placer site (AZ N:11:19[ASM]), the Princes Placer site (AZ N:11:20[ASM]), the Montezuma and the Eagle Fraction claims at the Huron Station site (AZ N:11:23[ASM]), and the Smelter Placer at the Treadwell/Great Western Smelter site (AZ N:12:30[ASM]). These five mining claims were located in 1900, 1898, 1898, 1909, and 1904, respectively. Four of them eventually went to patent; the fifth (Bay View) never did. Site AZ N:11:25(ASM) may also have been related to mineral extraction, although the evidence was not clear.

Prospectors sought different minerals in the region. Two placer claims on Post Office Gulch and a third along Big Bug Creek were valued initially for the gold they were suspected to contain. The two lode claims at Huron Stations were believed to hold not only gold but silver and copper as well. Archival records, particularly those of the Arizona Department of Mines and Mineral Resources, indicated that none of these claims was notably productive. They contained low-grade ores that needed massive capitalization to develop. The only claims that indeed attracted "massive capitalists" were the Eagle Fraction and Montezuma properties, acquired by George "Make-a-Million" Hull in 1910 and 1911, and the Smelter Placer, located by George Treadwell in 1904. Hull became embroiled in controversy surrounding his Jerome mines and died before his dream of developing the Huron properties could be realized. Treadwell lost interest in the Smelter Placer when his namesake smelter floundered in 1906. In summary, lode claims fared no better than placer claims in the project area, and both fared rather poorly indeed.

In addition to mineral-extraction sites, the project area contained two mineral-processing sites: the Treadwell/Great Western Smelter [AZ N:12:30(ASM)] and the Gray Eagle Reduction/Mayer Custom Plant [AZ N:12:39(ASM)]. Owners of both facilities hoped to be able to efficiently handle the low-grade ores of the region by incorporating state-of-the-art technologies and upgrading their equipment to provide better service to customers. The Gray Eagle Reduction/Mayer Custom Plant in particular employed innovative technology to attempt to process low-grade ores bearing all types of metals. For a variety of reasons, including mechanical difficulties, the inability to secure adequate shipments of ore, the ending of World War I, and corporate turmoil, both facilities ultimately failed, and their impact on the economic development of the Mayer-Dewey area was short and negligible.

The project area also contained two properties that provided the *infrastructure* for mining: the Prescott & Eastern Railway and the Poland Junction Substation. These sites played vital roles in the local mining industry. The railroad, built in 1898, opened new markets for local ores and made the rapid and economical transportation of ores possible. The substation, constructed in 1909–1910, provided electrical power to run machinery cheaply and permit deeper excavation in search of new mineral wealth.

The important roles of the railroad and substation in the local mining industry provide insight into a concept that might be called "the miner's equation." A multitude of factors fed into the miner's equation, the mental calculation by a miner of many factors to determine if a particular mining property might be successful or unsuccessful. Archival sources such as *Yavapai Magazine* indicate that Yavapai County miners (like other miners of the West) were risk-takers who usually trod a fine line between profitability and financial ruin. They were ever-mindful of the "cut-off point," the point below which it became impossible to run a mine profitably. Any number of factors—the arrival of a good means of transportation, the development of a new technology, the delivery of electrical power, a decrease in labor costs, the discovery of a valuable new mineral vein—could raise the cut-off point and make a previously unprofitable mine profitable.

FINDINGS RELATED TO TRANSPORTATION AND COMMUNICATION

From linear resources in the project area, SWCA researchers assembled an interesting and valuable body of information regarding historic railroad and highway construction methods and materials. Previous writers (such as Sayre 1985) had provided much information about the history of the Prescott & Eastern Railway but little information about its material culture. Documentation of sections of the railroad (as well as sections of historic roads) during the present investigations thus began to provide insight into a neglected aspect of history.

A surprising finding of the investigations was that some of the features along the railroad were apparently built long after the heyday of the rail line. With a decline in mining around 1910, the railroad witnessed a decrease in activity. Transportation services increased during World War I but then declined again at the end of the war. Therefore, it was surprising that various trestles and culverts along Segments 3, 5, and 6 bore inscriptions or date nails suggesting construction activities in 1925 and 1927. In the 1920s few mines in the area were operating; the Iron King, McCabe, and Arizona National mines were among them. Information collected during the investigations would suggest that mining along the project area was substantial enough in the 1920s to warrant the maintenance and improvement of the Prescott & Eastern line. It is also possible that other types of customers developed in this decade, such as livestock shippers, warranting the continued use of the line. The data also suggest that features originally built along the line in 1898 may have had less than 30-year life spans and needed to be replaced by the mid 1920s.

In developing research goals for the SR 69 project, SWCA researchers hoped to test the notion that railroads and roads were agents of culture change. Using archival records and historic artifacts, SWCA proposed to date each historic site closely and tightly and to compare pre-railroad and post-railroad sites. If the data did not allow a division of sites along this temporal scale, then SWCA proposed to compare pre-automotive and post-automotive sites. The hypothesis to be tested was that artifact diversity would increase and supply networks would expand as transportation systems were improved.

In analyzing the archival and archaeological data, SWCA archaeologists determined that none of the sites in the project area clearly dated to the pre-railroad era (that is, to the period before 1898). Most of the sites had been settled in the decade following the arrival of the iron horse. This fact was itself interesting, for it suggested a direct relationship between the arrival of the Prescott & Eastern Railway and the development of the surrounding countryside. Specifically, it suggested that the railroad played a catalytic role in drawing a variety of people—homesteaders, miners, merchants, and entrepreneurs—to the area. Finding that the study area lacked pre-railroad sites, the researchers then attempted to test the culture-change hypothesis in association with the presence of automobiles. However, the historical literature of the area indicated that this could not reliably be done, as the horseless carriage was introduced to the area very gradually beginning around the turn of the century (Rodda 1993). The automobile was essentially a rich man's toy for the first decade of the twentieth century; it grew in popularity in the 1910s and became the most popular means of conveyance in the 1920s. A meaningful division of the sites into pre-automotive and post-automotive categories was thus not possible either.

The investigations did provide a revealing look at a train station along the Prescott & Eastern Railway. Excavation of Site AZ N:11:23(ASM), Huron Station, provided the opportunity to learn specific details about the buildings and structures that comprised the station and to understand how the work space was organized to accommodate various activities. Detailed archival work succeeded in locating a rare historical map and photograph of the facility. Archaeological work, combined with historical research, produced the surprising finding that the Huron saloon was located within the train depot, a rare arrangement indeed among stations along the Prescott & Eastern and Bradshaw Mountain railways. Investigations at the station also identified a previously undocumented but undoubtedly important activity there, blacksmithing.

Mining activity comprises an important part of our state's heritage; the quest for mineral wealth continues in contemporary Arizona. In each of the state's 246 mining districts, decades of mining activity have produced a legacy of historic properties that characterize and often define the cultural landscape. The State Route 69 investigations provided the opportunity to study mining and related activities within one such district, the Big Bug. Using archival and archaeological data, SWCA archaeologists were able to shed light on the complex and tenuous nature of mineral extraction and processing within that district and the factors that made those activities moderately successful in some localities and less successful in others. The study of "mining the Big Bug" confirmed the valuable role that historical archaeological sites play in illuminating the past and underscored the importance of examining a variety of data sets to gain a balanced understanding of that past.

GLOSSARY OF HISTORICAL ARTIFACT TERMINOLOGY

Careful descriptions of artifacts are important because known dates or periods of manufacture allow temporal assignment of sites, and identification of contents provides information on diet and site activities. Cans and bottles, in particular, have many datable variations, and certain types are closely associated with specific contents. Nearly all provide some chronological limits, if not exact date ranges. This is not an exhaustive glossary; the terms listed below are those that appear in this report. For further information, please consult the references cited in the artifact analyses.

CANS

Types

Hole-in-cap: The common food can of the nineteenth century. In the earliest versions, seams were lapped, and soldered both inside and outside; in later versions the seams were crimped. The top was attached before filling, with a large enough hole left in the center to accommodate the contents. After filling, the top was closed with a soldered-on cap with a small hole left in the center for steam to escape during processing. This small hole was then closed with a drop of solder.

Sanitary can: Also a food can, introduced in the 1890s. Seams were crimped, and soldered on the outside only, which was more sanitary, hence the name. (The Sanitary Can Company was established in 1904.) The solid top was attached after filling.

Closures

External-friction: Lid with a rim or lip that fits tightly over the outside of the can's top.

Score-strip: Can is opened by use of a key that removes a scored strip of metal from around the top of the can.

BOTTLES

Parts

Lip: The top of the bottle finish, where the closure is attached.

Finish: The portion of the bottle above the neck, including the lip.

Neck: The slender portion of the bottle above the body, joined at the curved shoulder.

Body: The main portion of the bottle below the neck and shoulder; usually cylindrical or rectangular.

Base: The bottom of the bottle, often bearing an embossed manufacturer's mark, sometimes with a date.

Types

Lip: *Hand-applied*: Added by hand (with a lipping tool) to molded bottle and finish. 1850s to early 1900s.

Ring-bead: Ring of glass around finish or upper neck; can have one, two, or more. 1850s to early 1900s.

Finish: *Brandy*: The common type on brandy, whiskey, and beer bottles.

Continuous thread: Molded with a spiral thread to receive a threaded cap.

Crown: The common type on beverage bottles, to fit the crimped crown cap. Introduced 1892.

Friction: Closed with a lid fitting closely around the inner or outer lid, or with a stopper.

Hand-applied: Entire finish added by hand (with a lipping tool) to neck of molded bottle. 1850s to early 1900s.

Sheared: Top of neck sheared off, sometimes smoothed, with no lip or finish. Likely to be early.

Body: *French Square*: Square with beveled edges. Commonly used for bitters.

Panel: Various shapes, with a panel impressed on each side. Commonly used for patent medicines.

Picnic Flask: Small refillable oval bottle, an early version of a hip flask; *pumpkin-seed* flask is one type. Most commonly used for whiskey, but also for other beverages.

Color: *Aqua*: Commonly used before and throughout the nineteenth century.

Black: Actually a very dark amber or green, commonly used for beer, bitters, and cider in the nineteenth century.

Sun-colored amethyst (SCA): Glass with manganese added to make it clear (natural glass has a pale green color), turns lavender or purple when exposed to sunlight. Made from approximately 1880 to 1920.

Closures

Bernardin: Formally the *Bernardin Metal Cap with Neckband,* a metal cap with an attached band fitted closely around the neck of the bottle with a buckle fastened into a slot. Overcame problem of corks blowing out of beer bottles under high pressure produced during pasteurization, enabled bottlers to use shorter, less expensive corks, took less time to apply than wiring (Lief 1965:15). Patented by Alfred L. Bernardin on March 12, 1885 (Herskovitz 1978:74).

Club sauce: Like today's Worcestershire sauce bottle stopper. Glass, with a roughened, tapered shank to provide a tight fit within the bottle finish, also roughened on the inside.

Continuous-thread: The common screw-on lid.

Crown Cap: The common crimped closure for beverage bottles.

NAILS

Types

Cut: Stamped from thin plates of iron, with the head either attached separately or continuous with the shank. In use throughout the nineteenth and early twentieth centuries, and for special uses until mid-twentieth century.

Wire: Cut from strands of wire, with a stamped head. Today's common round nail, invented in Europe in the mid-nineteenth century. Became the most popular type in the U.S. in the 1890s, after invention of automatic machine.

Size

Sizing of nails is based on the number of nails of a given type in one pound and is expressed in pennyweights (symbol "d"). A 2d nail is 1" long, with sizes increasing by increments of ¼" to 10d (3"); 12d, 16d, and 20d are 3¼", 3½", and 4", respectively; then each additional 10d equals another ½" in length, to 60d (6").

BUTTONS

Ligne: Unit of measurement of button width, pronounced and sometimes spelled *line*; 40 lignes = 1 inch.

230

REFERENCES

American Finance & Trust Company

1901   *At Least Seven Per Cent.* Prospectus published by the American Finance & Trust Co., Philadelphia. Copy on file, Western History Department, Denver Public Library, Denver.

Anderson, C. A., and P. M. Blacet

1972   *Precambrian Geology of the Northern Bradshaw Mountains, Yavapai County, Arizona.* Geological Survey Bulletin No. 1336. U.S. Government Printing Office, Washington, D.C.

Arizona Business Directory

var.   *The Arizona Business Directory.* On file, State Library, Archives, and Public Records, Phoenix.

Arizona Department of Mines and Mineral Resources (ADMMR)

var.   Resources File (RF): Hull-Huron Mining Property. On file, ADMMR, Phoenix.

var.   Resources File: Montezuma & Huron MES 1673. On file, ADMMR, Phoenix.

var.   Resources File: Princes Placer Claim. On file, ADMMR, Phoenix.

var.   Resources File: Star Patented MES 1292. On file, ADMMR, Phoenix.

Arizona Department of Transportation (ADOT)

1954   Project map, ADOT Project S-38(9). On file, ADOT, Phoenix.

1993   Request for Proposals for Contract 94-08. ADOT Engineering Consultants Services, Phoenix.

Arizona Journal-Miner (AJM)

var.   *The Arizona Journal-Miner.* Microfilmed copies on file, Sharlot Hall Museum, Prescott, Arizona.

Atchison, Topeka and Santa Fe Railway

1925   Map of Huron Station, Arizona. On file, AT&SF, Winslow, Arizona.

Ayres, James E.

1984   *Rosemont: The History and Archaeology of Post-1880 Sites in the Rosemont Area, Santa Rita Mountains, Arizona.* Arizona State Museum Archaeological Series No. 147, Vol. 3. Tucson.

Barnes, Frank C.

1985   *Cartridges of the World.* 5th ed. rev. DBI Books, Northbridge, Illinois.

Barnett, Franklin

1970   *Matli Ranch Ruins: A Report of Excavation of Five Prehistoric Indian Ruins of the Prescott Culture in Arizona.* Museum of Northern Arizona Technical Series No. 10. Flagstaff.

1974   *Excavation of the Main Pueblo at Fitzmaurice Ruin: Prescott Culture in Yavapai County, Arizona.* Museum of Northern Arizona Special Publication, Flagstaff.

1975   *Excavation of the Main Pueblo at Fitzmaurice Ruin (NA4031)*. Yavapai College, Prescott, Arizona.

Barry, John Wolfe
1876   *Railway Appliances: A Description of Details of Railway Construction*. Longmans, Green, London.

Bartlett, Katharine
1943   Oñate's Route across West-Central Arizona. *Plateau* 15(3):33–39.

Berge, Dale
1966   Camp Grant Horseshoes. Ms. on file, Arizona State Museum, Tucson.

1980   *Simpson Springs Station: Historical Archaeology in Western Utah 1974–1975*. Utah Bureau of Land Management Cultural Resource Series No. 6. Salt Lake City.

Biddle, Walter A.
1976   Childs and Irving Hydro Project. In *The Childs-Irving Hydro-Electric Project, Irving, Arizona: A National Historic Mechanical Engineering Landmark*. American Society of Mechanical Engineers, Phoenix.

Bolton, Herbert E.
1919   Father Escobar's Relation of the Oñate Expedition to California. *Catholic Historical Review* V(1):19–41.

Brandes, Ray
1960   *Frontier Military Posts of Arizona*. Dale Stuart King, Globe, Arizona.

Bryant, Ralph Clement
1913   *Logging: The Principles and General Methods of Operation in the United States*. John Wiley & Sons, New York.

Butler, John R.
1994   Letter report from John R. Butler of Scott, Allard & Bohannan, Inc., to Thomas J. Sullivan, Arizona Department of Transportation. 26 January. On file, ADOT, Phoenix.

Cantley, Garry J.
1988   *An Archaeological Assessment of the Arizona Public Service Company's Poland Junction Substation (AR-03-09-03-238), Bradshaw Ranger District, Prescott National Forest, Arizona*. Archaeological Consulting Services, Ltd., Tempe, Arizona.

Caywood, Louis R.
1936   Fitzmaurice Ruin. In *Two Pueblo Ruins in West Central Arizona*, edited by E. H. Spicer, pp. 87–115. University of Arizona Social Science Bulletin No. 10. Tucson.

Cleland, Robert G.
1952   *A History of Phelps Dodge, 1834–1950*. Alfred A. Knopf, New York.

Conneaut News-Herald
    1946   Conneaut: The Story of Its Growth. *Conneaut News-Herald* 2 July. On file, Conneaut Carnegie Library, Conneaut, Ohio.

Conneaut Telephone Directory
    1957   *Conneaut Telephone Directory.* On file, Conneaut Public Library, Conneaut, Ohio.

Cross, Jack L., Elizabeth H. Shaw, and Kathleen Scheifele
    1960   *Arizona: Its People and Resources.* University of Arizona Press, Tucson.

Cunningham, Jo
    1982   *The Collector's Encyclopedia of American Dinnerware.* CB Collector Books, Paducah, Kentucky.

Dosh, Steven G.
    1988   *An Archaeological Survey of Construction Impact Zones Associated with Improvements to State Route 69 near Mayer and Poland Junction, Yavapai County, Arizona (ADOT Contract 86-40).* Museum of Northern Arizona, Flagstaff.

Dunning, Charles H.
    1951   Information from C. H. Dunning. Resources File (RF): Hull-Huron Mining Property. On file, Arizona Department of Mines and Mineral Resources, Phoenix.

Dunning, Charles H., and Edward Peplow
    1959   *Rocks to Riches.* Southwest Publishing Company, Phoenix.

Effland, Richard W., Jr., and Barbara S. Macnider
    1991   *National Register of Historic Places Registration Form: Childs-Irving Hydroelectric Facilities.* On file, State Historic Preservation Office, Phoenix.

Electrical World
    1910a   A Remarkable Utilization of Water. Reprint. *Electrical World* 18 August.

    1910b   The Hydroelectric Generating System of the Arizona Power Company. *Electrical World* 11 August and 18 August.

Emmit, Boris (editor)
    1969   *Catalogue No. 57, Montgomery Ward & Co., 1895.* Dover Publications, New York.

Fagerberg, Dixon
    1989   The 1933–1941 Mining Boom East of the Bradshaws. Ms. on file, Sharlot Hall Museum, Prescott, Arizona.

Farish, Thomas E.
    1916   *History of Arizona.* 9 vols. Thomas E. Farish, Phoenix.

Federal Register
1983   *The Secretary of the Interior's Standards and Guidelines for Archeology and Historic Preservation.* Federal Register No. 48, Vol. 190. USDI National Park Service, Interagency Resources Division, Washington, D.C.

Federal Writers' Project (FWP)
1940   *Arizona: A State Guide.* Hastings House, New York.

Fike, Richard E.
1987   *The Bottle Book: A Comprehensive Guide to Historic, Embossed Medicine Bottles.* Gibbs M. Smith, Salt Lake City.

Fisher, J. J.
1898   Surveyor's notes and plat, Mineral Entry Survey 1292, Star Placer. Microfiche on file, USDI Bureau of Land Management State Office, Phoenix.

1902   Surveyor's notes and plat, Mineral Entry Survey 1673, Montezuma and Huron Claims. Microfiche on file, USDI Bureau of Land Management State Office, Phoenix.

Fontana, Bernard L., and J. Cameron Greenleaf
1962   Johnny Ward's Ranch: A Study in Historic Archaeology. *The Kiva* 28(102):1–115.

Gates, John M.
1967   General George Crook's First Apache Campaign. *Journal of the West* VI(2):310–320.

Gates, William J., Jr., and Dana E. Ormerod
1982   The East Liverpool Pottery District: Identification of Manufacturers and Marks. *Historical Archaeology* 16(1–2):1–358.

General Land Office (GLO)
1902   Mineral Entry Survey (MES) 1673. Microfiche on file, USDI Bureau of Land Management State Office, Phoenix.

1914   Map of Township 12 North, Range 1 East, Gila and Salt River Meridian, Arizona. On file, USDI Bureau of Land Management State Office, Phoenix.

1915   Mineral Entry Survey 3234. Microfiche on file, USDI Bureau of Land Management State Office, Phoenix.

1935   Map of Township 12 North, Range 1 East, Gila and Salt River Meridian, Arizona. On file, USDI Bureau of Land Management State Office, Phoenix.

var.   Homestead Entry Survey (HES) 41: William Murphy Homestead. Microfiche on file, USDI Bureau of Land Management State Office, Phoenix.

var.   Mineral Entry Survey 3991: Smelter Placer Mining Claim. Microfiche on file, USDI Bureau of Land Management State Office, Phoenix.

Gifford, E. W.
 1936   *Northeastern and Western Yavapai.* University of California Press, Berkeley.

Gilbert, B.
 1983   *Westering Man: The Life of Joseph Walker.* Atheneum, New York.

Glover, Vernon J.
 1984   *Logging Railroads of the Lincoln National Forest, New Mexico.* Cultural Resources Management Report No. 4. USDA Forest Service, Southwest Region, Albuquerque.

Godden, Geoffrey A.
 1964   *Encyclopedia of British Pottery and Porcelain Marks.* Bonanza Books, New York.

Goodman, John David, II
 1993   *Spring Rancheria: Archaeological Investigations of a Transient Cahuilla Village in Early Riverside, California.* Unpublished Master's thesis, Department of Anthropology, University of California, Riverside.

GPI Environmental, Inc.
 1991   *Archaeological Survey Report Cordes Junction-Prescott SR 69 Milepost 269.9 to M.P. 280.8 Yavapai County, Arizona.* Design Concept Study ADOT Contract No. 89-27 Tracs No. 69 YV 263 H-2369-02D. GPI Environmental, Inc., Phoenix.

Granger, Byrd H.
 1960   *Will C. Barnes' Arizona Place Names.* rev. University of Arizona Press, Tucson.

Hardesty, Donald L.
 1988   *The Archaeology of Mining and Miners: A View from the Silver State.* Society for Historical Archaeology Special Publication Series No. 6. Ann Arbor.

Harvey, Dale, and Bonnie Harvey
 1985   *National Register of Historic Places Inventory-Nomination Form: Robert W. Wingfield House.* On file, State Historic Preservation Office, Phoenix.

Hathaway, Jeffrey B.
 1992   *Cultural Resources Survey along an 11.1 Mile Segment of State Route 69 between Mayer and Dewey in Southeastern Yavapai County, Arizona (ADOT Contract 90-22).* Archaeological Research Services, Inc., Tempe, Arizona.

Heider, Karl G.
 1955   Fort McDowell–Yavapai Field Notes. Copy on file, Arizona State Museum Library, Tucson.

Henderson, Patrick
 1958   *A History of the Prescott Bradshaw Mining Districts.* Unpublished Master's thesis, Department of History, The University of Arizona, Tucson.

Henson, Pauline
1965   *Founding a Wilderness Capital: Prescott, A.T. 1864.* Northland Press, Flagstaff.

Herskovitz, Robert M.
1978   *Fort Bowie Material Culture.* University of Arizona Press, Tucson.

Hoffman, C. Marshall
1991   *Assessment of Archaeological Sites Identified during the SR 69 Survey between Cordes Junction and Prescott, Yavapai County, Arizona (ADOT Project No. F-029-1-310; Tracs No. 69 YV 263 H-2369 02D).* Archaeological Research Services, Inc., Tempe, Arizona.

Hoffman, Kathleen S.
1985   *An Archaeological Resource Inventory at the U.S. Veterans Administration Medical Center, Prescott, Yavapai County, Arizona.* Archaeological Research Services, Inc., Tempe, Arizona.

Hull-Walski, Deborah A., and James E. Ayres
1989   *The Historical Archaeology of Dam Construction Camps in Central Arizona. Volume 3: Laboratory Methods and Data Computerization.* Dames & Moore, Phoenix.

Israel, Fred L. (editor)
1968   *1897 Sears Roebuck Catalogue.* Chelsea House Publishers, New York.

Janus Associates Incorporated
1989   *Transcontinental Railroading in Arizona, 1878–1940: A Component of the Arizona Historic Preservation Plan.* Janus, Phoenix.

Jerome Miner News (JMN)
1909   *Jerome Miner News* 29 June. On file, Sharlot Hall Museum, Prescott, Arizona.

Jeter, Marvin D.
1977   *Archaeology in Copper Basin, Yavapai County, Arizona: Model Building for the Prehistory of the Prescott Region.* Anthropological Research Paper No. 11. Arizona State Museum, Tucson.

Jones, Richard D.
1969   *An Analysis of Papago Communities, 1900–1920.* Unpublished Ph.D. dissertation, Department of Anthropology, The University of Arizona, Tucson.

Keane, Melissa, and A. E. Rogge
1992   *Gold and Silver Mining in Arizona, 1848–1945: A Context for Historic Preservation Planning.* Dames & Moore Intermountain Cultural Resource Services Research Paper No. 6. Phoenix.

Keller, Donald R., and Pat H. Stein
1985   *Archaeological Study at Three Twentieth Century Yavapai Wickiup Sites, Prescott, Arizona.* Department of Anthropology Report No. A-84-61. Museum of Northern Arizona, Flagstaff.

Lehner, Lois
1980   *Complete Book of American Kitchen and Dinner Wares.* Wallace-Homestead Books, Des Moines.

Leshy, John D.
1987   *The Mining Law: A Study in Perpetual Motion.* Resources for the Future, Washington, D.C.

Lief, Alfred
1965   *A Close-Up of Closures: History and Progress.* Glass Container Manufacturers Institute, New York.

Lindgren, Waldemar
1926   *Ore Deposits of the Jerome and Bradshaw Mountains Quadrangles, Arizona.* U.S. Geological Survey Bulletin No. 782. U.S. Government Printing Office, Washington, D.C.

Lorrain, Dessamae
1968   An Archaeologist's Guide to Nineteenth Century American Glass. *Historical Archaeology* 2:35–44.

Lowe, C. H., and D. E. Brown
1973   *The Natural Vegetation of Arizona.* Arizona Resources Information System Cooperative Publication No. 2. Phoenix.

McKie, James M.
1988   Inventory·Standards and Accounting Form: Access Road to Poland Junction Substation (Project 1988-09-126). Ms. on file, USDA Prescott National Forest, Prescott, Arizona.

Macnider, Barbara S.
1990   *An Archaeological Assessment of the State Route 69 Right-of-Way between Mileposts 262.9 and 270.0, Cordes Junction to Mayer, Yavapai County, Arizona.* Archaeological Consulting Services, Ltd., Tempe, Arizona.

Macnider, Barbara S., Richard W. Effland, Jr., and George Ford
1989   *Cultural Resources Overview: The Prescott National Forest.* Prescott National Forest Cultural Resources Inventory Report No. 89-062. Archaeological Consulting Services, Ltd., Tempe, Arizona.

Macnider, Barbara S., Richard W. Effland, Jr., and Ann Valdo Howard
1988   *An Archaeological and Historical Assessment of Arizona Public Service Company's Childs and Irving Hydroelectric Facilities, Coconino National Forest, Beaver Creek Ranger District.* Archaeological Consulting Services Cultural Resources Report No. 55. Tempe, Arizona.

Macnider, Barbara S., and Monique Sawyer-Lang
1990   *An Archaeological Assessment of the APS Lonesome Valley–Dewey 69 kV Realignment Right-of Way.* Archaeological Consulting Services, Ltd., Tempe, Arizona.

McPherson, O. M.
    1914   Report to the Honorable Cato Sells, Commissioner of Indian Affairs, Washington, D.C., Concerning the Purchase of Lands for Camp Verde Indians. Ms. on file, Middle Verde Reservation, Middle Verde, Arizona.

Masson, Raymond S.
    1910   The Arizona Power Company. *Electrical World* 11 August and 18 August.

Merritt, William H.
    1901   Surveyor's notes, Mineral Entry Survey (MES) 1538, Princes Placer Claim. Microfiche copy on file, USDI Bureau of Land Management State Office, Phoenix.

    1909   Surveyor's notes and plat, Homestead Entry Survey (HES) 41, William P. Murphy Claim. Microfiche on file, USDI Bureau of Land Management State Office, Phoenix.

    1915   Surveyor's notes and plat, Mineral Entry Survey 3234, George W. Hull Mining Claims. Microfiche on file, USDI Bureau of Land Management State Office, Phoenix.

    1926   Surveyor's notes and plat, Mineral Entry Survey 3991, Smelter Placer Mining Claim. Microfiche on file, USDI Bureau of Land Management State Office, Phoenix.

Michael, Sam
    1986   *Trade Token Place Names of Arizona.* Sam Michael, Mesa, Arizona.

Mining Reporter (MR)
    1906   *The Mining Reporter* 22 February. Copy on file, Sharlot Hall Museum, Prescott, Arizona.

Mining and Scientific Press (MSP)
    1903   *Mining and Scientific Press* 31 January. Copy on file, Sharlot Hall Museum, Prescott, Arizona.

Mitchell, Douglas R. (editor)
    1994   *Archaeological Testing at Three Prehistoric Sites along State Route 69, Mayer and Dewey, Yavapai County, Arizona.* SWCA Archaeological Report No. 94-102. Scottsdale.

    1995   *Archaeological Investigations at Three Prehistoric Sites along State Route 69 between Mayer and Dewey, Yavapai County, Arizona.* SWCA Archaeological Report No. 95-114. Phoenix.

Moore, R.
    1879   *The Universal Assistant and Complete Mechanic.* J. S. Ogilvie, New York.

Morris, Clyde P.
    1971   A Brief Economic History of the Camp and Middle Verde Reservations. *Plateau* 44(2):43–51.

Munsey, Cecil
    1970   *The Illustrated Guide to Collecting Bottles.* Hawthorn Books, New York.

Myrick, David F.
  1968   *Pioneer Arizona Railroads*. Colorado Railroad Museum, Golden, Colorado.

National Archives (NA)
  var.   Homestead Case File 01352: William Murphy Homestead. On file, Suitland Reference
          Branch, Textual Reference Division, National Archives, Washington, D.C.

Nininger, H. H.
  1956   *Arizona's Meteorite Crater*. World Press, Denver.

Noble, Bruce J., Jr., and Robert Spude
  1992   *National Register Bulletin 42: Guidelines for Identifying, Evaluating, and Registering Historic
          Mining Properties*.   USDI National Park Service, Interagency Resources Division,
          Washington, D.C.

Pape, Richard F.
  1987   Big Bug Lead-Zinc District. In *History of Mining in Arizona*, edited by J. Michael Canty and
          Michael N. Greeley, pp. 77–97. Mining Club of the Southwest Foundation, Tucson.

Peele, Robert (editor)
  1927   *The Mining Engineers Handbook*. 2nd ed. Wiley, New York. Originally published 1918,
          various editions.

Periodical Publishers Association
  1934   *Nationally Established Trademarks*. Periodical Publishers Association, New York.

Peterson, Arthur G.
  1968   *400 Trademarks on Glass*. Washington College Press, Takoma Park, Maryland.

Phoenix Gazette
  var.   *The Phoenix Gazette*. Microfilmed copies on file, Arizona State Library, Archives, and Public
          Records, Phoenix.

Prescott Courier
  1971   *The Prescott Courier* 23 March. Copy on file, Sharlot Hall Museum, Prescott, Arizona.

Prescott Journal Miner (PJM)
  var.   *The Prescott Journal Miner*. Microfilmed copies on file, Arizona State Library, Archives, and
          Public Records, Phoenix.

Prospect
  var.   *The Prospect*. Newspaper occasionally published in Prescott, Arizona. Copy on file, Sharlot
          Hall Museum, Prescott, Arizona.

Randall, Mark E., and Dennis Webb
  1988   *Greenberg's Guide to Marbles*. Greenberg Publishing, Sykesville, Maryland.

Richards, Robert H.
  1903   *Ore Dressing: Volume II*. The Engineering and Mining Journal Press, New York.

Richardson, Gladwell
  1968   *Two Guns, Arizona*. The Press of the Territorian No. 15. Santa Fe.

Rickard, Forrest R.
  1987   History of Smelting in Arizona. In *History of Mining in Arizona: Volume II*, edited by J. Michael Canty and Michael N. Greeley, pp. 191–228. American Institute of Mining Engineers and Southwestern Minerals Exploration Association, Tucson.

Robertson, Donald B.
  1986   *Encyclopedia of Western Railroad History: The Desert States*. Caxton Printers, Caldwell, Idaho.

Rock, Jim
  1981   *Tin Cans: Notes and Comments*. USDA Forest Service Klamath National Forest, Region 5, Yreka, California.

  1987   *A Brief Commentary on Cans*. USDA Forest Service Klamath National Forest, Region 5, Yreka, California.

  1992   Tin Can Chronology. In *User's Guide: Instructions and Computer Codes for Use with the IMACS Site Form*, prepared by University of Utah, USDI Bureau of Land Management, and U.S. Forest Service, Sec. 471, pp. 4–6. Salt Lake City.

Rodda, Jeanette
  1993   Chug Wagons and Benzine Buggies: Arizona's Automotive Pioneers. *Journal of Arizona History* 34(4):391–418.

Rogers, James B., and Donald E. Weaver, Jr.
  1990   Preliminary Testing Report and Data Recovery Research Plan for Six Archaeological Sites along State Route 69 near Dewey in Yavapai County, Arizona. Plateau Mountain Desert Research, Flagstaff. Draft.

Rogge, A. E., Melissa Keane, and D. Lorne McWaters
  1994   *The Historical Archaeology of Dam Construction Camps in Central Arizona, Volume 1: Synthesis*. Dames & Moore, Phoenix.

Sayre, John W.
  1979   *Mines, Men, and Machinery: A Study of Copper Mining in the Bradshaw Mountains, 1875–1979*. Unpublished Master's thesis, Department of History, Northern Arizona University, Flagstaff.

  1985   *A Journey through Yesteryear: Ghost Railroads of Central Arizona*. Red Rock Publishing, Phoenix.

1990   *The Santa Fe, Prescott & Phoenix Railway: The Scenic Line of Arizona.* Pruett Publishing, Boulder, Colorado.

Schroeder, Albert H.
1974   *A Study of Yavapai History.* Garland Publishing, New York.

Servin, Manuel P., and Robert L. Spude
1975   Historical Conditions of Early Mexican Labor in the United States. Arizona: A Neglected Story. *Journal of Mexican American History* V:43–56.

Sharlot Hall Museum (SHM)
var.   Document Book. Archival material on file, Sharlot Hall Museum, Prescott, Arizona.

var.   Obituary Book. Archival material on file, Sharlot Hall Museum, Prescott, Arizona.

Simonis, Donald E.
1992   Condensed/Evaporated Milk Cans: Chronology for Dating Historical Sites. In *User's Guide: Instructions and Computer Codes for Use with the IMACS Site Form,* prepared by University of Utah, USDI Bureau of Land Management, and U.S. Forest Service, Sec. 471, pg. 9. Salt Lake City.

Simpson, Claudette
1975   Mayer's Smokeless Smokestack. *Prescott Courier* 7 March. Copy on file, Sharlot Hall Museum, Prescott, Arizona.

Sparkes, Grace M.
1926   Outline of Mining Properties in Yavapai County, Arizona: Montezuma Mine. Ms. on file, Grace M. Sparkes Collection, Arizona Historical Collection, Tempe.

Sprague, Roderick
1981   A Functional Classification for Artifacts from 19th and 20th Century Historical Sites. *North American Anthropologist* 2(3):251–261.

Spude, Robert L.
n.d.   The Poland Branch of the Bradshaw Mountain Railroad. Ms. on file, Arizona Historical Foundation, Tempe.

1976   *Mineral Frontier in Transition: Copper Mining in Arizona, 1880–1885.* Unpublished Master's thesis, Department of Anthropology, Arizona State University, Tempe.

Spude, Robert L., and Stanley W. Paher
1978   *Central Arizona Ghost Towns.* Nevada Publications, Las Vegas.

Stein, Pat H.
1994   *Archaeological Testing at Twelve Historic Sites along State Route 69 between Mayer and Dewey, Yavapai County, Arizona.* SWCA Archaeological Report No. 94-91. Flagstaff.

1995   *Interim Report: Data Recovery at Two Archaeological Sites along State Route 69 between Mayer and Dewey, Yavapai County, Arizona.* SWCA Archaeological Report No. 95-67. Flagstaff.

Stephens, Fannie Wingfield
1955   A Pioneer of the Verde Valley (W. G. Wingfield). In *Echoes of the Past: Tales of Old Yavapai*, pp. 129–135. Yavapai Cow Belles, Prescott, Arizona.

Steward, Frank H.
1969   *Shotgun Shells: Identification, Manufacturers and Checklist for Collectors.* B&P Associates, St. Louis.

Stone, Connie L., and Joann E. Kisselburg
1991   *Archaeological Testing at Five Sites along State Route 69 from Cordes Junction to Mayer.* Archaeological Consulting Services, Ltd., Tempe, Arizona.

SWCA, Inc., Environmental Consultants
1993   Proposal for Archaeological Investigations along State Route 69, Mayer to Dewey, Yavapai County, Arizona (ADOT Contract 94-08). Ms. on file, SWCA, Flagstaff.

1994   Cost Proposal, Data Recovery Plan for SR 69, Mayer to Dewey. Ms. on file, SWCA, Flagstaff.

Swenson, Helen (editor)
1988   *We Remember Humboldt and Dewey, Arizona.* Humboldt Publishing and Advertising, Humboldt.

Teague, George A.
1980   *Reward Mine and Associated Sites: Historical Archeology on the Papago Reservation.* Western Archeological Center Publications in Anthropology No. 11. USDI National Park Service, WAC, Tucson.

Theobald, John, and Lillian Theobald
1961   *Arizona Territory Post Offices & Postmasters.* Arizona Historical Foundation, Phoenix.

Thorn, C. Jordan
1947   *Handbook of Old Pottery and Porcelain Marks.* Tudor Publishing, New York.

Thorpe, Winifred L.
1978   Joe Mayer and His Town. *The Journal of Arizona History* 19(2):131–168.

Toulouse, Julian H.
1971   *Bottle Makers and Their Marks.* Thomas Nelson, Nashville.

Townsend, Jan, John H. Sprinkle, Jr., and John Knoerl
1993   *National Register Bulletin 36:   Guidelines for Evaluating and Registering Historical Archeological Sites and Districts.*   USDI National Park Service Interagency Resources Division, Washington, D.C.

Treadwell, George A.
n.d.   *Prospectus of the George A. Treadwell Mining Company.*   On file, State Library, Archives, and Public Records, Phoenix.

U.S. Department of Commerce, Bureau of the Census
1910   *U.S. Census Enumeration Records, 1910.*   Microfilm copy on file, Special Collections and Archives, Northern Arizona University, Flagstaff.

U.S. Department of the Interior, Bureau of Land Management (BLM)
var.   Homestead Entry Survey 42.   Microfiche on file, BLM State Office, Phoenix.

var.   Phoenix Serial Record 028509.   Microfiche on file, BLM State Office, Phoenix.

U.S. Department of the Interior, National Park Service (NPS)
1991a   *National Register Bulletin 15:   How to Apply the National Register Criteria for Evaluation.*   NPS Interagency Resources Division, Washington, D.C.

1991b   *National Register Bulletin 16A: How to Complete the National Register Registration Form.*   NPS Interagency Resources Division, Washington, D.C.

Walker, Henry P., and Don Bufkin
1986   *Historical Atlas of Arizona.*   University of Oklahoma Press, Norman.

Ward, Albert E., Emily K. Abbink, and John R. Stein
1977   Ethnohistorical and Chronological Basis of the Navajo Material Culture.   In *Settlement and Subsistence along the Lower Chaco River: The CGP Survey*, edited by Charles A. Reher, pp. 217–278.   University of New Mexico Press, Albuquerque.

Weaver, Donald E., Jr.
1989   *Archaeological Survey of 3.2 Miles of Right-of-Way along State Route 69 near Dewey, Milepost 280.8 to Milepost 284.0, Yavapai County, Arizona.*   Plateau Mountain Desert Research, Flagstaff.

Weber, David J.
1982   *The Mexican Frontier, 1821–1846: The American Southwest under Mexico.*   University of New Mexico Press, Albuquerque.

Weed, Carol S., and Albert E. Ward
1970   The Henderson Site: Colonial Hohokam in North Central Arizona, A Preliminary Report. *Kiva* 36(2):1–12.

Weekly Reflex
  1899   Treadwell's Smelter at Mayer. Copy on file, Sharlot Hall Museum, Prescott, Arizona.

Wilson, Eldred D., J. B. Cunningham, and G. M. Butler
  1967   *Arizona Lode Gold Mines and Gold Mining.* Arizona Bureau of Mines Mineral Technology Series No. 37, Bulletin No. 137. University of Arizona Press, Tucson.

Wilson, Rex
  1981   *Bottles on the Western Frontier.* University of Arizona Press, Tucson.

Wilson, W.L., and B. Wilson
  1971   *19th Century Medicine in Glass.* 19th Century Hobby and Publishing, Amador City, California.

Wingfield, William G.
  1954   Autobiography of W. G. Wingfield. In *Pioneer Stories of Arizona's Verde Valley*, pp. 30–32. Verde Valley Pioneers Association, Camp Verde, Arizona.

Yavapai County Recorder (YCR)
  var.   Book of Deeds (BD). Series on file, Yavapai County Recorder, Yavapai County Courthouse Annex, Prescott, Arizona.

  var.   Book of Mines (BM). Series on file, Yavapai County Recorder, Yavapai County Courthouse Annex, Prescott, Arizona.

  var.   Book of Wills (BW). Series on file, Yavapai County Recorder, Yavapai County Courthouse Annex, Prescott, Arizona.

Yavapai Magazine (YM)
  var.   *Yavapai Magazine.* Copies on file, Sharlot Hall Museum, Prescott, Arizona.

Young, Herbert V.
  1972   *They Came to Jerome: The Billion Dollar Copper Camp.* Jerome Historical Society, Jerome, Arizona.

  1974   *Ghosts of Cleopatra Hill: Men and Legends of Old Jerome.* Jerome Historical Society, Jerome, Arizona.

Zumwalt, Betty
  1980   *Ketchup, Pickles, Sauces: 19th Century Food in Glass.* Mark West Publishers, Fulton, Missouri.